Patterns of Information Management

By Mandy Chessell and Harald C. Smith
ISBN: 978-0-13-315550-1

Use Best Practice Patterns to Understand and Architect Manageable, Efficient Information Supply Chains That Help You Leverage All Your Data and Knowledge

Building on the analogy of a supply chain, Mandy Chessell and Harald Smith explain how information can be transformed, enriched, reconciled, redistributed, and utilized in even the most complex environments. Through a realistic, end-to-end case study, they help you blend overlapping information management, SOA, and BPM technologies that are often viewed as competitive.

Using this book's patterns, you can integrate all levels of your architecture—from holistic, enterprise, system-level views down to low-level design elements. You can fully address key non-functional requirements such as the amount, quality, and pace of incoming data. Above all, you can create an IT landscape that is coherent, interconnected, efficient, effective, and manageable.

Analytics Across the Enterprise

How IBM Realizes Business Value from Big Data and Analytics

By Brenda L. Dietrich, Emily C. Plachy, Maureen F. Norton
ISBN: 978-0-13-383303-4

How to Transform Your Organization with Analytics: Insider Lessons from IBM's Pioneering Experience

Analytics is not just a technology: It is a better way to do business. Using analytics, you can systematically inform human judgment with data-driven insight. This book demystifies your analytics journey by showing you how IBM has successfully leveraged analytics across the enterprise, worldwide. Three of IBM's pioneering analytics practitioners share invaluable real-world perspectives on what does and doesn't work and how you can start or accelerate your own transformation.

Whatever your industry or role, whether a current or future leader, analytics can make you smarter and more competitive. *Analytics Across the Enterprise* shows how IBM did it—and how you can, too.

Related Books of Interest

The Art of Enterprise Information Architecture
A Systems-Based Approach for Unlocking Business Insight

By Mario Godinez, Eberhard Hechler, Klaus Koenig, Steve Lockwood, Martin Oberhofer, and Michael Schroeck
ISBN: 978-0-13-703571-7

Architecture for the Intelligent Enterprise: Powerful New Ways to Maximize the Real-Time Value of Information

Tomorrow's winning "Intelligent Enterprises" will bring together far more diverse sources of data, analyze it in more powerful ways, and deliver immediate insight to decision-makers throughout the organization. Today, however, most companies fail to apply the information they already have, while struggling with the complexity and costs of their existing information environments.

In this book, a team of IBM's leading information management experts guide you on a journey that will take you from where you are today toward becoming an "Intelligent Enterprise."

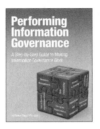

Performing Information Governance
A Step-by-step Guide to Making Information Governance Work

By Anthony David Giordano
ISBN: 978-0-13-338565-6

Make Information Governance Work: Best Practices, Step-by-Step Tasks, and Detailed Deliverables

Using case studies and hands-on activities, Anthony Giordano fully illuminates the "who, what, how, and when" of information governance. He explains how core governance components link with other enterprise information management disciplines, and provides workable "job descriptions" for each project participant.

Giordano helps you successfully integrate key data stewardship processes as you develop large-scale applications and Master Data Management (MDM) environments. Then, once you've deployed an information asset, he shows how to consistently get reliable regulatory and financial information from it.

Performing Information Governance will be indispensable to CIOs and Chief Data Officers...data quality, metadata, and MDM specialists...anyone responsible for making information governance work.

 Listen to the author's podcast at:
ibmpressbooks.com/podcasts

IBM Press.

Related Books of Interest

Enterprise Master Data Management
An SOA Approach to Managing Core Information
Dreibelbis, Hechler, Milman, Oberhofer, Van Run, Wolfson
ISBN: 978-0-13-236625-0

The New Era of Enterprise Business Intelligence:
Using Analytics to Achieve a Global Competitive Advantage

By Mike Biere
ISBN: 978-0-13-707542-3

A Complete Blueprint for Maximizing the Value of Business Intelligence in the Enterprise

The typical enterprise recognizes the immense potential of business intelligence (BI) and its impact upon many facets within the organization— but it's not easy to transform BI's potential into real business value. Top BI expert Mike Biere presents a complete blueprint for creating winning BI strategies and infrastructure and systematically maximizing the value of information throughout the enterprise.

This product-independent guide brings together start-to-finish guidance and practical checklists for every senior IT executive, planner, strategist, implementer, and the actual business users themselves.

Decision Management Systems
A Practical Guide to Using Business Rules and Predictive Analytics
Taylor
ISBN: 978-0-13-288438-9

IBM Cognos Business Intelligence v10
The Complete Guide
Gautam
ISBN: 978-0-13-272472-2

IBM Cognos 10 Report Studio
Practical Examples
Draskovic, Johnson
ISBN: 978-0-13-265675-7

Data Integration Blueprint and Modeling
Techniques for a Scalable and Sustainable Architecture
Giordano
ISBN: 978-0-13-708493-7

Beyond Big Data

Using Social MDM to Drive Deep Customer Insight

Beyond Big Data

Using Social MDM to Drive Deep Customer Insight

Martin Oberhofer, Eberhard Hechler,
Ivan Milman, Scott Schumacher, and
Dan Wolfson

IBM Press
Pearson plc
Upper Saddle River, NJ • Boston • Indianapolis • San Francisco
New York • Toronto •Montreal • London • Munich • Paris • Madrid
Cape Town • Sydney • Tokyo • Singapore • Mexico City

ibmpressbooks.com

IBM Press Program Managers: Steven M. Stansel, Ellice Uffer

Cover design: IBM Corporation
Associate Publisher: Dave Dusthimer
Marketing Manager: Stephane Nakib
Executive Editor: Mary Beth Ray
Publicist: Heather Fox
Senior Development Editor: Christopher Cleveland
Managing Editor: Kristy Hart
Designer: Alan Clements
Project Editor: Andy Beaster
Copy Editor: Chuck Hutchinson
Indexer: Tim Wright
Compositor: Gloria Schurick
Proofreader: Sarah Kearns
Manufacturing Buyer: Dan Uhrig

Published by Pearson plc
Publishing as IBM Press

For information about buying this title in bulk quantities, or for special sales opportunities (which may include electronic versions; custom cover designs; and content particular to your business, training goals, marketing focus, or branding interests), please contact our corporate sales department at corpsales@pearsoned.com or (800) 382-3419.

For government sales inquiries, please contact governmentsales@pearsoned.com.

For questions about sales outside the U.S., please contact international@pearsoned.com.

Library of Congress Control Number: 2014942802

ISBN-13: 978-0-13-350980-9
ISBN-10: 0-13-350980-X

Text printed in the United States on recycled paper at R.R. Donnelley in Crawfordsville, Indiana. First printing: October 2014

To my wife Kirsten and my sons Damian and Adrian—
You are the great love and joy of my life.

—Martin Oberhofer

To my wife Irina and my sons Lars and Alex—
Who so greatly encouraged me in this endeavor.

—Eberhard Hechler

To my wife Janie, for making my heart dance with joy.
To Jenica and Ryan, for showing me how a heart can grow.
And to Bill, for joining the club.

—Ivan Milman

I would like to dedicate this to my wife Julie,
who supports me in everything I do.

—Scott Schumacher

To my family, especially my wife Danelle, for their
understanding and support.

—Dan Wolfson

Contents

Foreword I

Every leader makes decisions. And every decision depends on information. That's been true whether someone has led a company, a government, an army, a team, or a household.

The ultimate value of the information technology industry has never been about chips, computers, and software. The industry has always sought to help leaders know with confidence all that has happened, is happening, and might happen to every aspect of the enterprise. But the ante is upped by the volume and variety of information and the velocity of decision making. We're entering the age of Big Data where knowledge and expertise are minimal stakes for survival, and the traditional data centers are becoming the coffins. In this new era of Big Data, continuous reinvention, relevance, and engagement are all that matter. Context is king, and contextual understanding of those you serve becomes absolutely critical to transforming your organization, industry and profession.

As a result, a systematic approach to engagement is now required. You will need to leverage new technology capabilities and business concepts—this is *Social Master Data Management*—to harness data both inside and outside your organizations. Social, mobile, and data together are empowering people with knowledge, enriching them through networks and spawning expectations for real value in return for their information and services, with enterprises they trust. You will want to personalize every meaningful interaction, make transparent those interactions, and continuously earn the right to serve customers. This demands privacy, security, and trust. You need to use mobile and social to increase speed and responsiveness—and meet customers, partners and employees where they are.

Look, data is becoming the world's new natural resource and it is inspiring organizations to take action differently. This book shares best practices in how to think and act differently about your customer data. I encourage everyone to read it!

Inhi Cho Suh
IBM Vice President
Big Data, Integration & Governance

Foreword II

Personal relationships are key to successful business. What if it was possible to provide your customers with the same personal touch they would expect from their favorite local mom-and-pop store when they visit your website, engage in live chat, or speak with technical support? Intuitively, we all know it is a huge competitive advantage because it would improve the quality of every interaction they have with your company.

In the virtual world, how do you provide a personalized experience when there is no physical interaction with people? You can't read their facial expressions as they view one of your products. You can't watch the body language as they are going through the checkout process. The answer is there is still plenty of information to be gleaned from a person's behavior online. You just need the right tools to capture and understand it.

In today's "always-on" society, people provide a wealth of information about their preferences and interests through the websites they visit, the products they rate, the people they follow, and the online communities they engage in. The challenge, of course, is sifting through all this information and making sense of it. Thankfully, advances in analytics and Big Data technologies are making it possible to sift through enormous volumes of information that is known about prospects and customers as well as providing insight into things that can be inferred from their behavior.

This challenge applies to B2C and B2B companies alike as companies of all types and sizes are striving to adopt a "Business to Individual" approach in all their customer interactions. However, it is compounded for B2B companies that must take the extra step of aggregating the interests and preferences for many individuals in a client company in order to infer the preferences and interests of the company at large.

Customers expect a high degree of personalized interactions at every stage of their relationship with a company. As such, quality information about an individual is needed by all the functions in a company; from the marketer working to deliver personalized messages to a technical support representative on the phone with a customer and every process in between.

In this book, you will learn how Master Data Management and Big Data technologies are being combined to arm you with the tools you need to attack this challenge. You will learn how to combine information you know about people with information you can only infer from their behavior. Further you will learn how to organize it in a way that will enable you to act on it and provide a personalized touch to your customers through all their interactions with your company.

I encourage anyone wrestling with this challenge to take full advantage of the wealth of information in *Beyond Big Data*. It will equip you with the knowledge you need to successfully take on this challenge.

Brian Mackey
Director, Marketing Transformation in IBM's BT/IT organization

Preface

What Is This Book About?

Social Master Data Management (Social MDM) is the new revolution in business data processing that marries customer and product centricity with big data to radically improve customer experiences and product strategy. Traditional master data management (MDM)—the set of processes, practices, and technologies for creating a single view of common core business objects shared across multiple business processes and multiple systems (such as *customer, product, vendor, and location*)—is widely used by enterprises to improve the marketing, operational, and support processes for their customers. However, the focus of traditional MDM is structured data—and today, valuable information about customers and products is locked inside of vast amounts of unstructured, transactional, and social data such as tweets, blogs, Facebook, email, call center transcripts, call data records, and so on. There has been an explosion in technology like Hadoop and BigInsights to extract that information, but often those efforts have limited reach because they are not tied into the existing insight about customers and products contained in MDM systems.

In *Beyond Big Data: Using Social MDM to Drive Deep Customer Insight*, we explain how the union of social, mobile, location, and master data:

- Creates a richer relationship with existing customers
- Improves how you find and target new customers with the right products
- Delivers deeper understanding of how your customers think and feel about your products
- Brings the immediacy of mobile technology to create new ways to engage with customers

Chapter 1, "Introduction to Social MDM," explains the basic concepts of master data and MDM. It describes how disparate data is linked together as cleansed and standardized master data in a master data management system. We show the typical use cases for MDM of customer care and insight (as well as product catalog management), and then introduce the concepts of how social data can extend and enhance MDM into a more powerful system of Social MDM.

Chapter 2, "Use Cases and Requirements for Social MDM," dives into a set of use cases for Social MDM related to improved customer experience, improved target marketing, deeper product understanding, regulatory issues, and the role of location in Social MDM. We then explore requirements and capabilities for the new types of insight and relationships that can be gleaned through integration of master data and social, mobile, and location data. These relationships cover person to person relationships, person to product relationships, person to organization relationships, and others.

Chapter 3, "Capabilities Framework for Social MDM," describes the different data domains that are in scope of a Social MDM environment, and then gives an overview of the core information capabilities needed to deliver a Social MDM solution.

Chapter 4, "Social MDM Reference Architecture," builds on the capabilities described in Chapter 3, and places them as components in a reference architecture. The reference architecture shows the interaction, layers, and relationships between the components.

Chapter 5, "Product Capabilities for Social MDM," links the capabilities described in Chapter 2, and the architectural components described in Chapters 3 and 4, with actual products and technologies that provides those capabilities.

Chapter 6, "Social MDM and Customer Care," looks in detail at how to create a more compelling customer experience using Social MDM. A specific reference architecture for Social MDM and Customer Care illustrates how to create customer centricity through offline, online and real-time capabilities of analyzing social and other enterprise data, linking it to MDM, and then delivering a more tailored experience through a variety of channels.

Chapter 7, "Social MDM and Marketing," shows how the move from traditional broad-based marketing to target marketing is accelerated through Social MDM. This chapter illustrates how to get a deeper understanding of your customers and products to create compelling offers, and how to create more effective (and different types of) marketing campaigns that yield appropriate offers based on Social MDM, identify influencers to expand the market, and use contextual marketing to deliver the right offer at the right time.

Chapter 8, "Mobile MDM," takes Social MDM in a different direction, by showing how MDM can inform and improve mobile applications, and how Social MDM can incorporate mobile data to improve customer experience and grow employee productivity. This chapter looks at the characteristics of mobile data, and modifies the Social MDM architecture to accommodate mobile data and mobile channels.

Chapter 9, "Future Trends in MDM," reveals how the traditional MDM capabilities for entity resolution and matching can be scaled out and enhanced with a Big Data platform. We also look at an emerging technology in the MDM space known as Semantic MDM. Semantic MDM uses new ways of representing the knowledge we have through MDM and social data along with semantic technology to derive new insights and relationships, giving us a better understanding of our customers. Finally, this chapter looks at the privacy and ethical considerations of how we gather, analyze, and use the Social MDM ecosystem, and what are the ethical considerations we must address at every step of Social MDM projects.

Who Should Read This Book

Beyond Big Data: Using Social MDM to Drive Deep Customer Insight has information and insight for a range of practitioners and roles in the enterprise. For business leaders looking to understand how to combine social and master data to create new business opportunities and improve their existing business, this book has excellent material on MDM, Social Data, business value, privacy concerns, and approaches to the new world of Social MDM.

For technical leaders such as Enterprise Architects, Information Architects, and System Architects, this book explores the technologies and use cases in detail, and specifically includes a reference architecture along with domain-specific guidance about best practices to drive a Social MDM project. It also includes a product mapping that gives direction on which technologies and products to adopt to solve particular scenarios.

What You Will Learn

This book provides a wide-ranging exploration of the business, technical, and ethical landscape of Social MDM. We cover the basic concepts of master data and master data management, and the same concepts for social data. You'll learn how Social MDM mediates the relationship of customers to the business, yielding greater insight about customers (so you can serve them better) and providing better service and value to customers (so they will have a greater incentive to buy more of your products and services).

We look at the different types of insight (cultural awareness, sentiment, detailed customer segmentation, influence of individuals) you can derive from social, underused enterprise, and mobile data and show how that is incorporated into a Social MDM platform. You will understand the architecture and capabilities of a Social MDM system, with a mapping to specific technologies and products. This book articulates how that architecture and those capabilities can be used to drive enhanced customer care and to build advanced marketing campaigns leveraging deep and broad insight of your customers, targeting them with the right offers and incentives (and avoiding the wrong ones). You will learn the new technologies brought about through mobile systems and how that extends and modifies the capabilities of a Social MDM system.

You will get a peek into new technologies to scale out and extend traditional MDM services in entity resolution and linking, as well as semantic technologies that add a learning and reasoning layer on top of Social MDM. Finally, you will be challenged to understand that just because you have all of this data and insight does not mean you have the right to use it. Privacy laws and customer expectations will be at the heart of a socially responsible MDM.

How to Read This Book

Beyond Big Data: Using Social MDM to Drive Deep Customer Insight is logically structured into three sections:

Concepts, Business Value Capabilities, and Ethics: These are targeted at business leaders who want to understand Social MDM and how it differs from traditional master data and analytics, delve into the new business opportunities derived from Social MDM, explore the capabilities required for Social MDM, and finally, reflect on the legal, ethical, and business implications of using Social MDM.

This section includes the following chapters:

- Chapter 1, "Introduction to Social MDM"
- Chapter 2, "Use Cases and Requirements for Social MDM"
- Chapter 9, "Future Trends in MDM"

Capability, Architecture, and Product Mapping: These chapters are aimed at technical leaders who need to understand the overall technical approach to Social MDM and the roles of the underlying components in the Social MDM architecture. This section includes:

- Chapter 3, "Capability Framework for Social MDM"
- Chapter 4, "Social MDM Reference Architecture"
- Chapter 5, "Product Capabilities for Social MDM"

Social MDM Domains: These chapters are for both business and technical leaders who want to understand the specific technical details about how Social MDM enhances business opportunities in these areas:

- Chapter 6, "Social MDM and Customer Care"
- Chapter 7, "Social MDM and Marketing"
- Chapter 8, "Mobile MDM"
- Chapter 9, "Future Trends in MDM"

Conventions

Following is a short list of key conventions that are used throughout this book:

- **Abbreviations**—Abbreviations are used across the book chapters, where all abbreviations are spelled out when they are used the first time in the book.
- **References**—This book includes quite a number of references for further study, where all references are listed at the end of each individual chapter. This way, you will find relevant information for further study in the context of the topics of each chapter. Footnotes are used to link the relevant statement in the chapter to the corresponding reference(s).
- **Footnotes**—Additional footnotes provide further background information, for example in regards to products or tools mentioned.
- **Italic type**—Key terms, new concepts, and important aspects within a statement, a list, and also in tables are emphasized through use of italic type.
- **Figures and tables**—Figures and tables are numbered consecutively in each chapter.

Acknowledgments

Social MDM as a practical concept has evolved dramatically since we first started thinking about this book in 2012. We've had the help of a great number of people in capturing the ideas, business values, architecture and approaches to Social MDM in that time. First and foremost, we'd like to thank Inhi Cho Suh and Brian Mackey for setting the tone of the book with their insightful forewords. We've had the pleasure of working directly with Brian and his team on defining and implementing the vision of Social MDM within IBM: that work has proven invaluable to us. We'd also like to thank our management—Martin Wildberger, Dave Wilkinson, Gudrun Zeller, and Armin Stegerer—for their support during this project. We've had quite a bit of help from the technical leadership at IBM, in particular, Mandy Chessell, Harald Smith, Sriram Padmanabhan, Tim Vincent, Sekar Krishnamurthy, Shiv Vaithyanathan, Lena Woolf, Bhavani Eshwar, Craig Muchinsky, Dmitry Drinfeld, Wei Zheng, and Upwan Chachra. We owe a special debt of gratitude to Vanessa Wilburn and Kevin Hackett—Vanessa gave us some great ideas about how to sharpen our writing for the different target audiences and Kevin gave us a huge hand in improving the quality of our artwork. The teams at Pearson: Mary Beth Ray, Andy Beaster, and the ever-patient Chuck Hutchinson, and at IBM Press: Steven Stansel, Ellice Uffer, and Susan Visser, went above and beyond to bring this book to life—we are extremely grateful for all their good work.

Undoubtedly we have missed recognizing some of the folks who helped us along this journey—for this, we apologize, because we know you made this a better book. Thanks for all the help, and we hope you enjoy seeing how your ideas and friendship helped fuel *Beyond Big Data: Using Social MDM to Drive Deep Customer Insight.*

About the Authors

Martin Oberhofer works as Executive Architect in the area of Enterprise Information Architecture with large clients world-wide. He helps customers to define their Enterprise Information Strategy and Architecture solving information-intense business problems. His areas of expertise include master data management based on an SOA, data warehousing, Big Data solutions, information integration, and database technologies. Martin delivers Enterprise Information Architecture and Solution workshops to large customers and major system integrators and provides expert advice in a lab advocate role for Information Management to large IBM clients. He started his career at IBM in the IBM Silicon Valley Labs in the United States at the beginning of 2002 as a software engineer and is currently based in the IBM Research and Development Lab in Germany. Martin co-authored the books *Enterprise Master Data Management: An SOA Approach to Managing Core Information* (IBM Press, 2008) and *The Art of Enterprise Information Architecture: A Systems-Based Approach for Unlocking Business Insight* (IBM Press, 2010) as well as numerous research articles and developerWorks articles. As inventor, he contributed to more than 70 patent applications for IBM and received the IBM Master Inventor title. Martin is certified by The Open Group as a Distinguished Architect and holds a master's degree in mathematics from the University of Constance/ Germany.

Eberhard Hechler is an Executive Architect who works out of the IBM Boeblingen R&D Lab in Germany. He is currently on a three-year assignment to IBM Singapore, working as the Lead Architect in the Communications Sector of IBM's Software Group. Prior to moving to Asia, he was a member of IBM's Information Management "Integration and Solutions Engineering" development organization. After a two-and-a-half year international assignment to the IBM Kingston Development Lab in New York, he has worked in software development, performance optimization and benchmarking, IT/solution architecture and design, and technical consultancy. In 1992, he began to work with DB2 for MVS, focusing on testing and performance measurements. Since 1999, he has concentrated on Information Management and DB2 on distributed platforms. His main expertise includes the areas of relational database management systems, data warehouse and BI solutions, IT architectures and industry solutions, information integration, and Master Data Management (MDM). He has worked worldwide with communication service providers and IBM clients from other industries. Eberhard Hechler is a member of the IBM Academy of Technology, the IBM InfoSphere Architecture Board, and the IBM Asset Architecture Board. He coauthored the books *Enterprise Master Data Management* (IBM Press, 2008) and *The Art of Enterprise Information Architecture: A Systems-Based Approach for Unlocking Business Insight* (IBM Press, 2010). He holds a master's degree (Diplom-Mathematiker) in Pure Mathematics and a bachelor's degree (Diplom-Ingenieur (FH)) in Electrical Engineering (Telecommunications).

Ivan Milman is a Senior Technical Staff Member at IBM working as a security and governance architect for IBM's Master Data Management (MDM) and InfoSphere product groups. Ivan co-authored the leading book on MDM: *Enterprise Master Data Management: SOA Approach to Managing Core Information* (IBM Press, 2008). Over the course of his career, Ivan has worked on a variety of distributed systems and security technology, including OS/2® Networking, DCE, IBM Global Sign-On, and Tivoli® Access Manager. Ivan has also represented IBM to standards bodies, including The Open Group and IETF. Prior to his current position, Ivan was the lead architect for the IBM Tivoli Access Manager family of security products. Ivan is a member of the IBM Academy of Technology and the IBM Data Governance Council. Ivan is a Certified Information Systems Security Professional and a Master Inventor at IBM, and has been granted 14 U.S. patents. Ivan's current focus is the integration of InfoSphere technology, including reference data management, data quality and security tools, and information governance processes.

Scott Schumacher, Ph.D., is an IBM Distinguished Engineer, the InfoSphere MDM Chief Scientist, and a technology expert specializing in statistical matching algorithms for healthcare, enterprise, and public sector solutions. For more than 20 years, Dr. Schumacher has been heavily involved in research, development, testing, and implementation of complex data analysis solutions, including work commissioned by the Department of Defense. As chief scientist, Scott is responsible for the InfoSphere MDM product architecture. He is also responsible for the research and development of the InfoSphere Initiate matching algorithms, and holds multiple patents in the entity resolution area. Scott has a Bachelor of Science degree in Mathematics from the University of California, Davis, and received his Master of Arts and Doctorate degrees in Mathematics from the University of California, Los Angeles (UCLA). He is currently a member of the Institute for Mathematical Statistics, the American Statistical Association, and IEEE.

Dan Wolfson is an IBM Distinguished Engineer and the chief architect/CTO for the Info-Sphere segment of the IBM Information Management Division of the IBM Software Group. He is responsible for architecture and technical leadership across the rapidly growing areas of Information Integration and Quality for Big Data including Information Quality Tools, Information Integration, Master Data Management, and Metadata Management. Dan is also CTO for Cloud and Mobile within Information Management, working closely with peers throughout IBM.

Dan has more than 30 years of experience in research and commercial distributed computing, covering a broad range of topics including transaction and object-oriented systems, software fault tolerance, messaging, information integration, business integration, metadata management, and database systems. He has written numerous papers, blogs, and is the coauthor of *Enterprise Master Data Management: An SOA Approach to Managing Core Business Information* (IBM Press, 2008). Dan is a member of the IBM Academy of Technology Leadership Team and an IBM Master Inventor. In 2010, Dan was also recognized by the Association of Computing Machinery (ACM) as an ACM Distinguished Engineer.

CHAPTER 1

Introduction to Social MDM

In this chapter, we discuss how enterprises are looking to gain new insights on their customers and products from non-traditional data sources. We look at the role of traditional MDM in providing a single source of information on customers and products along with the business value derived from traditional MDM. Finally we show that incorporating the new insights available from external sources into MDM—leading to Social MDM—allows organizations to achieve a new level of customer interaction.

Social MDM represents a significant milestone in the ongoing quest of companies to improve customer relationships and service through a deeper understanding of their customers—extending that understanding beyond the traditional boundaries of the enterprise.

Definition of Social MDM

As companies have adopted customer-centric approaches, such as Master Data Management (MDM), to their information systems and processes, they have also begun exploring new techniques for developing actionable insights about their customers. We use the term customer to refer to both individuals and organizational customers. Employees working for organizational customers are treated as individuals, with customer-employee relationships also identifying the role they have at such an organization. In-house employees such as sales representatives are also represented as individuals with appropriate roles and relationships to customers. Traditionally, insights have come from customer interaction data such as purchasing history and web viewing patterns, or segmentation information from third-party marketing firms. Whatever the source of these insights, centralizing these insights in MDM ensures that they are available at operational touch points to support directed marketing, buying suggestions, or improved customer service.

The emergence of Big Data technologies has many companies looking to exploit the data outside their firewalls—that is, to take advantage of information on social media, blogs, Twitter, Facebook, and other sources of customer-provided public data. Big Data capabilities allow functions such as sentiment analysis based on natural language processing to be employed at the scale required for these data sources. Examples include measuring sentiment for a particular movie before and after a specific advertising campaign, or measuring trending of sentiment leading up to and subsequent to an event, such as the Oscars or an official product offering.

> The marriage of these two pieces, customer centricity and Big Data analysis, form the core of what we call Social MDM. The goal of which is to move beyond just Big Data analyses to active use of this information to improve the customer experience. As an example, companies wishing to move from macro, or population-based, sentiment analysis to micro, or customer-based, sentiment; or companies wish to understand which of their specific product attributes resonate with the public at large. Social MDM is the integration of these new Big Data technologies with MDM to operationalize these derived insights based on Social Media data.

Customer Insight and Opportunities with Social Data

Customer-facing enterprises have long used data to derive customer insight—insight that is used to improve customer service, to drive up-sell and cross-sell opportunities, or to perform targeted marketing. Data to support these efforts falls into two broad categories. Internal data such as customer interaction history or support logs forms the first category. This data can be used to alert call-center operators to an unhappy customer or be mined for remediation actions. This data is also used in determining product placement either through customer micro segmentations (for example, "customers like you also viewed...") or complex predictive models (such as used by Netflix to suggest the next movie to rent). In the latter example, models are developed by analyzing historical purchase information and then are deployed to customer-facing systems for real-time use. This illustrates a common pattern used for operational customer insight, mining historical data in an "analytical sandbox," and then deploying that insight in operational systems.

Enterprises also know that their internal data presents a very narrow view of the customer. Many seek to augment information on their customers by purchasing third-party information that they can associate with individual customers. This data aids in their segmentation but is typically quite coarse (for example, average income by ZIP Code). This supports macro-level marketing but does nothing for individual customer insight. Thus, until recently, data for developing a detailed, rich profile for each customer came only from internal data sources.

Social media—and consumer willingness to create public data on themselves—changes that. Now key life events (birthdays, anniversaries, graduations), demographics (age, location), interests, relationships (spouse, child), and even influence (followers) exist in public or opt-in sources for growing segments of the populations. Pew [1] estimates that 27% of Internet users in the 18–29 age range use Twitter. In addition, blog posts and replies along with online product reviews provide a rich source of customer sentiment on a wide variety of issues and products.

Exploiting social media for establishing customer insight poses significant technical challenges such as extracting relevant information from unstructured or semistructured data and associating the social media author with a particular customer. Entity extraction, sentiment analysis, and entity resolution deployed on a Big Data platform to handle the volumes of data generated in the social world allow us to tackle these challenges. However, Big Data alone doesn't solve the entire problem. After we've developed these customer insights, they need to become operational so that they are available throughout the enterprise. Enterprises already use MDM to store and distribute deep customer insights, and although social media data brings new challenges, extending MDM to Social MDM provides the final operational step.

Legal and ethical challenges are two additional dimensions for social media exploitation. For example, in some countries, customers might have the legal right to see their full customer information stored in IT systems. It might be a surprise for customers to see the stored customer record enriched with social media information without explicit consent to use that information.

Product Insight and Opportunities with Product Reviews

Retailers and manufacturers use MDM to master product information in addition to customer information. The data typically kept on products in traditional MDM systems tends to be structured and limited to describing the product and its physical attributes (dimensions, weight, and so on). However, social media, product review blogs, and online retail sites provide a new source of information generated by consumers. Today's consumers use technology to research products, compare products from different manufacturers, and compare prices. As they do this, shoppers are generating their own content about products and their shopping and support experiences. The review sections of online retailers, such as Amazon, provide a good example of consumer-generated product information. Here, consumers rank products from one to five and provide a text description of their experience with the products. The following paragraph illustrates a typical review:

> This thermostat is just great. It works well with the Nexia system as would be expected, but also works great with other home automation systems like MiCasaVerde and their Mi Casa Verde VeraLite Home Controller, White and Green, and Mi Casa Verde Vera3 flexible, powerful, and affordable Home Controller (both of which have no monthly fee). It is an easy install if you have a common neutral wire and looks nice when installed. Responds instantly to your command over Z-Wave and is a terrific way to save a lot of money on your electric bill.

This review contains two types of product attributes useful to retailers and manufacturers. The first of these are functional attributes of the product: the thermostat integrates well with multiple home automation systems in addition to the one recommended by the manufacturer, installs easily, and responds instantly. Functional attributes derived from these reviews would augment similar attributes provided by the manufacturer. The review also contains nonfunctional requirements of interest to the retailer. These represent consumer sentiment about the product such as attractiveness ("looks nice") and economy ("terrific way to save a lot of money").

A second review on the same product may yield a different set of attributes as illustrated by the following:

> Purchased this thermostat since seemed to have decent reviews for use with Nexia Z-wave home automation system. Subsequently realized the Mi Casa Verde offered similar Z-wave utility without the monthly fee. Purchased three and the install went smoothly. Was able to control both on device and remotely via iPhone app.

> I was surprised to learn that the device doesn't allow onboard scheduling. Even controlling the thermostat via the Mi Casa Verde requires complex setup with multiple "rules" in order to create a simple schedule. There is no user friendly network interface.

This review also indicates multiple home automation systems and easy install, along with nonfunctional attributes such as complex setup and not being user friendly.

These two examples demonstrate two technical challenges in extracting product attributes from social media data. The first, similar to finding customer insights, is that the information is available in unstructured text. This requires advanced natural language processing capabilities. The second challenge, different from the customer insights problem, is that these attributes cannot be reliably derived from a single review. This means that extracting usable attributes requires that they be accumulated across many reviews and many review sources, and that the statistics associated with these attributes be retained with the attribute (for example, 80% of reviews claim "easy install," 5% of reviews claim a "difficult install," and 15% of reviews do not mention "install").

Retailers would gain advantage in using these additional attributes primarily in determining product placement and advertising ("easy to install"). Manufacturers would gain significant customer insight from these attributes to support product development, support changes, and improved documentation. Incorporating these attributes into the MDM solution supports their use by all parties.

Traditional Master Data Management

In this section, we introduce (or for some, reintroduce) the concept of *master data*—the core business objects that are reused across multiple business processes in an enterprise. Then we discuss the problems that enterprises have with the proliferation of master data in today's enterprise information systems. Finally, we describe how these problems can be addressed with Master Data Management. For a complete discussion of traditional Master Data Management from an architecture, data quality, and tool selection perspective, please consult the references in the "Additional Reading" section.

Master Data Defined

The easiest way to understand master data is to look at some classic examples of master data. Examples of master data include (but are not limited to):

- **Parties or members:** Individuals or organizations. These are the customers, vendors, suppliers, employees, business partners, patients, employees, and citizens whom your enterprise serves and interacts with. The details of what is associated with a party vary by industry, but the data typically includes demographic information: name, address, phone, email, privacy preferences, and so on. More sophisticated systems (such as customer relationship management [CRM] systems) will have information on customers that is seeded from an analytical system (whether this is a gold customer, for example).

- **Products:** These are the goods and services offered by your enterprise. The information associated with these products can include information such as product description, size, color, price, catalog number, and UPC. Often these products are also grouped and organized in particular ways, such as bundles (Internet service plus telephone plus cable TV from a telecommunication or cable TV provider), or in a hierarchy, such as you would find in an online catalog (for example: electronics ==> phones ==> wireless ==> smart phones).

- **Location:** These are locations of core enterprise assets, which can include your offices, stores, classrooms, loading docks, and so on. Location master data can also be where a customer lives, or where a product is offered for sale, hence tying the location to other master data.

- **Account or contract:** Accounts are a common way to associate customers with the product or service they have purchased (or suppliers with the products or services they deliver to you). Accounts can have information about the terms and conditions associated with the products purchased, who is the primary contact for an account, how the different products are related, and so on.

As you can tell from the different types of master data, it is ubiquitous in an enterprise; indeed, master data is sometimes called the *nouns* or *domains* of the business. But it is the widespread occurrence of master data that is a major problem that enterprises have with master data; the same logical information is present in multiple systems, represented differently, with the data having varying degrees of completeness and accuracy across the different systems.

For example, Figure 1.1 shows four enterprise applications with information about two different customers.

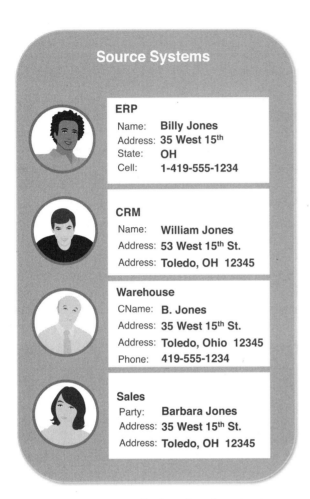

Figure 1.1   Typical application silos of master data

These customers—William Jones, and his spouse, Barbara Jones—are stored in four different repositories (one for ERP, one for CRM, one for a warehouse, and one for sales), with each repository being accessed by a single distinct application, and with the information about William and Barbara Jones varying in a significant fashion across each system:

- **Variation in the values of individual attributes:** William Jones is represented as Billy Jones in the ERP system, William Jones in the CRM system, and B. Jones in the warehouse system. The address is "35 West 15th St" in two systems, just "35 W. 15th" in the ERP system, and incorrect in the fourth as 53 West 15th St..

- **Variation in the format of attributes:** The address for this customer sometimes includes a full street address and postal codes, and other times the address includes just the state. One system includes a country code in the phone number; another does not.

- **Variation in the names of attributes:** The name attribute is different across the systems. It is called "Name" in ERP and CRM, but "CName" in the warehouse and "Party" in the Sales systems. The phone attribute also is named differently ("Cell" vs. "Phone") in two different systems.

- **Variation in the overall set of attributes:** Two systems contain phone numbers; however, two systems do not.

Furthermore, none of this information is shared between systems, because each system has its own repository, so updates made in one system are not available to any of the other systems. So we have multiple systems but no system of record (a single authoritative source for the master data). Finally, there is no guarantee that any of the systems follow a consistent set of rules and policies for governing the correctness and accuracy of updates, nor the privacy and security of the master data (especially crucial with customer data that may be subject to privacy regulation and breach notification laws). What is needed is a way to bridge all of these systems into a logically consistent system, and that's where the technologies and processes of *Master Data Management (MDM)* have emerged. Figure 1.2 illustrates how an MDM system can rationalize the disjoint, inconsistent, and redundant master data records from the various sources into a trusted record in the MDM system.

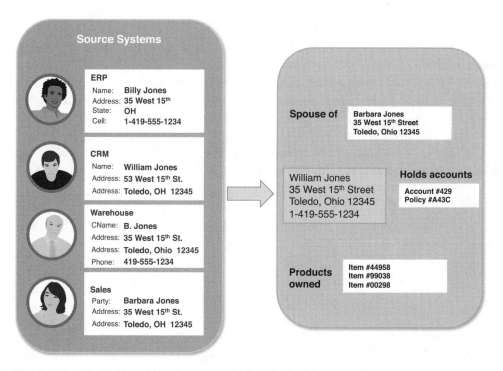

Figure 1.2   Master Data Management providing the "golden record"

Master Data Management—Today

Enterprises employ MDM solutions as a central place to manage core business data—the master data—used by multiple stakeholders. MDM provides the tools and processes around master data, allowing the enterprise to achieve key operational goals: that master data is consistent, for example, ensuring that each department uses the same customer name or product description; that master data is governed so that it is updated or changed in accordance to business policies; and that master data is seamlessly available wherever needed. Essentially, MDM solutions exist as the authoritative source for these core data elements across different lines of business and across multiple business processes.

Traditionally, MDM has focused on key master data needed to run an enterprise. This varies by industry but typically includes the domains of master data discussed earlier, in particular, customer demographic information, supplier or vendor information, product information, and employee information. This scope of master data is often generated internal to the enterprise and flows to the MDM solution where it may be reconciled with other information, verified and corrected, and made available to operational systems. In addition to managing data from these domains (customer, product, supplier), MDM also manages relationship information among these domains. For example, MDM may store links between customers and the products they've purchased, or between employees and the suppliers they manage, or between hierarchies of an organization. Relationships support both operational use cases, such as supporting call centers, and analytical use cases, such as determining credit exposure.

The authoritative information collected, correlated, and managed by MDM is a valuable resource to not only operational systems but also analytic systems. Successful analytics relies on the kind of relevant and current information that MDM provides. Consequently, master data is delivered to data warehouses, marts, and other analytics systems to represent core dimensions in star schemas and to serve as the basis for many forms of analysis—from financial risk analytics to marketing campaign analysis.

As shown in Figure 1.3, MDM systems use a set of layered services, components, and repositories to receive master data from source systems, and then rationalize that data to deliver clean, consistent, deduplicated master data to consuming applications.

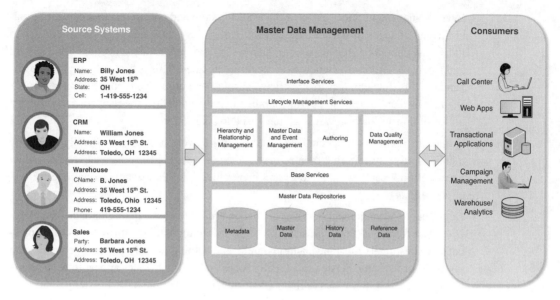

Figure 1.3   Architecture overview for Master Data Management

Let's briefly review each set of services and repositories and discuss how consumers use master data:

- Interface Services are generally the programming interfaces and protocols used by applications to query and update the MDM system. MDM systems typically support a variety of methods, including web services, RESTful calls, messaging interfaces, batch processes, as well as custom protocol translators to enable consistent access to MDM. Custom protocol translations allow applications written to use a specific protocol (such as HL7 for health-care systems) to interact with master data systems without changing the applications. It is important for applications to use the interface services (rather than going directly to the repositories), because MDM maintains the integrity of the master data at a level above the repository.

- Lifecycle Management Services control how master data evolves over time. Master data objects are created, merged, updated, validated, distributed, versioned, and deprecated through the lifecycle services.

- Hierarchy and Relationship Services are used to organize master data in different relationships. For example, people belong to departments, departments belong to organizations, and so on. That is a typical hierarchy. Other types of relationships can be layered on master data; our earlier example shows that William Jones is the spouse of Barbara Jones. People can also have a role in the organization (support specialist). All of this is managed through Hierarchy and Relationship Services.

- Event Management Services allow the MDM system and consumers to receive information about changes in master data and act on them. Systems can register for updates to individual data (a particular person), data types (people, products, accounts, and so on), and receive a notification when those items are updated. This is typically used for governance events (like changes to a restricted account or a duplicate reported for a person) or events based on some business rule or other activity, and allow the recipients to enforce a policy or notify a data steward that they need to take action.

- Authoring Services are specialized instances of lifecycle services specifically for use by a collaborative system that creates master data—systems like those that create product masters (think catalogs at a store) and hierarchies (like the organizational one we discussed earlier).

- Data Quality Management Services are the ones used to clean up master data—standardizing data formats ("Street" instead of "St"), enforcing that key attributes must be present ("All customers must have a last name"), and helping identify and reconcile different instances of the same master data ("Billy Jones and William Jones appear to be the same person—here's how we merge them into a single record in the MDM system.").

- Base Services are the security, privacy, data storage and retrieval, business rules, and other services that MDM uses to deliver clean, consistent, secure master data.

MDM systems store and process the following aspects of master data:

- Metadata describes the structure and format of the master data, and the rules used to apply consistency and validity to individual records and the linkage between them.

- Master data is the underlying set of database tables that store instances of the master data and can potentially store the original source data used to link individual records from a source system to a single master data instance.

- History data is used to store the set of changes to master data so you can re-create how it was changed over time. Audit data is the complement to history data, enabling you to see who changed the master data.

- Reference data, described in some detail later in this chapter, is used to provide meaning to master data. Reference data is critical to customer and product insight because you use it to characterize master data ("John is a **GOLD** customer," "This Samsung Galaxy S4 is **BLACK**, and is **NEW**").

Business Value of Traditional MDM

Discussions about the business value of traditional MDM (see [3] for more information) focus primarily on providing a consistent understanding of customer or product data to enterprise consumers. MDM is the trusted source of complete, relevant, accurate customer or product data. Traditional MDM empowers operational processes, such as customer on-boarding applications, order-to-cash operations, shipping applications, customer service applications, and marketing applications.

Customer Service

In multichannel enterprises, MDM is a critical component in a customer service organization. It provides service operators with a single system to search for a customer and provides them with the complete customer profile that has been synthesized from the multiple systems in the enterprise that contain customer data. Having a single, easily searchable system greatly improves the efficiency in the call center. More importantly, because operators have a complete and accurate picture of the customer, they are able to better react to the customer issue, which enhances the customer experience.

Marketing and Targeted Product Offers

MDM systems have grown to support business marketing operations. A common example is up- and cross-sell campaigns. Because the MDM system contains the fullest picture of customers (but not necessarily complete, which is the theme of this book), it is used to identify customers who, for example, have an automobile insurance policy but not a homeowner's policy nor a life insurance policy. This allows the marketing campaign to target likely purchasers (that is, those familiar with the company but who do not have a particular product). Companies also use MDM to screen third-party marketing lists so that they do not offer products to customers who already have them.

Compliance

Compliance has always been a key business driver for MDM systems. In health-care organizations, MDM is used to track personal health information about patients and who has accessed that information. This capability supports the reporting requirements under the Health Insurance Portability and Accountability Act (HIPAA) [1], which requires organizations to provide this information to patients on demand. In financial services organizations, MDM provides the central repository for privacy consent information for the customer.

Hidden IT Costs

Finally, there are IT and business cost and complexity issues with unmanaged master data. Maintaining incomplete, inaccurate data across multiple systems leads to higher expenses and bad business decisions. As organizations go through mergers, acquisitions, and divestitures, the number of systems that get thrown into the mix only increases, exacerbating these problems.

Case Study: Financial Institution

One of the major MDM success stories is a large North American bank that was experiencing all these problems. It had multiple customer information files (CIFs) with millions of overlapping customer records as a result of mergers and acquisitions. The bank was unable to execute on its compliance initiatives related to "Know Your Customer" and new business processes such as customer-centric product recommendations, consistent information across all channels, and new product innovation. Furthermore, the costs of maintaining the existing diverse infrastructures, copying data between silos, and overall inflexibility were a major drain on profit.

The bank opted to retire the existing CIFs with a single MDM system for its customers, as shown in Figure 1.4.

Financial Institution Case Study

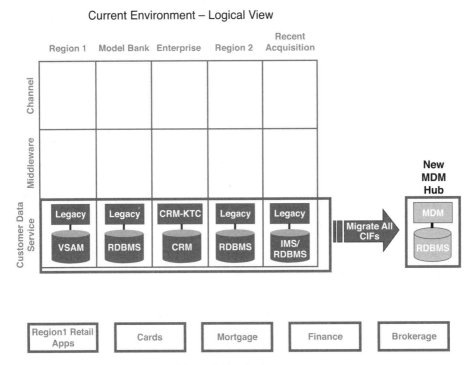

Figure 1.4   MDM case study of financial institution

After implementing an MDM solution, this financial institution experienced a dramatic reduction in IT infrastructure costs due to the consolidation to a single source for customer data. With a consolidated, accurate, complete repository of customer information, it has been able to increase revenue and product-to-customer ratio with targeted (customer-centric) offers. Customer service is now consistent across all regions and lines of business with updates being made in just one system, and the effort and costs of regulatory reports have dropped. New CIFs from other acquisitions have been integrated into the MDM system, expanding the reach of the business. Clean data from MDM is now powering new opportunities (product offers) and business processes (reusing customer profiles for creating different types of accounts).

In each of the preceding examples and in the case study, the business value of MDM is derived from its being the primary source for complete, accurate, timely information. In the following sections, we describe how this information is enhanced by new data about customers from external sources and by the timeliness for using this data through mobile applications.

Social MDM

Available information on either customers or products falls into three broad categories—asserted facts, observed facts, and derived information—as shown in Figure 1.5. Asserted facts include those tracked by traditional MDM that have been pulled from source systems and perhaps verified and modified by data stewards. For customers, these facts include demographic information (name, address, phone, and so on), privacy preferences, account information, and relationships. Asserted information for products would be product description, product attributes (color, weight, and so on), product hierarchies, and identifiers (for example, UPC). This data comes from sources internal to the enterprise or trusted external reference sources (such as Dun & Bradstreet).

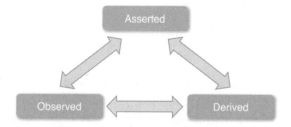

Figure 1.5 Simple model of master data information

Observed facts come from observing customer behavior or product experience, or in general activity data. They can be from internal sources and include data such as buying history or website navigation for customers or product sales data by area. Observations can also be from external data such as Twitter, blogs, or product reviews.

Information derived from asserted and observed facts makes up the third category. Data in this category is used to support customer centricity efforts, fraud detection, and Next Best Action programs. Examples of information in this category include "high value" customer indicators (based on purchasing or account history), "at risk" customer indicators (based on sentiment analysis), fraud scores, key life events (based on social media analysis), micro segmentation information (based on purchase history, viewing history, and social media analysis), and functional and nonfunctional attributes for products.

Traditional MDM focuses on asserted information, basically that which is required to run the enterprise. Social MDM extends this to observed and derived data. Social MDM provides a platform for gathering, integrating, and stewarding the expanded set of customer and product facts and for making them available throughout the enterprise.

One very public (and legitimately controversial) example of combining observed, asserted, and derived information is how the retail giant Target identified pregnant customers and built a custom marketing program for them [2]. Target fed in transactional records of purchases (observed) and information about the gender of the purchaser (asserted information from the Target loyalty cards) into an analytical algorithm that deduced whether a purchaser was pregnant (derived), and her approximate due date (derived). If so, Target would send coupons for pregnancy-related products to the purchaser. This algorithm worked too well: some of the women who received coupons had not told their family that they were pregnant.

Data for operational use has a different set of requirements than data for analytical use, and the Social MDM solution needs to support them:

- The data needs to be distilled to provide structured information.

- The extracted profiles need to be linked to a particular customer or product.

- These insights need to be made available broadly throughout the enterprise.

- The solution needs to support on-the-edge data governance

These are described further below.

Data Distillation

Users of the data are performing real-time activities and do not have the time to read extensive textual information. This structuring of data is accomplished by applying text analytics tools with rule sets designed for social media data. Social data analytics takes text segments, as illustrated in Figure 1.6, and creates structured information, as shown in Table 1.1, for further processing.

This example points out a key aspect of using social media data. This data accumulates over time. Initially, it can be integrated only around social media handles. However, as data accumulates in these profiles, it becomes rich enough to support matching to customer profiles or other social media profiles. Thus, continuous ingestion forms a key part of the Social MDM architecture.

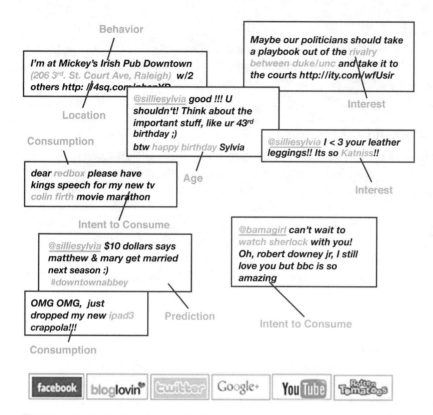

Figure 1.6   Sample social media data

Table 1.1   Information Extracted by Social Data Analytics

Personal Attributes	Buzz/Sentiment	Interests/Behavior
Sylvia Campbell, female, in a relationship	Retweets best friends' comments	Watch movies and TV shows
32 years old, birthday on 7/17	Interest in BBC shows, *Downton Abbey, Sherlock, Fringe*	Romance plots, "hero types," strong women
Lives near Raleigh, NC	Sherlock Holmes, Robert Downey Jr.	Uses iPad2, Redbox, Hulu
College graduate, income 80–120K	*Hunger Games,* J. Lawrence	Shopping, interest in sales/deals
		Duke/UNC basketball

Profile Linking

These extracted profiles need to be linked to a particular customer or, in the case of product sentiment, to a particular product skew. Although normal social media data analytics centers on micro segmentation for marketing purposes, its use in Social MDM targets specific customers or products.

Available Throughout the Enterprise

To be operational, these insights need to be widely available throughout the enterprise. This requirement argues for including derived social media profiles as part of the enterprise customer profile stored in MDM. However, this approach concerns many users in that their MDM solution contains data in which they are highly confident, and the data that is first derived from social data analytics and then linked with matching algorithms lacks the same confidence. Matching solutions for master data typically operate with six nines of precision and recall in high the 90% range. These numbers are not achievable in the social media data realm. This places a requirement on Social MDM to maintain multiple domains of data with varying confidence and to indicate that confidence to consuming systems.

Governance

This leads to the final requirement for a Social MDM solution: governance. Due to the volume of data, proactive data stewardship is infeasible; no resources are available to manually review suspect matches between the social profiles and the customer profiles or to review data where the social data analytics encountered ambiguous text. However, Social MDM can support a "governance at the edge" model. In this architecture, the end user who views the social data and the customer data simultaneously can flag or change incorrect decisions and overwrite the linkages between the data sets or modify the social media profiles (correcting an erroneous text extraction).

The social data analytics, the building of the social profiles, and the matching of the profiles to the customer data all occur in the Big Data environment. Here, two continuous update loops are operating. The first is the continuous ingestion of the social media data. As a profile is added or updated, the system evaluates or re-evaluates the matches to the customer data. Similarly, as customer data is added or updated in MDM, the matches are also re-evaluated.

MDM maintains the linkages between the customer profiles stored in MDM and the social media profiles stored on the Big Data platform, enforcing separation of high and low confidence data.

Business Value of Social MDM

The business value of Social MDM is discussed in detail in the following chapter. At a high level, Social MDM extends and enhances the values brought by traditional MDM and perhaps is best expressed as transitioning from *know the customer* to *know the individual*. This leads to two fundamental benefits to the business, improved customer experience, and improved target marketing.

In Social MDM, external data allow the business an expanded view of the individual customer. Incorporating insights derived from the data, such as culture, life changes, sentiment on particular products, and influencer information into MDM allows the business to personalize each customer interaction. This personalization allows the organization to be more responsive to the customer needs and to provide a uniform experience across all channels.

The second key business benefit to Social MDM is precise target marketing. Knowing the customer's culture, life events, interests, etc., provide the information needed to target customers with offers and information they are likely to use and, as importantly, not extend offers and information that they are unlikely to use

Conclusion

In this chapter, we introduced Master Data Management and the new concept of Social MDM. We showed that Social MDM solutions need new dimensions to think about master data values such as observed, asserted, and derived. Finally, we showed Social MDM solutions require new components in the MDM ecosystem, such as mobile extensions.

References

[1] Pew Research Center's Internet & American Life Project Post-Election Survey, November 14–December 9, 2012. http://www.pewinternet.org/files/old-media/Files/Reports/2013/PIP_SocialMediaUsers.pdf.

[2] Duhigg, C. "How Companies Learn Your Secrets." Retrieved 7/13/2013 from nytimes.com: http://www.nytimes.com/2012/02/19/magazine/shopping-habits.html.

[3] Dreibelbis, Allen, Eberhard Hechler, Ivan Milman, Martin Oberhofer, Paul Van Run, and Dan Wolfson. *Enterprise Master Data Management: An SOA Approach to Managing Core Information* (IBM Press, 2008).

Additional Reading

For this book, we assume in some areas that the reader has some knowledge of Master Data Management, and provide some relevant pointers in case you would like to refresh or review some of the basics for MDM.

For an in-depth discussion on the MDM reference architecture and the embedding of MDM solutions in the broader enterprise information architecture context, we recommend:

Dreibelbis, Allen, Eberhard Hechler, Ivan Milman, Martin Oberhofer, Paul Van Run, and Dan Wolfson. *Enterprise Master Data Management: An SOA Approach to Managing Core Information* (IBM Press, 2008).

Godinez, Mario, Eberhard Hechler, Klaus Koenig, Steve Lockwood, Martin Oberhofer, and Michael Schroeck. *The Art of Enterprise Information Architecture: A Systems-Based Approach for Unlocking Business Insight,* (IBM Press, 2010).

The following books provide an overview on Master Data Management with a focus on data quality specifically for the customer master data domain:

Berson, Alex, and Larry Dubov. *Master Data Management and Customer Data Integration for a Global Enterprise.* (McGraw-Hill, 2007).

Berson, Alex, and Larry Dubov. *Master Data Management and Data Governance,* 2nd edition. (McGraw-Hill, 2010).

This reference provides an overview on implementation and tool selection strategies:

Roebuck, Kevin. *Master Data Management.* (Tebbo, 2011).

CHAPTER 2

Use Cases and Requirements for Social MDM

Social MDM augments traditional MDM by mining and integrating social, mobile, location, and under-utilized enterprise data, creating new capabilities for understanding customers and products. These capabilities enhance both the traditional business benefits of MDM and provide new business benefits. We start by looking at a customer value approach to assessing the relationship between the customer and the business, and then describe in detailed scenarios the two primary drivers for Social MDM—improved customer experience and improved target marketing. We finish by exploring the impact of "social" aspects for MDM to identify the new capabilities a Social MDM–enabled MDM system must provide. The underlying use cases drive changes to the feature set of the MDM system itself (for example, data model enhancements), whereas others arise through the integration of the MDM system with Big Data platforms (for example, analytics-derived relationships that contain uncertainty versus relationships that have been explicitly declared in traditional use cases). Finally, you see how Social MDM can help to transform business models such as the well-known business-to-business (B2B) model into a person@organization model

Business Value of Social MDM—Use Cases and Customer Value

It is often said that the best customer is one you already have. If you treat that customer well, he or she will not only provide an ongoing revenue stream for your business but also can be your best advocate with family and friends. Chief executive officers (CEOs) and chief marketing officers (CMOs) are already realizing this; as one CEO (described in [1]) said, "In the next few years we want to build deep, strategic relationships with our customers, enterprise-to-enterprise relationships where the 'customer is for life.'"

From a business perspective, this is embodied in the concept of *customer lifetime value (CLTV)* [2]—the overall net profit that can be attributed to customers across the lifetime of their relationship (past, present, and future) with the business. Different CLTV formulas use their own components and metrics, but typically they include:

- Base profit
- Profit from increased purchases (cross-sell)
- Profit from price premium (up-sell)
- Profit from reduced costs
- Profit from referrals

Identifying and aggressively pursuing those customers with a high CLTV has a major effect on the bottom line. Reichheld [3] claims that if companies could increase their customer retention rates by only 5%, they could grow their profits by 25%–100%. From a business perspective, it makes sense to take concrete actions to raise the CLTV of your customers in addition to honing your marketing campaigns for drawing in new customers.

Customers, however, initially take a different view of their relationship with the business. Per [4], customers are seeking an experience that delivers "...tangible value in return for customers' time, attention, endorsement, and data." This "tangible value" is embodied in the "Improved Customer Experience" use cases described in the sections below. After you deliver that tangible value, you can build that tighter, more profitable relationship that increases CLTV, as described in the "Improved Targeted Marketing Use Cases" section of the chapter. Social MDM mediates this two-way negotiation between customers and your enterprise so that your business can better match what the customers want with the products and services you offer. This builds trust and confidence with the customers, giving that increase in CLTV.

Improved Customer Experience Use Cases

The first part of enhancing the customer lifetime value is making your business valuable to them through improving their customer experience. By mining and analyzing everything the business knows about a customer (traditional master data, social data, unstructured engagement data like email and chats, transactional data like call data records, and so on), you can create that insight into the customer that delivers a truly effective, personalized experience. Personalization also includes not asking for information you should already have (eliminating buying barriers and speeding time to purchase) and guiding customers to what your analysis shows they will be interested in purchasing. In the following sections, we explore the different aspects of how Social MDM creates that personalized experience.

Showing Cultural Awareness

To personalize interactions with customers in their local markets, you need to know the cultural context of your customers. By interacting with people as they expect to be dealt with by people in their own culture, you personalize the interaction and make them more receptive to dealing with you. Culturally aware Social Master Data Management can help with:

- Cultures in which people have different names: official names, religious names, and work names (for example, Anglicized names for non-European people: RB for Ruo Bo and Jack for Joaquim).

- Honorifics (how they like to be addressed), which can also imply role.

- Different dates that are culturally relevant—religious birth dates along with standard calendar birth dates and local holidays. For example, in some rural areas of India, on a child's first day in elementary school, the government tracks the date of birth computed as the current date minus six years. This date might be different than the religious birth date. Dates can be used as triggers for personalized greetings and offers (more on this later in the chapter).

- Gender that can be inferred through names and other data.

- Language.

Cultural data can be gleaned from social media such as Facebook postings and tweets:

- "You go, girl" implies gender.

- "Congratulations on the birth of Gila Channa, aka Georgia Anne" can imply both religion (Jewish, from the alternate name Gila Channa) and gender (from the name 'Georgia Anne').

Simple ways to use this cultural awareness include greeting customers with the right title and name ("Guten Tag, Herr Doktor Schumacher!"), using their own language, and recognizing events relevant to them ("Happy Chūnjié, RB!" for the Chinese New Year).

Knowing the Important Changes in a Customer's Life

As you can infer from the examples in the preceding section, state-of-the-art MDM systems allow the definition of events on master data. For example, to maintain the customer relationship, you might want to send your customer a happy birthday message along with a personalized offer. The new challenge within a culture-aware MDM system is on which date of birth you want to send the happy birthday message if the receiving person supposedly has multiple dates of birth—a government-related and a religious date of birth. Consequently, some of the event rules need to be defined with a cultural perspective. Events can also be used for target marketing, which we discuss later in this chapter.

Master data with relationships may add anniversaries, spouse's birthday, and children's birthdays. This data can be gleaned through social media or other entity resolutions. We also tend to see other life-cycle events on social media: job changes (LinkedIn), travel, retirement, and new baby. The reality we all face is that we are growing older every day, and our needs, interests, relationships, physical condition, income, home, and so on change as we age. Thus, how companies approach us needs to change over time as well. Acting on these events and changes creates a relationship with people as they are, not as they were.

Knowing Location

Where customers live; where they work; and their favorite places to shop, eat, and hang out all provide opportunities to create a personalized experience tailored to the customers that reduces barriers to purchase, making it almost more difficult for customers *not* to buy your products. Furthermore, knowledge of your customers' habitual locations helps identify potentially fraudulent transactions, saving you and your customers time, money, and inconvenience. Based on master data about a person's home and office location, and social data such as restaurant reviews on Yelp, check-ins on Foursquare, systems of engagement can derive a number of location-specific accelerators, including:

- Shipping costs and times for online orders
- Lists of potential addresses to ship a product (usually seen in an address book)
- Directions to the nearest of your business locations from one of those known customer addresses

Immediate in-person shopping experiences can be greatly enhanced with the combination of master data, personal devices, and location-based services that know your favorite places (and what you think of these places, through online reviews and tweets). These can be driven through the high-quality GPS systems found in most cell phones and tablets, along with in-store positioning devices that can link personal devices to store promotional activities. Some examples include:

- Arriving in the airport boarding area puts your boarding pass on the phone screen without unlocking the phone (faster service by airline personnel). Furthermore, the airline can tweet you an offer for an upgrade, especially if you tweet a comment like, "Man, it is going to be really cramped on the last flight to Dallas tonight!"
- Recognizing your "favorite" coffee store tells the baristas to queue up your favorite drink ("Hey, Ivan, do you want your usual grande mocha with nonfat milk and sprinkles?") and tell your phone when the drink is ready. You can order from the app, pay on the app, and be told when it is done.
- In-store systems can remind you to pick up preordered goods [5]. Or, they can use regular shopping lists plus knowledge of last purchases to guide you to stock up on items you usually buy, or can be used to have your food delivered directly to your table from a restaurant that has counter service.

Finally, from an improved experience perspective, location master data combined with social data can prove effective in fighting fraud. Risk-based authorization and authentication can leverage knowledge about your regular locations to identify suspicious transactions (for example, for Amanda, who lives in London, buying electronics in Brazil coming in through a website in Iran would raise a red flag as a fraudulent transaction). At the same time, social data could show that Amanda posted a picture from Rio, indicating that she really is in Brazil, and incorporating that information into the risk assessment would make it less likely this transaction is bogus.

Knowing if They Are Influencers: Networks and Relationships

One of the aspects of CLTV is the ability of customers to generate more business for you. In Chapter 6, "Social MDM and Customer Care," and Chapter 7, "Social MDM and Marketing," we describe the architecture and concepts behind *influencers* (people who can encourage others to take an action, in particular a purchasing decision) and how the interest groups and social networks broaden the impact of a particular influencer. This extends the common business notion of identifying high-value customers. From a business perspective, we can entice influencers in every interaction across all channels and also understand that members of the influencer networks (for example, relationships) should be treated specially. Some ways the business may act include:

- Encouraging and rewarding positive reviews on social media
- Treating people in a network or relationship well (son of the bank president)
- Putting people at the top of an upgrade list or the front of a line to change planes when the incoming one is late

Knowing What They Have Purchased and What They Think and What They Are Doing

Businesses lose customers if the businesses do not really understand how customers truly *feel* about their products and services, or if customers have a terrible experience with customer support. A typical example cited in [10] is of a high-value customer of 15 years who complained about a delivery process, and was forced through a pre-canned script that just stated the delivery policy. The customer was then further infuriated when a vice president of customer service offered a gift card, paltry compensation when the customer was really trying to help the business fix their broken processes.

For retention, it is crucial to know what products the customers have, how they feel about them, and how to act appropriately. MDM can help with tying customers to products, but Social MDM delivers the *sentiment analysis* from social media and internal data (call records, transcripts of support calls, and so on) that guides customer support and other interactions to make better decisions, not only about those customers, but about given products. From a support perspective, Social MDM delivers a broader view than just the typical structured data for customers, allowing support personnel to understand the customers' true needs and pain points. An example of this is shown in Figure 2.1.

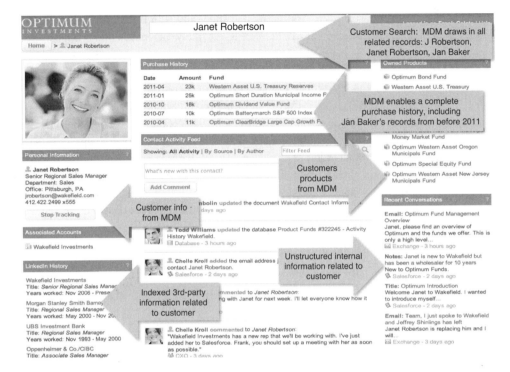

Figure 2.1   Social MDM enhanced support portal

In this portal, the support engineer can see the core customer information (merged across multiple profiles) and products (typical MDM information). But the Social MDM difference is the addition of customer life events from LinkedIn (so the call center might make a different offer because Janet has just changed jobs) and the facts about inquiries the customer has made about other products ("Janet, I see that you've asked about Optimum Funds. Do you need any more information? Would you like to talk to a specialist about those funds?"). This enhanced view of the customer leads to better support and greater retention, cross-sell, and up-sell.

Providing Next Best Offer and Next Best Action

Traditional marketing campaigns struggle with creating a high rate of return (attracting new customers or drawing more profits through existing ones). This is true for both inbound marketing (through customers coming in person, calling a business, or accessing through a website) and external campaigns (direct mail, email, phone, and others). Part of the problem is that the broad brushstrokes with which these campaigns are created makes it difficult to craft a personalized offer likely to entice a customer. Canned scripts by salespeople or contact people who don't understand the details of a product or what the customer really needs are ineffectual.

Logically, a more personalized approach would have a higher chance of success. Amazon has long been a leader in this area through its use of simple analytics ("customers who bought this item also were interested in..."), but now technology has evolved to take this to the next level. As described in [6], one of the hottest trends in personalized marketing is *next best offer* (NBO), or using information we know about the customer, about our products, and advanced analytical models to deliver the right offer, at the right price, for the right person, at the right time through the right channel, in real time. A well-executed NBO can enhance customer loyalty and improve profitability, but a poorly executed one (let's call it the *next worst offer*) can alienate customers and turn them away. Examples of a next worst offer (or action) are trying to sell more products to customers unhappy with your current set, reaching out using an inappropriate contact method, or selling them something they already have or something you should know they don't need.

Improvements in conversion (offer to sales) and profitability are reported in numerous cases (see [5]):

- The grocery chain Tesco used engagement information to target regular customers with special offers on products they usually purchase, but also with analytics-based offers (new parents buy beer at the grocery store because they don't go out to pubs with a new-born) and with flash offers (in-store offers to high-value customers that expire in a short period of time). These next best offers achieved redemption rates ranging from 8% to 14%, a vast improvement over the 1%–2% typically found in the grocery industry.

- International clothing retailer H&M partnered with the online game MyTown. Customers playing the game in an H&M store get bonus points and offers (entry into a sweepstakes) if they check in and scan an item. More than 40% of those who checked in online actually entered the store and scanned an item.

Next best offer can be broadened into *next best action (NBA)* to include activities that (1) are not immediate offers, such as reaching out to a customer related to a complaint or life event; and (2) are related to other forms of action, such as suggesting predictive maintenance. For example, this includes servicing parts that are likely to fail before they do, and what parts should be serviced at the same time to minimize downtime. One manufacturer saved $1 million in two weeks this way. For details on NBA and results, see [7] and [8].

Davenport [9] prescribes four key elements to an effective NBO program:

- **Defining objectives:** Trying to be all things to all people will sink an NBO program. Businesses have to decide if they are focusing on loyalty, attracting new customers, cross-selling/up-selling, and so on.

- **Gathering data:** In this respect, Social MDM drives an NBO program. NBO programs are driven by three types of data:

  - **Customers:** NBOs start with the demographic data found in traditional MDM (gender, age, home location, culture, and so on), but to be truly effective, they need to augment that information with social (Facebook profile, tweets, and so on), mobile,

location, and unstructured data (online reviews, chat transcripts, emails, and so on)—
to know the customers' interests, previous purchases, where they are to make an
immediate offer, and so on.

- **Products:** This is the other value point of MDM to an NBO program. Without standardized master data about your product and services, you can't know the right product to offer customers. You can't mine previous purchases unless the product data is
consistently represented.

- **Context:** This determines how, where, and when are you interacting with the customers. Certain offers are less effective based on channel and circumstances (inviting
someone by SMS to visit a restaurant for a 10% discount during a hurricane is not a
good idea).

- **Analyzing and executing:** This the heart of an NBA/NBO system, using all the social
MDM data plus other engagement data, models, and business rules to create the next
best action. The derived data needed for NBA/NBO (segments, customer lifetime value,
loyalty, and so on) can be stored in MDM for use by the NBA system. Furthermore, any
implementation may have to factor in privacy policies and regulatory requirements; such
information can be sourced from MDM.

- **Learning and evolving:** Associating the responses for NBOs with the master data lets
a business gauge the effectiveness of a program and further refine the target market program in general and for specific customers.

In conclusion, using next best action/offer to increase customer lifetime value is a growing
part of any large enterprise's marketing model, and Social MDM is mandatory for an NBA/NBO
project to be successful.

Improved Target Marketing Use Cases

Marketing support is a key business value of MDM. In traditional MDM, where data about customers is limited to data internal to the enterprise, this support focuses on two use cases. The first
is up-sell and cross-sell campaigns in which marketers query the MDM for existing customers
who do not have a particular product. The second use case is as a repository for customer privacy
preferences that need to be respected during marketing activities.

Social MDM, with its expanded information about customers, greatly expands marketing
support. This new data, combined with mobile data gathering and delivery, creates new opportunities for marketers. As one CMO expressed in an IBM CMO study (see [6] for details):

> The key thing is the ability to proactively use data to understand the needs of a
> specific client and customize and present relevant services and products.

Marketing efforts are undergoing a fundamental shift to focus on individual customers. In
the same study, another CMO said:

> The perfect solution is to serve each consumer individually. The problem? There
> are 7 billion of them.

As a repository for customer information, Social MDM supports this shift to the individual. As we discussed previously, cultural awareness, location, and influencer information as part of the MDM solution lead to improved customer experience. These capabilities also are key to improved target marketing. When combined with sentiment analysis and richer information from social media analysis, they enable the marketing department to provide highly individualized, and often real-time, campaigns.

Micro Segmentation

Folding information extracted from social media greatly enhances the customer profile that can be used in target marketing. Social data analytics can determine additional personal attributes such as gender, relationship status, employment, number of children, anniversary dates, college or university, and many others. This capability can also extract customer interest in sports teams, movies, books, games, theater, outdoor activities, and others. Also available are life events such as weddings, births, job changes, and moves, along with planned travel or other activities.

Figure 2.2 illustrates how even basic segmentation from social media can enhance the customer view. In this example, a bank integrated a set of 11 million social media profiles with its customer MDM data. This figure compares the distribution of different credit card ownership for all bank customers to the distribution of just those customers who are active on social media. The change in the distribution may lead the bank to target customers who have credit card 3 with a different set of offers, tailored to active social media users, than to holders of the other cards.

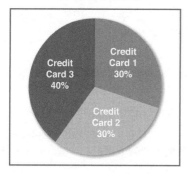
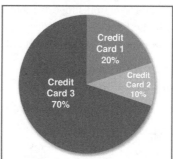

Figure 2.2   Using social media in customer segmentation

This new data provides the marketing team with a more detailed picture of the customers. Social information can be used to include or exclude customers in particular campaigns (don't market baby clothes to a person without children, even if they have recently purchased baby clothes from an online baby shower registry) or provide information for just-in-time marketing.

One large bank used this capability to determine, via processing Facebook and Twitter data, which of its customers were traveling in the near future to offer them travel protection coverage (see Table 2.1). Integrating the social data with the customer data in MDM, creating a Social MDM store, enabled this campaign.

Table 2.1   Use of Travel Records in a Customer Targeting Campaign

Customer ID	Date	City	State	Gender	Lead Type	Stage	Destination City	Destination State
1234	04/29/14	New York	NY	F	Travel	Intent	Boston	MA
1224	04/29/14	Boston	MA	M	Travel	Ontrip	Philadelphia	PA
5234	04/29/14	San Francisco	CA	F	Travel	Intent	Tucson	AZ

Cultural Awareness

As mentioned earlier, cultural information as part of the Social MDM profile is key to treating customers as individuals, which enables the business to establish trusted relationships more quickly. This relationship can be harmed if the cultural information is not considered in marketing campaigns and conversely can enhance the relationship if it is considered. This is especially true for companies that sell cultural-specific items, such as books or artwork that might contain culturally offensive material.

Target Based on Location

Master data on location information supports target marketing in two ways. The first uses static location information, home location, and office location to advertise for local events or services. Examples of this use of location for marketing include:

- Providing notification of sales events near your home targeted to products of interest gleaned from social and other data
- Offering services, such as a mobile car wash, that cover your office location
- Offering products in real time specific to a customer location and, perhaps more importantly, not offering inappropriate items (telling customers in Maui about a sale on snow blowers doesn't leave them with the impression that the company understands them)

Again, using expanded data from a Social MDM system allows more effective targeting and thus increases the share of the customer's wallet, but it also creates a more personalized relationship with customers by making only relevant offers. This makes them feel that the company understands them and thinks of them as individuals.

The second way that location information supports marketing is through interaction with mobile devices. Applications on mobile devices can allow the company to target individuals with fine-grained push notifications. Several customers are experimenting with indoor positioning systems that allow smart push advertisements directing them to nearby sales. This topic is explored further in Chapter 8, "Mobile MDM."

Target Based on Personal Network

One key piece of information available to support marketing is information about the customers' social network. This information can range from basic items, such as the number of followers or friends that a particular customer has, to advanced analytics that determine the customer's influence. Companies are using the number of retweets or reblogs to gauge the influence of an individual customer. Using Social MDM, you also can determine the extent that an influencer has on your existing customer base. The key to enabling a business to make social media data actionable is by integrating it with customer master data.

This information can be leveraged in marketing campaigns, primarily to ensure that influencers receive priority offers and information. A side benefit from Social MDM is that by analyzing if the influencer purchased and how many customers in his network also purchased, you can easily measure the effectiveness of these campaigns.

Target Based on Sentiment on Another Product

Target marketing based on prior purchases is an approach that many companies use ("Customers like you who have purchased product X have also shown interest in Y"). Businesses use purchasing patterns to classify customer by interests, sophistication within those interests, and personality (early adopter and so on). A new dimension added by Social MDM is product sentiment. So now businesses can base the indicators not only on what was purchased, but also what consumers thought about the product and the buying experience.

This data, available from blogs and tweets, provides a means to target individual customers by brands with which they had a good experience and to avoid targeting them for brands for which they have expressed negative sentiment. Again, Social MDM allows businesses to know the customers as individuals and to market accordingly.

Another side benefit of Social MDM is brand protection and brand reinforcement. As noted in Avery [10], brands offer specific types of relationships with their customers (which they characterize in terms of friends, acquaintances, and romantic partners), and if businesses violate the implicit rules that govern such relationships, they can jeopardize the business. Additionally, businesses want to understand the type of relationship the customer has with the brand, so they can create opportunities to move the customer to a higher-margin (or generally more appropriate) relationship. Linking traditional product master data with sentiment analysis on social and enterprise data on those products enables a business to see if they are indeed creating the expected type of relationship with customers. Sentiment analysis combined with traditional master data on a customer reveals the underlying relationship, and helps drive a target campaign to reinforce that relationship, or change to a more profitable one.

Underlying Capabilities Required for Social MDM

The business use cases described above drive a new set of technology capabilities into an underlying MDM system. Some of the social requirements drive changes for the feature set of the MDM system itself (for example, data model enhancements), whereas others arise through the integration of the MDM system with Big Data platforms (for example, analytics-derived relationships that contain uncertainty versus relationships that have been explicitly declared in traditional use cases). Logically, we can group these new capabilities as follows:

- **Location in a very broad sense**—Social MDM needs to understand the culture of a customer (which may be tied to location), the characteristics of the home location of the customer, and then awareness of where the customer is, has been, and where that customer may be going.

- **Relationship discovery, management, and mining**—Customers can have a variety of relationships that are useful to Social MDM: relationships with other people, with your enterprise, with specific products, and with other organizations (in this last case, an employee is acting on behalf of their company). The capability to first understand that a relationship exists and then to represent the nature of the relationship is the underpinning of enhanced targeted marketing.

Cultural Awareness Capabilities for Social MDM

As we have worked with customers around the world, we have encountered numerous situations that have taught us to broaden our understanding, handling, and use of information about people—once again reminding us of the diversity and richness of human nature. Following are some of the things we have learned:

- Birth dates can be surprisingly tricky. In some cultures, people have a religious birth date that is different from the birth date tracked by the government. This could be due to differences between religious calendars and secular calendars, or it could be that the religious birth date is selected for other reasons. Depending on how you ask people for their birth date, you may get either their actual or religious birth date. In other situations, the government may assign a birth date. For example, in some rural areas of India, children are assigned a legal birth date based on their first day in elementary school. So you need to exercise caution in using birth date as an attribute in matching individuals, and you also have to consider how information is gathered.

- Names can also be challenging. In some cultures, people have official and religious names. So again, it is important to understand how and why an individual might give one or the other and perhaps provide the capability to support both.

- In some countries, there are multiple government identification systems for taxation, social services, military service, and other purposes. In some of these schemes, an individual may, for instance, have multiple tax ID numbers: one that represents the individual and another that might represent individuals in their role as head of household or head of clan.

- Different languages and cultures represent family relationships in different ways. In some languages, specific terms and honorifics reflect relationships that don't have equivalents in other languages. Therefore, as you look at understanding relationships and householding, you have to accommodate these nuances.

- Address information is country-specific and, in some cases, also region-specific within a country. Not all countries have postal codes. Many countries allow an address to be descriptive, such as "3rd house behind the church." We have found this in parts Europe as well as other parts of the world.

These examples are not just interesting; they represent new kinds of challenges (and opportunities) in how we represent, manage, and use master data. State-of-the-art MDM solutions have a model-driven approach that enables implementors to change the out-of-the-box data model and regenerate the MDM services based on the data model changes very quickly. So you might wonder: What is the big deal about requirements making an MDM solution culturally aware? Consider the following implications:

- **Matching procedures:** In MDM, matching procedures to detect duplicate records for persons usually use the name, address, and date of birth fields as part of the matching attribute set. If people have multiple names, addresses with different structures for the same country, and multiple dates of birth in some countries, this requires a much more flexible matching procedure. If your MDM system needs to support customer records from multiple countries with different cultures with different attribute set usage, you might need to implement the matching procedures by culture, which in some cases might be aligned with country boundaries and in other cases span across countries.

- **Information governance:** The intent of an MDM system is to be a corporate system. However, if an enterprise operates across regions with different cultures, the organization of the information governance needs to be considered. We have found that information stewards have a social-cultural background based on the culture in which they primarily grew up. Thus, it might be necessary to train information stewards regarding cultural differences in various regions of the world to be able to make informed decisions when processing suspected duplicate records[1] if they are organized in a centralized information governance organization. Alternatively, for globally operating enterprises, having a decentralized or a federated information governance organization with local staff might be advantageous. In such a scenario, local staff with awareness of the local culture can process suspected duplicates for the culture in which they grew up. Of course, this might require stewardship processes that are adapted to the needs for each culture they need to support.

---

1. These are records that may represent the same customer or same organization.

- **Actionable master data:** State-of-the-art MDM systems allow the definition of events on master data. For example, to maintain a customer relationship, perhaps you might want to send your customer a birthday message with a personalized offer. The new challenge within a culturally aware MDM system is on which date of birth you want to send the birthday message if the person receiving it has multiple dates of birth—that is, a government-related and a religious date of birth. Consequently, some of the event rules need to be defined with a cultural perspective.

Locale, Location, and Location Awareness in Social MDM

Working with customers around the world, we also have learned that understanding the different facets of *location* is another key capability for Social MDM. Let's start with a couple of simple observations that are related to the format in which any particular piece of master data is presented. For example, in U.S. culture, a date is presented in the MM/DD/YYYY format, such as 06/24/2014; whereas in the German culture, the preferred date representation is DD/MM/YYYY, so the same date would be shown as 24/06/2014. Similarly, time in U.S. culture is often shown using a 12-hour format with the *a.m.* or *p.m.* suffix, whereas in the German culture, time usually follows a 24-hour representation without the *a.m.* or *p.m.* suffix. *Locale* settings covering preferred presentation language on the screen, preferred keyboard layouts, and so on are part of the *user preferences.* Depending on the culture, locale settings might be more or less complex. For example, in Germany, the only official language is German. In Switzerland, the official languages are German, French, Italian, and Romansh. Given that German and French, for example, have different special characters, such as the German letters ä, ö, and ü, there are already a number of different keyboard layouts to support if an enterprise has information stewards who need to support customers in various regions in Switzerland and Germany. Additional examples include currency, sort order, and so on, which might vary depending on location. A bank in the United States implemented locale settings for its ATM machines. Instead of asking a customer each time for the preferred language shown onscreen such as English or Spanish, reflecting the preferred languages for the various minorities in the United States, the bank decided to allow its customers to set their preferred locales. After a customer makes this decision, each time that customer swipes a credit or debit card at one of the bank's ATMs, the screen presentation automatically shows the preferred locale settings that are part of the user preferences.

A different concept from locale is *location.* Location has multiple aspects. First, it might be necessary to know where the user is located because this information might affect how and how much master data the user might be able to access. For example, a salesperson in an office at work might be able to use a business laptop or business mobile to interact with master data. Outside the company premises, however, access to master data might be possible only with the business mobile. Given the different screen sizes, the combination of user location and device affects the presentation user interface of the master data. Also, the consumption of master data through mobile devices yields new requirements for the MDM system. Sales representatives should have access to customer information only for clients assigned to them. Using *geolocation* services, sales representatives might want to browse the list of contacts of assigned enterprise customers who are within a few kilometers or miles of a current location. For such a feature, the address information within MDM needs to be enriched so that it includes fields for longitude and latitude information and distance calculations based on spherical trigonometry[2] to reflect distance measures on the surface of the earth.[3] For marketing to customers on mobile channels, you might want to send them advertisements based on their current location—for example, shortly before they enter a shopping mall to direct them with special offers to certain stores within the shopping mall. For these scenarios, you need a Mobile MDM architecture, which we discuss in detail in Chapter 8, "Mobile MDM."

Different locations can also mean different cultures or very different socioeconomic status. On a country level, for example, compare the socioeconomic status in terms of sophistication of government, economy, infrastructure, housing, and health care between the United States and countries in Eastern Europe. Even within a country, different demographic groups may represent unique markets served by specialized products. For example, in banking, this might require banking offerings reflecting the requirements of Islam. As a consequence, to effectively run market campaigns, you need to appropriately tailor and offer the products to the right customers. These observations originate from an MDM perspective involving the requirement for location-aware, complex cross-domain relationship management.

Another dimension of location is the political dimension, which is usually expressed in laws and regulations.[4] Examples include data privacy regulations (for example, Federal Data Protection Act [Bundesdatenschutzgesetz][5] in Germany) that are applicable across industries. Industry-specific regulations include the Health Insurance Portability and Accountability Act (HIPAA)[6] in the United States and the consent regulation in banking in Canada. Consent regulation in Canada requires that a financial institution not share customer data across different lines of business unless the customer explicitly gives consent to do so. Other regulations might affect professions. For example, in the U.S. health-care system, a doctor might have a license in two states, but the license in each state allows him or her to offer only different subsets of certain procedures and treatments. Thus, depending on whether a patient visits the doctor in an office in state A or state B, the procedure and treatments received might differ due to the scope of the license applicable in that state.

2. Distance between two points on a spherical object can be calculated using the *Harvesine* formula. You can find an example in [11].

3. If you have access to real-time geocoding services that scale, perform, are cost-effective, and so on, you might be able to avoid storing longitude and latitude in MDM by computing these values each time on request.

4. You should not infer binding legal advice from any of the notes in this section. As an introduction on how to deal with regulations, we recommend [12] and [13].

5. Details can be found in [14].

6. The HIPAA regulation can be found at [15].

Regulations in countries or regions might also affect products a company can or cannot sell. For example, banking products across the various countries in Europe need to comply to the laws in the country in which they are offered and sold. For the telecommunication industries, the EU decided to limit the amount of fees telecommunication providers can charge a customer if they make cross-country calls—an example of a cross-country regulation. From an MDM perspective, these requirements drive additional fields in the data model and sometimes also cross-domain relationships; for example, which product (medical treatment) is permitted by which doctor license (by state) and can be thus offered at which locations (which have to be in the state for which the doctor license is applicable) to a patient (the customer).

Advanced Relationships in Social MDM

In the traditional world of MDM, relationships are usually explicitly known and declared. Examples include spouse of, child of, grandfather of, employed by, lawyer for person, doctor for person, friend of, and so on. Relationships are either entered through self-service functionality in applications like online banking or captured by customer-facing employees.

Social MDM can change this pattern as more and more relationships augmenting master data become *analytics-derived*. For an example, look at Figure 2.3.

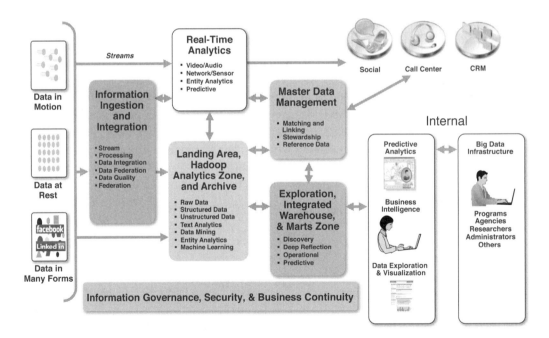

Figure 2.3   Social MDM: Intersection of MDM and the analytics world

With the rise of Big Data, new analytical systems arrived; they can be roughly divided into systems analyzing data in motion (streaming analytics) and into systems analyzing data at rest (usually Hadoop[7]-based). Social MDM integrates streaming analytics and Hadoop-based analytics with the MDM system as shown. Hadoop-based analytics can benefit from trusted master data from the MDM system. Aggregated results such as analytics-derived relationships, sentiment ratings for products owned by customers, and so on, might be operationalized through MDM after the analytics process is done. These two types of analytical systems complement the traditional analytical systems such as data warehouses (DW), data marts, and decision support systems (DSS). The major differences between these two new analytical system types and the existing in-house analytical systems are as follows:

- They process semistructured or unstructured data extremely well. This includes in-house data (for example, voice-to-text translated call-center recordings, log files, emails) as well as external sources (YouTube, Facebook, Twitter, and so on).
- They process many data sources external to the enterprise such as social media platforms.

Person-to-Person Relationships

Social MDM that is integrated with Big Data processing increases the breadth and depth of our understanding of leads, prospects, and customers through these additional data sources and analytics. For example, we can infer relationships that represent an individual's influence as well as where people may have shared interests. Persons and organizations in the real world can have one or multiple representations in the online world. Making matters even more complicated is that there might be a single online representation related to multiple real-world people—for example, a Facebook account used by a household. Depending on the purpose of the online representations, it's more or less difficult to link the online representation to the real-world entity. For example, people are more likely to use their real names and more accurate and complete details such as address or contact details on professional networks such as LinkedIn and are less likely to do so on other less formal social media or online platforms. We call the online representations *social personas*. With this background, Social MDM must have the capability to derive the social personas and their relationships. In addition, Social MDM needs to determine how the social personas are related to the real-world entities represented as persons or organizations in the MDM system. This is a nontrivial step because the information quality of the external online sources might not be as good as the information quality of in-house master data.

Due to the lack of information quality, there also might be confidence issues regarding this information. Linking social personas to customer records in MDM is particularly interesting because if there is a relationship between two social personas such as *social persona x is a Twitter follower of social persona y,* it is possible that you can relate social persona x to a master data

---

7. Hadoop is an open-source platform based on the map-reduce processing paradigm. You can find more information at http://hadoop.apache.org/.

record in MDM but not yet social persona y. This implies you might be able to add a Twitter ID to an existing *customer record x* but not yet a *person-to-person relationship* because you might not yet know who social persona y relates to in the real world. Now with this background, consider the following scenarios:

- By analyzing posted comments related to a blog entry, you can create informal relationships such as *social persona x is blog reader of social persona y*.

- By analyzing *Twitter* streams, you can create informal relationships such as *social persona x* is Twitter follower of social persona y.

    Now assume a person x is on Facebook, LinkedIn, and Xing. On each of these platforms, person x has relationships with other members of the platform, forming a *relationship network*. Given three platforms in this example, there are three relationship networks. First, you can obviously start to derive informal relationships such as *social persona x "Facebook-knows" social persona y* in case you cannot determine more about the relationship or maybe something more concrete such as *person x is friend of person y*. Where it gets even more interesting is if you start to compare the relationship networks across platforms to see if you can identify more information for any particular relationship from one relationship network with information found in another relationship network.

- Now assume *social persona x knows first-degree social persona y* on Facebook. And further assume *social persona y knows first-degree social persona z* on LinkedIn. You can then derive the relationship *social persona x knows second-degree social persona z*. This would be an example for an analytics-derived, *inferred relationship*.

Because the relationship networks are between people, they are also referred to as *social networks,* and today there is a dedicated analytics discipline known as *Social Network Analysis (SNA).*[8] SNA techniques can be applied to external and internal sources. For example, there are techniques to analyze the importance of a person in a social network through analysis of internal email traffic.[9] SNA techniques have been also applied to external sources to discover relationship networks and social behavior from the blogosphere, Flickr,[10] and so on. Analyzing the relationships between people and drawing graphs for the visualization of networks are not the only types of analytics performed. Identifying influencers, experts, and social butterflies[11] is another set of common analytics applied to social networks. Analysis of who is sharing data with whom based

8. Due to the importance of this subject, there are even dedicated research conferences on this topic today. You can find one example at http://www.asonam2014.org/.

9. This is discussed in detail in [16].

10. For more details regarding how social networks and relationships can be derived or used to study behavior, see [17] and [18].

11. *Social butterflies* are also known as *celebrities.* You can find a method regarding how they can be identified in [19].

on close versus less close relationships on social media platforms[12] is one example studied to understand privacy behavior. SNA is also applied to the domain of corporate governance, where researchers study how interlocking directorates[13] and company profitability are related to each other.

Not surprisingly, deep understanding of social networks is one of the most valuable information assets for companies such as Facebook which make money through smart placement of advertisements. However, in other industries such as telecommunication,[14] SNA is also done because insight into social relationship networks helps to improve business results in two areas. First, targeting friends of existing customers could help to gain new customers. Second, SNA is useful in the area of churn analytics. If all friends of a person switch from your telecommunications company to a competitor, for example, it's statistically likely that that person will churn soon as well. So by monitoring if a lot of relationships for a person go away, you know that this customer is becoming a candidate for churn. You can find more details regarding this topic in Chapter 7, "Social MDM and Marketing."

For Social MDM, a rich set of analytical capabilities to analyze all dimensions of relationships between people is a necessity. The analytical capabilities used are often deployed on streaming and Hadoop-based analytical systems that are integrated with the MDM system. The results of the social analytics are operationalized through the MDM system, which is already integrated with operational systems such as call centers, order entry systems, and sales systems.

Person-to-Product Relationships: Sentiment

From 2000 to 2007, MDM had two primary implementation types: customer data integration (CDI) focused on customer master data and product information management (PIM) focused on product master data. Looking back, we can see there were two primary reasons for this. First, the early adaptors of MDM settled on the master data domain and started to validate if the MDM concept really works. Second, most commercial software vendors during that era focused their efforts in one master data domain at the expense of the other master data domains. Today, most major commercial software vendors for MDM offer software for multidomain implementations. Critical features include:

- Enabling relationships within a domain, such as product bundles for the product master data domain. Depending on the industry, product bundles might be quite different things. In the telecommunications industry, a product bundle might be composed of a smart phone and a certain subscription plan. In the automotive industry, a product bundle might be a repair kit composed of several parts that need to be replaced at the same time if any one of them breaks.

12. For an example on photo sharing among Facebook users and the influence of how close people know each other, see [20].
13. See [21] on this topic.
14. For an introduction to SNA in the telecommunications industry, see [22]. Identifying and using local communities in social networks for churn prediction is discussed in [23].

- Enabling relationships across master data domains such as customer-product relationships and supplier-product relationships.

Now let's explore this issue a little bit further. In Figure 2.4, a customer named John Smith purchased two products—a tablet and a digital camera—from the same consumer electronics company. This purchase creates two customer-product relationships in the MDM system. As you saw in the previous section, Big Data analytics are useful to better understand relationships between people. Let's now explore what we can do for customer-product relationships using Social MDM scenarios.

Figure 2.4   Customer-product relationships

In traditional approaches, unstructured data analytics used annotators, dictionaries, or regular expressions to extract names, dates, email addresses, and so on, and tried to link them together to create a record for a person. Now, with an MDM system, each master data record can be treated as a magnet, attracting relevant information from unstructured information where the master data records become the input for Big Data analytics such as entity extraction, annotation, matching, and sentiment analysis. Applying this to the product domain and integrating MDM with Hadoop-based analytics on unstructured data, we can create scenarios such as shown in Figure 2.5. First, online product reviews are loaded into a Hadoop cluster. In addition, product information from MDM also is loaded. Second, with text analytics,[15] the sentiment[16] of the customer posting the product review is analyzed. Sentiment is the expression of an opinion, which can be favorable or not favorable. In the example shown in Figure 2.5, the customer assessed the digital camera as very satisfying, low-end, and cheap. Through fuzzy matching with KB-10 from the product review to the product master data record, the system detects that *low-end* and *cheap* are two attributes that are not yet part of the perception values of the corresponding product master data record and are thus added to it as shown.

15. We are well aware that this is a drastically simplified version of the overall process. For blogs from the blogosphere, for example, we can use a more detailed description regarding how blog spiders find blog entries, apply blog parsers, and then apply data formatting techniques before using blog discovery algorithms to answer questions related to topic detection, trends, and sentiment. For collective wisdom, see [24]. In addition, [24] provides an overview of many relevant algorithms for the blogosphere space.

16. There has been significant research in the area of sentiment analytics. You can find an interesting in-depth discussion in [25].

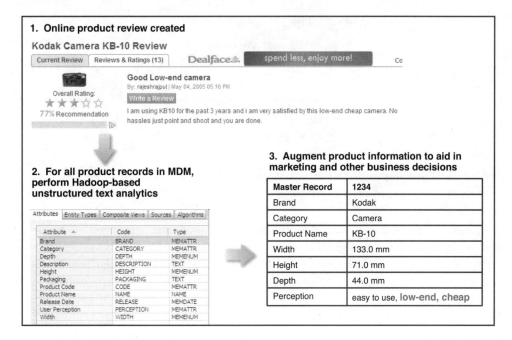

Figure 2.5 Product information in the product hierarchy can be enriched by analyzing customer postings related to the products.

If the social persona who posted the product review can be matched to a customer record in the MDM system, an even finer-grained sentiment linkage is possible, as shown in Figure 2.6. In this case, a multi-occurrence sentiment entity in the MDM data model can be used to track the sentiments of a customer in relationship to one or multiple products. This fine-grained approach is more seamlessly applicable in call-center scenarios where you know who calls through the customer identification process. Thus, sentiment analytics applied to voice-to-text translated call-center recordings is one instance in which this fine-grained approach to capture sentiment by customer per product is more easily established. Similar scenarios can be created by analyzing social interactions between your own employees and customers through the company presence on social media platforms and other online channels. The benefits of doing this are that you can trace by linking the unstructured sources (for example, a voice-to-text translated call-center recording) to the sentiment entry in MDM seamlessly where the customer raised positive or negative sentiments. By evaluating the most recent customer interactions, you can evaluate how satisfied or dissatisfied customers are with your products, which can be used as warning signals for customer churn.

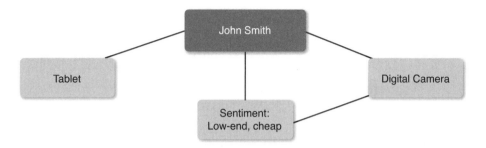

Figure 2.6   Customer-product cross-domain relationships can be enriched with sentiment information.

Finally, if you combine sentiment results in customer-product relationships with the deep understanding of the social network of a person, you can look for the customers who speak the most favorably about your products and who have the largest impact in social communities. These are the customers in the social business world you want to treat particularly well because if they go to the competition, they might influence a lot of others to go there as well. A Social MDM system is well suited to help establish this insight by integrating with Big Data analytics platforms and by acting on this insight by operationalizing it to the front-end applications.

Person@Organization: The Social MDM–Driven Evolution of the B2B Business Model

In the previous sections, we discussed the impact of Big Data analytics driving Social MDM for the B2C case. But this is just the beginning. An even more profound impact emerges on the B2B scenario. Traditionally, enterprises in B2B markets focused their efforts on trying to understand the organization they were doing business with. For that reason, many companies purchased third-party data from Dun & Bradstreet[17] and other providers to get access to a legal hierarchy, for example. However, receiving data from the third-party data providers poses challenges that surfaced while using them in the MDM context. These challenges are as follows:

- **The records purchased were not customer- or product-specific:** You had to process them to see how many matched your records in the MDM system before you could use them to enrich your master data.

- **The records purchased had a degree of staleness in them:** For example, when Daimler purchased Chrysler, requiring the merge of two globally operating enterprises into a single legal hierarchy, the third-party data providers needed time until they could make these changes available.

---

17. Find out more about Dun & Bradstreet at http://www.dnb.com/.

- **The records purchased might be incomplete:** You might not be able to purchase information for all attributes you may be interested in or for attributes you purchased. Values are not available for all records.

- **The records purchased are expensive:** Purchasing large volumes of third-party data for globally operating enterprises is very expensive for batch subscriptions (once a month or quarter) and even more so for real-time subscriptions.

These challenges have led organizations to search for additional data sources to improve marketing campaigns, to improve customer retention, to gain new leads, and to better address fraud and credit risk. And finally, the organizations started to look for third-party data that is either "free" or at least available at a lower cost. Studying information available on the Internet, some people realized that a lot of information is available around the employment history of people in professional network platforms, including when a person switched employers and so on. Furthermore, in forums, blogs, and other sources, people expressed whether they liked or disliked a product and why. Note that these sources have issues related to information quality, currency, and completeness; thus, any information from such sources might not provide the same confidence regarding accuracy, which poses a risk in using it that needs to be managed. Nonetheless, these sources currently drive a paradigm shift from an organization-centric to a people-centric sales model for the B2B case—the foundation for *social business*. Now look at Figure 2.7. In the traditional scenario at the center of the figure, there is the customer organization A for which Mark Miller is a sales representative. Mark added John Smith as his contact at organization A by creating an employed-by relationship between John and his employer.

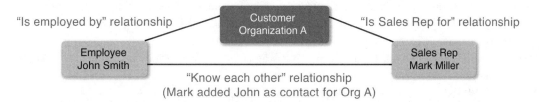

Figure 2.7   Managing person and organization master data: explicitly declared relationships

Now contrast this scenario with the one shown in Figure 2.8.

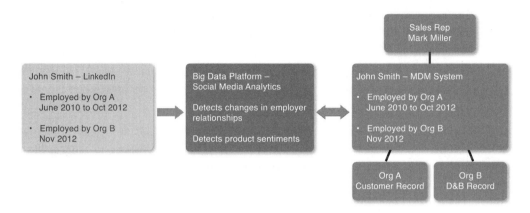

Figure 2.8   Managing person and organization master data: analytics-derived relationships

Here, John Smith is center stage in the MDM system and currently has an employed-by relationship with organization A. Assume that sales representative Mark Miller and John Smith have known each other for a while and have done good business together: Mark sold through John to organization A, and John got very good products and good services, allowing him to be successful at organization A. Periodically in this second scenario, a Big Data analytics platform processes input from social media sources. As part of these analytics, there is a search on whether or not John is still employed by the same employer or if he has a new employer, which occurs in this scenario. Consequently, in the MDM system, the relationship in which John is employed by organization A gets an end date, and a new relationship is created for John, linking him with an employed-by relationship to organization B. At this point, the scenario gets really interesting. If organization B is represented in the MDM system as a lead, prospect, or record from a third-party data source, but not yet a customer, you can now trigger the following events in the MDM system:

• Notify Mark that John switched employers. This information could be sent to Mark as a suggestion to congratulate John in his new role to maintain good relationship status.

• Notify Mark about the fact that the new organization B is not yet a customer. This information should be sent to Mark as notification to take an appropriate sales action.

• Notify Mark that he is now the responsible sales representative for organization B as well (and add the appropriate relationships in the MDM system). The creation of this relationship between Mark and organization B could be an automated rule in the MDM system based on a trigger event that John switched employers.

• Notify (optionally if applicable) that organization A is now assigned to another new sales representative unless Mark has additional strong relationships beyond John with other contacts at organization A (and remove the relationship between Mark and organization

A if applicable). This could be a notification to a human in the role of Sales Territory Manager to review who would be a good replacement candidate for Mark for organization A.

The idea behind this scenario is to reorganize the B2B paradigm into a person@organization paradigm. This is done by modeling the B2B case around human beings and their relationships with organizations over their (professional work) life. This entails collecting the history as well as a much broader profile of a person (and the following are just a view of the basic examples):

- Revenue through this person per employer
- Revenue through this person across his or her employment history
- Products sold through this person at previous employers
- Features of products this person likes or dislikes
- Employees in your own enterprise known by that individual
- Nature of the relationships (strong or weak) between your employees and that individual (analytics on email, voice-to-text translated call-center records, and other exchanges might help to determine this)
- Hobbies and preferences (restaurants, food, and so on)
- Preferred contact and interaction methods and times

Obviously, with this information available, you have a much better understanding of who your most powerful influencers are and with which of your employees they get along well so that you can optimize the relationship management. Also, by tracking individuals' employers, you might get leads not only in terms of new organizations you can start to consider doing business with but also in terms of whom to contact there.

For implementing a person@organization approach for B2B markets, you need to extend the reach of your MDM system by deeply integrating it with a Big Data platform.

Conclusion

In this chapter, we introduced the business value of Social MDM using multiple scenarios. Examples include scenarios such as next best action and next best offer. We also gave an overview of the data and capabilities that we need in a Social MDM system in order to achieve these business values. With a solid understanding of the Social MDM business value, we can now transition into the architectural and technical aspects of Social MDM solutions in the next chapter.

References

[1] IBM Institute for Business Value, "The Customer-Activated Enterprise: Insights from the Global C-suite Study." Retrieved 05/06/2014 from http://public.dhe.ibm.com/common/ssi/ecm/en/gbe03572usen/GBE03572USEN.PDF.

[2] Harvard Business School Publishing, "Customer Lifetime Value Tool." Retrieved 05/06/2014 from http://hbsp.harvard.edu/multimedia/flashtools/cltv/.

[3] Reichheld, F. *The Loyalty Effect: The Hidden Force Behind Growth, Profits and Lasting Value.* (Harvard Business School Press, 1996; revised 2001).

[4] Baird, C., and G. Prasnis, *From Social Media to Social CRM—What Customers Want, Part 1.* (IBM Institute of Business Value, 2013).

[5] Brian, Matt, "Waitrose and Tesco Begin Trialling iBeacons for In-Store Offers and Alerts." Retrieved 05/06/2014 from http://www.engadget.com/2014/05/06/waitrose-tesco-ibeacon-trial/.

[6] IBM, "From Stretched to Strengthened—Insights from the Global Chief Marketing Officer Study." Retrieved 05/06/2014 from http://public.dhe.ibm.com/common/ssi/ecm/en/gbe03419usen/GBE03419USEN.PDF.

[7] Chessell, M., and D. Pugh. "Smarter Analytics: Driving Customer Interactions with the IBM Next Best Action Solution." Retrieved 05/06/2014 from http://www.redbooks.ibm.com/abstracts/redp4888.html?Open.

[8] IBM, "Predictive Maintenance from IBM." Retrieved 05/06/2014 from http://www-01.ibm.com/software/analytics/infographics/predictive-analytics/fixed-before-broken.html.

[9] Davenport, T., L. Dalle Mulle, and J. Lucker. "Know What Your Customers Want Before They Do." *Harvard Business Review* (December 2011). http://www-01.ibm.com/software/analytics/infographics/predictive-analytics/fixed-before-broken.html.

[10] Avery, J., S. Fournier, and J. Wittenbraker, "Unlock the Mysteries of Your Customer Relationships," *Harvard Business Review, July—August 2014, p. 72—80.*

[11] Veness, C. "Calculate Distance and Bearing between Two Latitude/Longitude Points Using Haversine Formula in JavaScript." Retrieved 02/28/2014 from http://www.movable-type.co.uk/scripts/latlong.html.

[12] Tarantino, A. *Manager's Guide to Compliance: Best Practices and Case Studies.* (New York: John Wiley & Sons, 2006).

[13] Shackleford, D. "Regulations and Standards: Where Encryption Applies." Retrieved 02/28/2014 from www.sans.org/reading-room/analysts_program/encryption-Nov07.pdf.

[14] Federal Data Protection Act (Germany, Bundesdatenschutzgesetz). German version retrieved 02/28/2014 from http://www.gesetze-im-internet.de/bdsg_1990/. English version retrieved 02/28/2014 from http://www.gesetze-im-internet.de/englisch_bdsg/index.html.

[15] Health Insurance Portability and Accountability Act (HIPAA) of 1996. Retrieved 02/28/2014 from http://www.hhs.gov/ocr/privacy/.

[16] Lubarski, P., and M. Morzy. "Measuring the Importance of Users in a Social Network Based on Email Communication Patterns." *Proceedings of the 2012 International Conference on Advances in Social Networks Analysis and Mining* (ASONAM, 2012).

[17] Tang, J., J. Wang, T. Wang, and D. Wei. "Efficient Social Network Approximate Analysis on Blogosphere Based on Network Structure Characteristics." *Proceedings of the 3rd Workshop on Social Network Mining and Analysis* (SNA-KDD, 2009).

[18] Jones, L., and K. Lerman. "Social Browsing on Flickr." *Proceedings of International Conference on Weblogs and Social Media* (ICWSM-07), 2007.

[19] Forestier, M., A. Stavrianou, J. Velcin, and D. Zighed. "Extracting Celebrities from Online Discussions. *Proceedings of the 2012 International Conference on Advances in Social Networks Analysis and Mining* (ASONAM, 2012).

[20] Javed, Y., and M. Shehab. "How Do Facebookers Use Friendlists?" *Proceedings of the 2012 International Conference on Advances in Social Networks Analysis and Mining* (ASONAM, 2012).

[21] Chua, A. Y. K., and S. Balkunje. "Interlocking Directorates and Profitability: A Social Network Analysis of Fortune 500 Companies." *Proceedings of the 2012 International Conference on Advances in Social Networks Analysis and Mining* (ASONAM, 2012).

[22] Pinheiro, C. A. R. *Social Network Analysis in Telecommunications*. (New York: Wiley and SAS Business Series, 2011).

[23] Ngonmang, B., M. Tchuente, and E. Viennet. "Churn Prediction in a Real Online Social Network Using Local Community Analysis." *Proceedings of the 2012 International Conference on Advances in Social Networks Analysis and Mining* (ASONAM, 2012).

[24] Lakshmanan, G., and M. Oberhofer. "Knowledge Discovery in the Blogosphere. Approaches and Challenges." *IEEE Computer Society, IEEE Internet Computing,* 14, Issue 2, 2010.

[25] Gregory, M., and P. Hui. "Quantifying Sentiment and Influence in Blogspaces." *Proceedings of the First Workshop on Social Media Analytics* (SOMA, 2010).

CHAPTER 3

Capability Framework for Social MDM

Building solutions for Social MDM require a broad range of technical capabilities. Some of them are existing capabilities such as certain information integration techniques like name and address standardization services, while others like BigMatch are novel capabilities on the Hadoop platform enabling seamless matching between social personas and customers. This chapter provides a capability framework for all capabilities required for building Social MDM solutions.

As a reader, you will learn about all relevant capabilities for Social MDM using a structured approach. The presented capability framework is the key input for the Social MDM Reference Architecture in the next chapter.

Introduction

So far, we introduced the key concept of Social MDM and its business value. In this chapter, we switch gears from a business perspective to a technical perspective, entering the realm of the Social MDM Reference Architecture. This chapter introduces the capability framework for Social MDM and Chapter 4 provides the Social MDM Reference Architecture based on the capability framework. Let's approach this in two steps: First, we gather an understanding what architecture means which leads to the insight that architecture needs to address functional and non-functional requirements. Second, we will then introduce the capability framework which defines the scope for our Social MDM Reference Architecture.

"Architecture" is a term that means different things to different people and is used in a variety of domains such as construction, engineering, etc. For example, an architect constructing buildings applies architecture to houses, skyscrapers, or bridges, whereas an engineer might apply architecture to ships or software. We will use the following definition of architecture:[1]

---

1. Note that this is not the only definition of architecture for IT. You can find a definition from IEEE in [1]. You also can find a very good introduction to software architecture in [2].

The architecture of an IT system describes its elements, their static structure in terms of relationships, and their dynamic behavior in terms of their interactions. The architecture describes the externally observable characteristics of an IT system.

There are two aspects worthwhile pointing out. First, the scope of a system and its elements is a question of *scale*. Consider the following examples:

- A car (the system) is comprised of elements such as doors, wheels, an engine, etc.
- An engine (the system) is comprised of cylinders, pistons, etc.

Above the scale are the requirements for the system. In the example, above the scale of the engine would be the car defining the requirements for the engine like permissible size, required power, etc. *At the scale* of the engine, we would apply the architecture describing the static relationships and dynamic behavior between the elements of the engine system. *Below the scale* of the engine would be the internal design of its elements such as the internal structure of pistons. Using this analogy in a company enterprise architecture[2] would be the complete car, whereas the solution architecture for an eCommerce system might be the equivalent of an engine.

Secondly, creating or modifying an architecture requires balancing technical, business, and operational requirements. Decisions made while creating an architecture affect aspects such as implementation, administration, operation, and maintenance of IT system(s). Clear understanding and prioritization of the different kinds of costs and benefits is critical. Third, sharing and communicating any particular architecture between people requires a description of the architecture. Creating the architecture and its description is an iterative, collaborative process lead by the IT architect by considering:

- **Functional requirements:** What problem is the system solving?
- **Qualities** (also known as non-functional requirements): How well is the system solving the problem? Qualities include performance, availability, etc.
- **Assets:** What is known and available to solve the problem in terms of architecture assets, architecture patterns, etc.?
- **Viability:** Will it work? What is the time to value and total cost of ownership?

The description typically encompasses diagrams on various levels of granularity and a textual description. The description provides insight into:

- *Architectural building blocks (ABBs)* are coarse-grained IT components and technologies.

---

2. In [3], you can find a list of over more than 50 architecture frameworks. The Open Group Architecture Framework (TOGAF) [4], which also provides the Architecture Development Method (ADM), is among the most well-known enterprise architecture frameworks in the industry. More details on TOGAF can be found in [4].

- A *component* encapsulates a set of related and logically grouped functions. A component has well-defined interfaces describing its externally observable behavior. IT architects use the concept of components for modular design.[3]

Usually, the description of an architecture starts with a high level perspective of the solution and is incrementally decomposed into more fine-granular perspectives where each more detailed architecture deliverable is built on a previous higher-level deliverable. For example, the operational architecture for a solution describing software versions, configurations of servers, storage, and networks is based upon the functional architecture deliverable that describes the solution in terms of components and their relationships and interactions.

For the Social MDM Reference Architecture, we thus need to define how it fits into the broader enterprise architecture context (above the scale). We also need to identify the ABBs and components needed for the Social MDM Reference Architecture (at scale) and their relationships and interactions defining the behavior.

A *reference architecture (RA)*[4] encapsulates the reusable architectural aspects of many successful solution architectures implementations that address similar business problems. An RA incorporates valuable insights captured in patterns and best practices from many lessons learned. Thus using a reference architecture as a starting point for a solution design reduces risk, accelerates the architecture design and improves consistency across multiple solutions. RAs contain all relevant components for end-to-end solution design and help the IT architect for scope identification and fit-gap assessments.[5]

The *Social MDM Reference Architecture (Social MDM RA)* is a reference architecture that supports the implementation of multi-domain MDM solutions for Social MDM use cases. We developed it by analyzing deployed MDM solutions to identify best practices and patterns across multiple industries—the latter making it industry-agnostic.

Data Domains

For the capability framework for Social MDM, we need to define the functional scope through requirements. Enterprises have information assets such as data on customers, orders, etc. The various information assets used by an enterprise and how they need to be managed efficiently are the functional scope our capability framework needs to address. Information assets come in different shapes and forms—however, there are data domains by which we can group them. Information assets in a data domain have similar characteristics.

---

3. You can find another good definition for a component in [5].
4. For a good discussion on the subject, specifically in the context of enterprise information architecture, see [6].
5. A fit-gap assessment compares how well the reference architecture addresses the specific project needs (the "fit") and where project-specific additions (the "gap") must be made.

Figure 3.1 shows a classification of different information asset types into the following domains: metadata, reference data, master data, operational data, and analytical data.

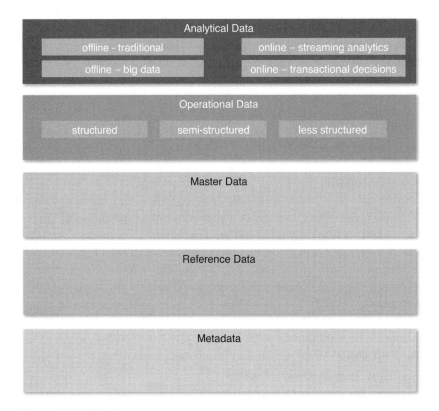

Figure 3.1   Data domains

Let's examine these elements starting from the bottom in Figure 3.1.

Metadata, also known as "data about data," is used to describe data assets and is usually considered to have the following three subcategories:

- **Business metadata:** Business terms, policies, data-quality key performance indicators, and so on all belong in the domain of business metadata. For an excellent book on the topic of business metadata, see [7].

- **Technical metadata:** Logical and physical data models and data model mappings are the most common examples in this subcategory.

- **Operational metadata:** Operations such as the execution of extract-transform-load (ETL) functions produce operational metadata such as duration of the function, number of records being moved, and success or failure status.

Typical functions applied on metadata are data lineage to understand where the data is coming from and impact analysis to understand where, for example, data movement or data-cleansing functions would be affected if a data model is changed.

Social MDM requires a new metadata capability to manage veracity values for certain master data attributes. Where applicable, the veracity values are part of the metadata values for an attribute. Social MDM introduces analytics-derived relationships which would be one example for attributes where veracity needs to be tracked as metadata information to describe confidence, context, and consequence.

Reference data examples include country codes, units of measure, and so on and are used to standardize the value range for an attribute on a predefined set of values. International organizations also provide reference data sets (for example, the International Classification of Diseases [ICD] by the World Health Organization [WHO]; see [8]). Reference data sets might be periodically updated either due to a standard update (for example, ICD9 to ICD10) or due to a need to support a new business requirement (such as a new unit of measure for a new product category). Thus, reference data sets have a lifecycle with versions over time. Until a couple of years ago, many companies did not really care about reference data as a data domain in its own right. This led to data inconsistencies that often surfaced in data warehousing (DW) environments. For example, a report such as revenue by country did not produce expected results if the country codes in the various order processing systems were different. Fixing these reference data inconsistencies in individual ETL processes feeding the DW is a costly exercise. In recent years, enterprises have started to treat reference data as a data domain in its own right, with central government and dedicated reference data management systems often also using commercial solutions that appeared on the market for this purpose. Overall, reference data management is still a relatively new citizen on information architecture.

You can think of *master data* as the golden nuggets of data in your enterprise because master data appears in all critical business processes. Typical examples include customer, vendor, supplier, product, citizen, account, contract, location, employee, and so on. Master data is usually referenced by operational data such as offers, orders, invoices, and bills. For example, an order references a customer entity and one or multiple products. Master data is usually the data domain with the highest data-quality demands because, due to its use in multiple processes, low-quality master data impacts business operations (for example, a wrong address causing a second shipment of a package drives up operational costs) as well as the ability to make the correct analytical decisions (for example, duplicated customer records might not allow proper customer segmentation based on revenue because the aggregation of orders is not working properly). Appropriate, central management of master data has become a common practice in many enterprises today, with a special focus on data quality. Social MDM drives changes for master data as previously introduced in Chapter 2 affecting data model, etc. and more technical aspects are discussed in subsequent chapters.

Historically, *operational data* was a binary distinction between structured (and usually interpreted as relational) and unstructured (and usually content) data. As shown in Figure 3.1, specifically in the domain of operational data, this is now seen as a spectrum from structured through semistructured to less-structured data. In recent years, the view of structured data centered on the relational model has been complemented through use of columnar processing models[6] which have become very popular. The widespread adoption of messaging systems as a communication backbone in SOA architectures over the past decade and specifically the recent adoption of the Internet of Things (IoT) have made XML data commonplace. As a consequence, XML as an example of semistructured data is supported in many major commercial databases. With the rise of the Semantic Web, triple stores became popular. The Resource Description Framework (RDF) for triple stores defined by the W3C (see [10]) became the industry-accepted standard adopted by many vendors.[7] Data processing with triple stores usually is done using SPARQL (a W3C standard; see [14]) instead of SQL. Today people choose the appropriate database engine from the various available engines based on the specific needs of the solution.

Speed for online transaction processing (OLTP) and online analytical processing (OLAP) is a key requirement for engines used for processing well- and semistructured data. Finally, with the rise of the Internet, there has been an explosion of less-structured information previously summarized as content. Examples include videos on YouTube; images on Flickr; maps delivered as images by services like Google Maps; audio content delivered through web radio; and all sorts of free text in blogs, forums, or social media platforms such as Facebook and LinkedIn. Managing less-structured information efficiently—and in an enterprise context also in compliance with regulations affecting retention, for example—requires appropriate capabilities as well.

Traditionally, *analytical data* was managed primarily in data warehouses (DWs) and data marts. A key characteristic of this use case is that it is *offline*. ETL feeds as well as trickle feeds using data replication techniques move a copy of the data from online operational systems such as order entry systems like SAP ERP to the DW. At a later point for daily, weekly, monthly, or quarterly reports, the data is analytically processed long after it has been created and business transactions have occurred.

Two drivers are reshaping the domain of analytical data. The first driver is the need for online analytics. An example is online analytics providing decision support on transactional systems. In a point of sales system, online analytics that deliver decision support functionality can be used to compute additional discounts per customer segment in real-time or provide a next best action to make the customer aware of a related product that also might be of interest based on contents currently in the shopping basket. This type of online analytics is primarily applied to structured or semistructured operational data. The second driver is Big Data with an online (streaming analytics) and offline (data at rest) use case sometimes also including unstructured

---

6. IBM DB2 v10.5 (see [9]) with the BLU technology combines the relational and columnar processing model into a single solution.

7. A commercial example is IBM DB2 v10.1 (see [11]) which added it to its relational database. Other examples, including open source, are SparkleDB (see [12]) and Soprano (see [13]).

data. Due to the size of data involved in some Big Data analytics, the data volume is distributed across large storage networks. For this scenario, a massively parallel processing framework known as MapReduce is applied. Key concepts of MapReduce were initially created by Google. For offline Big Data scenarios with data at rest, the open source Hadoop (see [15]) stack is a well-known runtime. Hadoop-based scenarios are like DW scenarios: the data is first stored on disk and analyzed thereafter. However, the volume of data streams in some Big Data scenarios is so large that it cannot be written to persistent disk storage anymore. In this case, the data stream has to do analytics online—on the spot where the data is created—in real-time to determine any relevant analytical insight and optionally whether this snippet of a data stream is worth persisting.

As you can see, different types of data domains require tailored sets of functions for efficient management of the data in that domain. And as you will see, dedicated engines are needed for each of the data domains and, in some cases, even multiple engines for various specialized purposes within a single data domain.

Differences Between Metadata, Reference Data, and Master Data

In Chapter 2, when we introduced the need to manage master data with cultural and location awareness for Social MDM, many of the examples showed that reference data is key to Social MDM because it is used to define aspects for culture, location, etc. Although there are practitioners[8] who have seen reference data as a data domain in its own right since 2006, others[9] have viewed it as just a relevant aspect of MDM. Today, many practitioners in the information management space see the disciplines of Reference Data Management (RDM) and Master Data Management (MDM) as two distinct capabilities for an enterprise that are related to each other in some areas. With Social MDM, the ability to manage reference data has become even more important—so let's explore what differentiates reference data from metadata and master data to have a good understanding why it needs a dedicated capability:

There are several major differences between reference data, metadata, and master data:

- **Reference data has meaning at the row level:** Each row in a reference data table has reference value, which has a meaning in its own right. For example, 62 might be the reference data value for Germany in one row, and 63 might be the reference data value for France in the next row. This property of reference data does not apply to master data. In a customer master data table, each row represents a customer and has no semantic difference because each record is a customer. However, the property to have meaning at the row level applies to reference data and metadata.

8. One example is Malcolm Chisholm, who published articles articulating the difference between reference data and master data in 2006. You can find more details in [16] and [17].
9. In [18], reference data is still considered a part of MDM.

- **Frequency of change:** Reference data usually changes less frequently compared to master data. Reference data such as country codes, ZIP codes, and titles is fairly slow changing compared to master data records, where customers update their contact details, address information, and the like more frequently.

- **Identification:** Reference data values usually don't need an identifier. A master data record, in contrast, might have multiple identifiers based on the lifecycle status of the entity (for example, a product in product research before it is mass manufactured versus the same product at a later lifecycle stage where it is sold on an eCommerce website) as well as different identifiers in each of the application systems the record is distributed to.

- **User roles interacting with the data:** Master data records are usually created and maintained by either operational business users (call-center employees, bank clerks, product specialists), the "owners" of the data such as customers using self-service portals, or information governance–related roles such as information stewards. In contrast, reference data and transcoding tables are created and maintained by business users and information stewards. Reference data tables are usually not exposed to customers for maintenance.

- **Table width and record counts:** Master data tables might have dozens of columns. In contrast, many reference data tables often have only a handful of columns. Master data tables can have millions of records (the largest we have seen is 1.5 billion records for a consumer electronics company), whereas reference data tables tend to be much smaller in terms of record counts.

Now look at Figure 3.2. Assume a Social MDM scenario where in a Hadoop-based analytics environment, relationships between social personas are derived which are then matched with customer information from MDM. The master data is then supposedly also shared with operational applications. The challenge with reference data arises because each application manages its own version of reference values for the same reference data domain. However, many processes span across application boundaries.

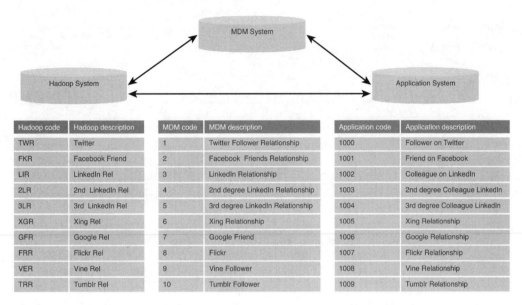

Figure 3.2   The Reference Data Management problem

To exchange product information, the systems must be integrated—often through batch interfaces based on an enterprise information integration platform using ETL techniques or an enterprise service bus (ESB). With unmanaged reference data, this integration need becomes a challenge because you need to define transcoding or mapping tables (see Figure 3.3) that are leveraged by the integration interface, which replaces the source reference data value with its corresponding target system reference data value. This problem becomes even harder because the semantic alignment of reference data values between systems is usually a task for business users, not for ETL or ESB developers. As you can, see business users need to decide if a *LinkedIn relationship* in MDM is semantically the same as a *colleague* in an application. Although it would be nice to just distribute the same set of reference values to all applications in the enterprise to avoid the transcoding problem entirely, doing so might not be possible in all instances due to different data types, field lengths, and so on used to store reference data in the various applications.

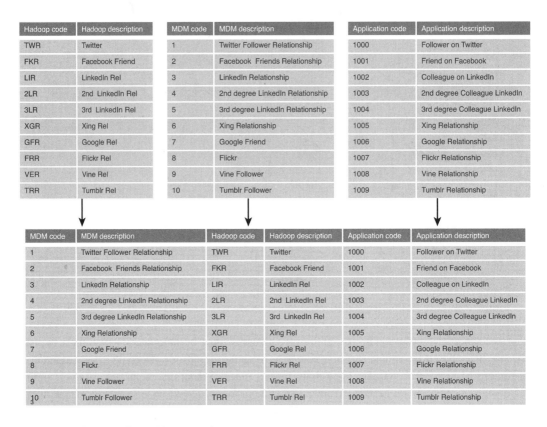

Hadoop code	Hadoop description
TWR	Twitter
FKR	Facebook Friend
LIR	LinkedIn Rel
2LR	2nd LinkedIn Rel
3LR	3rd LinkedIn Rel
XGR	Xing Rel
GFR	Google Rel
FRR	Flickr Rel
VER	Vine Rel
TRR	Tumblr Rel

MDM code	MDM description
1	Twitter Follower Relationship
2	Facebook Friends Relationship
3	LinkedIn Relationship
4	2nd degree LinkedIn Relationship
5	3rd degree LinkedIn Relationship
6	Xing Relationship
7	Google Friend
8	Flickr
9	Vine Follower
10	Tumblr Follower

Application code	Application description
1000	Follower on Twitter
1001	Friend on Facebook
1002	Colleague on LinkedIn
1003	2nd degree Colleague LinkedIn
1004	3rd degree Colleague LinkedIn
1005	Xing Relationship
1006	Google Relationship
1007	Flickr Relationship
1008	Vine Relationship
1009	Tumblr Relationship

MDM code	MDM description	Hadoop code	Hadoop description	Application code	Application description
1	Twitter Follower Relationship	TWR	Twitter	1000	Follower on Twitter
2	Facebook Friends Relationship	FKR	Facebook Friend	1001	Friend on Facebook
3	LinkedIn Relationship	LIR	LinkedIn Rel	1002	Colleague on LinkedIn
4	2nd degree LinkedIn Relationship	2LR	2nd LinkedIn Rel	1003	2nd degree Colleague LinkedIn
5	3rd degree LinkedIn Relationship	3LR	3rd LinkedIn Rel	1004	3rd degree Colleague LinkedIn
6	Xing Relationship	XGR	Xing Rel	1005	Xing Relationship
7	Google Friend	GFR	Google Rel	1006	Google Relationship
8	Flickr	FRR	Flickr Rel	1007	Flickr Relationship
9	Vine Follower	VER	Vine Rel	1008	Vine Relationship
10	Tumblr Follower	TRR	Tumblr Rel	1009	Tumblr Relationship

Figure 3.3   Transcoding table example

Today, in many cases, the reference data values are extracted from the databases, put into Excel spreadsheets, and given to the business users who do the alignment. When they are done, developers put the Excel spreadsheet content into transcoding tables. From that point onward, the business users don't really have access to the transcoding tables anymore without asking the developers. This makes the management of reference data and transcoding tables error-prone, time-consuming, and very cumbersome. And, of course, over time all governance aspects such as versioning and auditability of changes are also missing. For Social MDM, that is an issue because reference data values are added over time (for example, new relationship types, new location types, new religion types, new identifier types), and that information also needs to be reflected in the transcoding tables. Given that MDM systems often have dozens to hundreds of consuming application systems, that many master data attributes are supported by reference data tables, the importance of managing all aspects of reference data for an MDM solution is critical for successful MDM operations.

Now let's complete the picture: the aforementioned reference data issues are also present in initial load scenarios for the deployment of Big Data analytics systems, DW, MDM, or new application systems. In such projects, data that needs to be harmonized across source systems have their own reference data tables. Thus, as part of the data harmonization effort, reference data harmonization across the source systems must be completed using transcoding tables.

We thus see the need to have a full reference data management (RDM) capability in the capability framework providing all relevant features to manage reference data. In [19], [20], [21], and [22], you can see details on available technology and best practices for implementation. In [23], you can read a full problem description and a solution approach for business intelligence (BI) systems.

Embedding of the Social MDM RA in Enterprise Architecture

Enterprise architecture (EA) is the glue between business strategy for a company and the corresponding IT strategy. Over time, EA needs to adapt to changing business needs driving appropriate changes in the corresponding IT ecosystem. EA is usually a multi-layered model to facilitate the communication between business and IT for the strategic direction of the IT environment. New solutions need to align and oftentimes comply with architectural constraints and principles defined by EA. Within EA, usually the following four layers are identified:

- **Business architecture:** The business architecture is the decomposition of the enterprise into the key business functions identifying major process areas. Examples for process areas might be opportunity management, order entry, order fulfillment, or HR. Defining the BA is capturing the business blueprint for a company. On this level, a business capability such as customer centricity might be defined. This would be one of the areas where the Social MDM RA links to the BA.

- **Application architecture:** Unfolding the business architecture to the next level of detail is linking the business domain to the domain of IT. The application architecture provides a complete overview of how the various business processes areas identified in the business architecture are deployed using standard software packages, custom-developed applications, and software as a service (SaaS) solutions. For the definition of the application architecture, decisions define which processes are commodity processes and which ones are key to the enterprise to provide differentiating capabilities in a competitive market place. For example, for commodity processes, oftentimes standard software packages or, with the rise of cloud computing, SaaS packages are purchased. For business process areas that are key to the business, either customizable software packages and/or custom-developed solutions are preferred. CRM applications, eCommerce channels, sales applications, and so on in this space are often consumers of master data—and would benefit from an MDM system that can provide Social MDM capabilities. Chapter 6, "Social MDM and Customer Care," and Chapter 7, "Social MDM and Marketing," describe how Social MDM systems enhance marketing, customer care, and sales systems—typical applications in the application architecture.

- **Information architecture:** Parallel to mapping the process areas from the BA to applications, business objects comprised of tables, attributes, and so on need to be identified because data is used in all processes. This layer describes the data domain and their processing capabilities, data flows between systems, and so forth in support of the BA complementing the application architecture. For an enterprise, the capability to gain insight from data is delivered through this layer. The information architecture covers all the data domains introduced. Not surprisingly, the Social MDM RA is in major parts embedded in this layer.

- **Infrastructure architecture:** This layer provides the architecture for all hardware aspects of IT (server, storage, and network) as well as for many infrastructure software components such as Enterprise Service Bus (ESB), security (LDAP, firewall, and so on), operating systems, and database platforms, etc. Because master data requires appropriate security, the Social MDM RA has some overlap into this layer as well.

Figure 3.4 shows a conceptual intersection of the Social MDM RA in an enterprise architecture context.

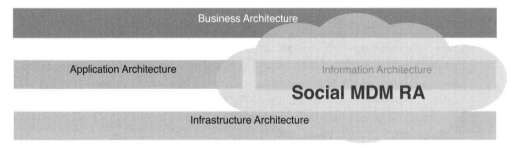

Figure 3.4   Embedding of Social MDM RA in enterprise architecture

With an understanding where the Social MDM RA intersects with enterprise architecture, we are now ready to define it in the following sections.

Capability Framework

Information architecture has functional and non-functional requirements. From a functional perspective, information architecture describes:

- Which data domains are managed by the enterprise
- Means to persist and store the data
- How data is moved between systems
- How human users can interact with the data

From a nonfunctional perspective, operational aspects such as administration, performance, and so on are also part of the information architecture. Figure 3.5 provides a high-level overview of the capability framework for information architecture with functional and nonfunctional capabilities that are in scope for the information architecture.

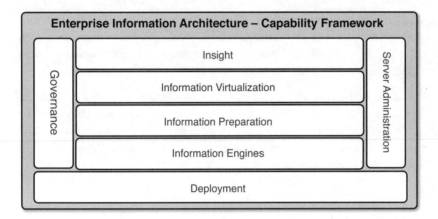

Figure 3.5   Enterprise Information Architecture—Capability Framework

- **Insight:** The insight capability describes the types of processing that accesses or creates information through analysis of existing information.
- **Information virtualization**[10]**:** The information virtualization capability delivers information to consumers in the most appropriate format and manner to match their processing needs, creating and provisioning information supply chains as needed.
- **Information preparation:** The information preparation capability enriches, aggregates, or otherwise enhances information before consumers use it.
- **Information engines:** This capability is composed of specialized server engines for managing information. These engines host the capabilities that sit above them.

10. Most readers are familiar with terms such as *enterprise information integration* as an umbrella term for techniques such as data replication, ETL, and federation. Although these techniques are part of IV, as you will see, IV also covers new aspects with concepts such as "Shopping for Data" and "Data Self-Service Provisioning." These new concepts are driven by observations that companies are not willing to wait six to nine months anymore until an information integration project delivers information assets into a new system such as a data mart for exploratory analytics. Rather, it is expected that business users can deploy a data mart with no (or at least little) IT involvement within minutes or a few hours at most. That requires a substantially higher abstraction around the traditional enterprise information integration techniques, hiding them entirely from the end users. These trends are the motivation for us to move away from the traditional terms.

- **Deployment:** The deployment capability describes the style of computing infrastructure for the capabilities that sit above it.

- **Information governance:** The information governance capability defines and controls how the organization protects, manages, and uses information assets.

- **Server administration:** The server administration capability has the management services for all platforms (software and hardware) to efficiently operate information platforms also fulfilling all nonfunctional requirements such as availability and disaster recovery. This capability is used by infrastructure management services such as those defined in ITIL.

As we explore these areas, you will notice that not every area is unfolded to the same degree of detail. There are two reasons: first, not all aspects of information architecture are equally important to discuss Social MDM use cases. Second, to focus the discussion in this chapter more on MDM-relevant capabilities, we have included some detailed discussions on relevant components in Chapter 5, "Product Capabilities for Social MDM."

Insight

The capabilities in the Insight area represent different operations invoked by users that can modify and enhance information—and often guide us in making decisions. We include both operations that can be performed on information as it flows, as well as at reset, when it is stored. This list is meant to be more suggestive than comprehensive; the capabilities called out in Figure 3.6 represent some of the more common operations that we encounter.

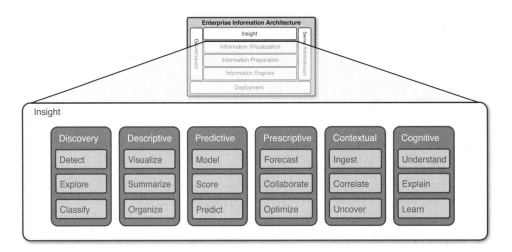

Figure 3.6   Insight—detailed capabilities view

Here are some brief descriptions of many of these capabilities, as shown in Figure 3.4:

- **Discovery:** Detect, explore, and classify information to find interesting patterns, anomalous events, and enrich situational understanding.

- **Descriptive:** Visualize, summarize, and organize information to gain visibility and recognition of what has and is happening.

- **Predictive:** Modeling or data mining is a set of analytical techniques that help us to find patterns within data sets; the resulting models can be codified as scoring functions that enable us to rate a prediction such as the likelihood of a customer remaining loyal. Predictive capabilities generalize this further by leveraging statistical techniques to predict future outcomes based on historical information.

- **Prescriptive:** Once we can predict what can happen, we can apply prescriptive analytics to understand and suggest what could happen if key parameters where changed. Utilizing techniques such as forecasting, collaboration, and mathematical optimization, new potential outcomes can be explored and recommendations for changes can be suggested and mathematically tested.

- **Contextual:** Correlating information ingested from multiple dynamic and static information sources helps us to uncover new relationships and behavior. For example, the situational context in which a marketing offer is received may help marketing determine the likelihood of the offer being accepted.

- **Cognitive:** Using a combination of machine learning, textual analytics, and semantic analysis, cognitive systems can learn, respond to questions and explain results.

The insight capabilities can be called directly through user interfaces or from automated processes. Any new insight created may also be stored for later reuse. The information virtualization capability that follows provides the mechanisms for accessing information and saving new insight.

Information Virtualization

Now let's explore these major components in a bit more detail, starting with the information virtualization capability set shown in Figure 3.7. Information virtualization delivers coherent views of information to the insight layer. The aim is to simplify the access to shared information for business users, particularly for information discovery, analytics, and ad hoc investigations. The information views are defined using the needs and terminology of the consumer and are implemented as a mapping to the real data stores.

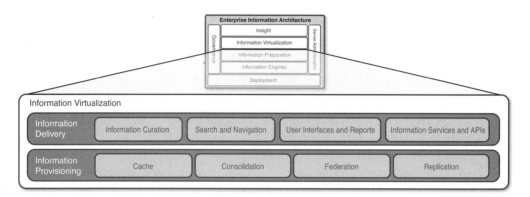

Figure 3.7   Information virtualization—detailed capability view

Information virtualization is divided into information delivery and information provisioning. Information delivery has a primary focus on information access from a consumer perspective.

- **Information Curation:** This capability provides a catalog of information assets. Through this catalog, we can advertise, understand, classify, locate, and request information assets. The catalog is the foundation for a novel concept which we call "Shop for Data." This allows business users, data scientists, and knowledge workers to browse for information assets they need and then make these assets available for their use. Given the pivotal nature of master data for an enterprise, browsing for the appropriate (slice of) master data is relevant for many users. Once the appropriate information assets have been identified in the catalog, business users can then check-out the information assets they need so they can be provisioned into a new mart or sandbox for analysis. The check-out and provisioning of information assets provides a "self-service" experience to business users. The self-service capability chooses the technical provisioning technique (such as ETL or replication) to be used based on the user's intent, the technical environment, and configuration policies that were administratively established beforehand. The job can then be executed. With this form of self-service, users no longer have to depend on IT to find and deliver the information they need—what previously took days, weeks, or even months can now be done in minutes or hours (depending on the size of the data).

  This self-service feature depends on initial configuration and governance of the environment to manage which information can be found and used by what users. An additional side benefit is that the automation provides visibility into who is using what information, and provides a basis for establishing the value of information sets.

- **Search & Navigation:** This capability allows consumers to search, browse, and navigate through information. For example, the ability to browse through a product catalog should be supported by faceted search functionality where keywords (either available to the user or entered by the user on the UI) slice and dice the product catalog accordingly.

- **User Interfaces (UIs) & Reports:** This capability visually presents information to the consumer. A UI can be a rich client UI, a Web UI, or a native UI on a mobile device. Similarly, the results of analytics are presented in reports with appropriate UI icons for bar charts, pie charts, and the like. Note that Social MDM exposes access to master data to customers using mobile devices requiring UIs on mobile platforms such as Android or iOS. Another aspect of Social MDM is that it needs to show master data in context. For example, this could be a composite Web user interface where some widgets receive master data from MDM, and other widgets retrieve related information about last customer interactions and sales figures through services from other application systems such as call-center and data warehousing applications.

- **Information Services & API:** In compliance with design principles such as function encapsulation, data consistency, and cost reduction, it's desirable to implement a given information processing function only once and make it reusable through appropriate services & APIs. Good examples are master data services enabling the seamless consumption of master data wherever needed or reusable data quality services such as name and address standardization services.

Information provisioning provides the technologies to bring information together for use by information delivery capabilities. Information may be physically materialized or just have the appearance of being locally available even though it is not moved. The following categories enumerate some of the most common information provisioning capabilities:

- **Cache:** A cache is a localized, often read-only copy of data. Caches can enhance performance or availability by providing a point-of-use copy of the information. For example, in some eCommerce environments, the customer and product master data is consumed from the eCommerce application through a local cache.

- **Consolidation:** This capability enables information harmonization across multiple sources by creating a copy of the source data, harmonizing it across multiple sources, and loading it to one or multiple targets. Extract-transform-load (ETL) processing is the most well-known example in this capability set.

- **Federation:** This capability hides multiple sources from an information consumer, making them look like a single source system that can be queried. Individual sources are registered with the federation server such that queries received by the federation server can be decomposed in queries on the registered sources.[11]

- **Replication[12]:** This capability is best used to maintain synchronized copies of source data in a scheduled or near real-time manner.

---

11. More details on the federation can be found in [24] and [25].
12. [26] provides an overview over several replication capabilities.

Note that many of these capabilities such as consolidation or replication are available as self-service capability to business users as well since generators have been added to the software platforms providing them, which completely automate their creation and deployment. For example, for consolidation using ETL, the complete function moving the data from source to target can be generated.[13]

The functionality usually provided through an interoperability and connectivity layer such as an enterprise service bus (ESB) is not part of the information virtualization capability set. These capabilities are part of the infrastructure architecture layer from an EA perspective. MDM solutions often use this part of the infrastructure architecture layer to apply publish/subscribe architecture patterns for efficient master data distribution. That's why in Figure 3.4, the Social MDM RA intersects with the infrastructure architecture layer.

Information Preparation

The information preparation capability has six subcapabilities, as illustrated in Figure 3.8 and described in the following list:

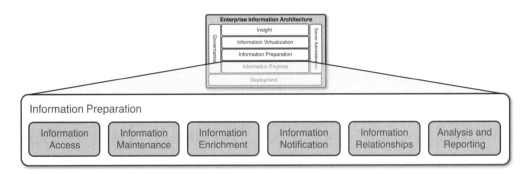

Figure 3.8   Information preparation—detailed capability view

- **Information Access:** Services to create, read, update, and delete (CRUD services) are the responsibility of this functional area. Making master data accessible through novel channels such as mobile providing CRUD capabilities for self-service is critical for Social MDM.

---

13. DataClick is the feature of IBM InfoSphere Information Server providing such a generation capability for consolidation and replication.

- **Information Maintenance:** These capabilities enable consistent maintenance of information by concurrent users, providing functions such as version and locking.

- **Information Enrichment:** Annotating information and enriching a record with values from third-party data sources are examples of this capability. For Social MDM, enrichment of master data from social media sources or call-center dialogs are good examples.

- **Information Notification:** Events, notifications, and alerts triggered on information being created or changed are the most relevant functions provided by this capability. For example, in the domain of master data, events could be life events (such as two customers getting married and forming a household), time events (such as a fixed time deposit being due in one month), or data quality events (such as the matching algorithm flagging two or more records as likely duplicates).

- **Information Relationships:** Linked data, relationships, and time series are typical examples of information relationships. Managing cross-domain relationships is a key area for multidomain MDM. For Social MDM, much richer social network relationships as well as analytics-derived relationships based on Big Data analytics are new important features.

- **Analysis and Reporting:** Before a consumer can read a report, tasks to prepare the report must be accomplished first. These preparation tasks include running analytics, filtering, aggregating, and visualizing the results (not the rendering on the UI, but the computational parts for pie charts, etc.). These preparation functions are provided in this capability.

Information Engines

Information engines are the specialist servers designed to manage information for a specific purpose in the most efficient manner. As you can see from Figure 3.9, we classified these engines into five major categories providing the specialist capabilities.

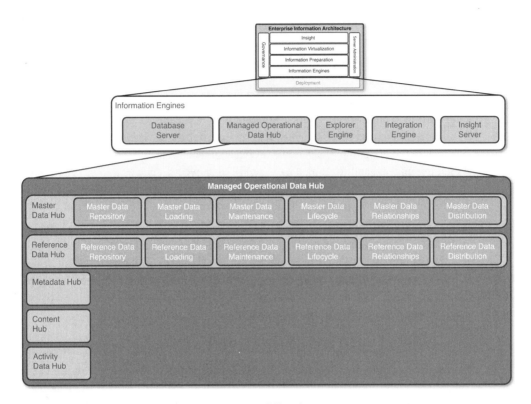

Figure 3.9   Information engines—detailed capability view

From the perspective of Social MDM, we will restrict our discussion to the most relevant capabilities, which means the information engines are discussed on different levels regarding details. As shown in Figure 3.9, we unfold only the Managed Operational Data Hub engine category, and within that, we only explore the Master Data Hub and the Reference Data Hub in detail. From the other information engine categories, we explore some more details for the information integration and the insight server engines in Chapter 5. Beyond what is covered in this section, we do not provide more details for database server and explorer engines for space reasons.

- **Database Server:** Summarized in this engine type are different kinds of database systems such as relational, triple store, columnar, in-memory, and XML databases. Further categories such as operational data stores, data warehouses (DW), data marts, and cubing capabilities are also included. Database server engines are primarily used to manage well-structured (e.g., relational) to semi-structured (e.g., XML, JSON) data. Database servers may be used for both operational and analytical situations.

- **Explorer Engine:** In this engine type, there are primarily three different engines: indexing engines, discovery engines,[14] and search engines. A search engine can be an engine to search the World Wide Web (WWW), such as the well-known Google search engine or an intranet engine able to search through an enterprise's internal wikis, portals, etc. For Social MDM, intranet engines are critical to provide social master data in the context of operational and analytical data from a broad variety of sources. This includes social media sources as well as internal sources such as email and call centers. An example for such an explorer engine is the Watson Explorer technology.

- **Integration Engines:** This engine type provides specialized engines for ETL, data replication, federation, and ESB. These components are discussed in depth in [15].

- **Insight Server:** MapReduce engines such as Hadoop and matching engines are two examples for engines in this category. Engines in this category are discussed in more detail in Chapter 5.

Managed Operational Data Hub

All engine types in the Managed Operational Data Hub category have the following characteristics: first, they usually manage widely shared information assets such as master data and reference data. Second, these information assets are often centrally managed. Third, they are strictly governed systems with appropriate information governance processes defining well-defined management procedures. Fourth, any hub in this category must be able to serve operational workload characteristics by providing real-time, concurrent access. Most of the data domains introduced in Section 3.2 have specialized engines in this category providing domain-specific functionality for appropriate management. The key engine types in the Managed Operational Data Hub category are:

- **Metadata Hub:** This engine type provides functions to discover, create, and maintain metadata for usage by a range of design, governance, and management tools. The engine also provides data lineage and impact analysis functionality and interfaces to seamlessly import and export metadata. A detailed discussion of metadata management capabilities can be found in Chapter 10 of [6].

- **Content Hub:** These engines manage content such as scanned contracts, product repair guide PDFs, emails, videos, product images, and many more less-structured content types within an enterprise. In practice, most of the time Content Hubs are implemented using commercial enterprise content management software solutions.

---

14. For example, IBM Watson Explorer (see [27]) indexes information from various sources using an index engine. Discovery engines can be used to reverse-engineer mappings between systems to identify data dependencies and/or redundancies. For example, InfoSphere Discovery provides such a capability.

- **Activity Data Hub:** Activity Hub engines manage operational data for an operational data store use case. An Activity Data Hub managing customer interaction information is a good example for an Activity Data Hub which is useful for Social MDM use cases. Traditionally, customer interactions in call-center applications, Web logs, sales applications, etc. are not integrated. Thus, if someone needs to understand the status whether or not the customer is likely to be happy, disgruntled, and so on based on the interaction history, a user would need to look into many applications. An Activity Data Hub that receives feeds from all applications where customer interactions occur can provide a consolidated view on all customer interactions. Furthermore, deploying analytics on such an Activity Data Hub scoring the current "customer happiness status" is seamlessly possible because the customer interaction data is in one place and each customer interaction is linked uniquely to a customer record in the MDM system. Based on the customer happiness status triggering appropriate events help to mitigate customer churn, to improve the customer relationship, and so on.

Reference Data Hub

This engine type is dedicated to manage reference data. We won't be able to cover everything relevant for it here—but the following excellent materials provide details from concept introduction to implementation in [19], [20], [21], and [22].

Reference Data Repository

The Reference Data Repository is usually a database server managing the reference data sets such as relationship types, identifier types, and data of birth types (remember—culturally aware customer master data might have more than one to manage).

Reference Data Loading

Reference data already exists in the enterprise in various applications—examples might include product type codes, units of measure, and titles. Also, reference data might come from third-party sources—e.g., country code values according to the ISO standard. In addition to internal and external reference data sets, there also transcoding tables that might already exist in ETL and ESB infrastructures. For reference data sets and transcoding tables, the Reference Data Loading capability provides batch load and delta load functionality to get them into the Reference Data Repository. Optionally, there might be also services to add reference and transcoding information to the Reference Data Repository.

Reference Data Maintenance

Reference Data Maintenance is a group of functions for CRUD processing of reference data, including abilities to approve, manage, and extend reference data sets and transcoding tables.

Reference Data Lifecycle

Reference Data Lifecycle is a group of functions orchestrating, for example, Reference Data Maintenance services, data quality services, and event management services. Approval management, versioning, and the related management of start and end date for reference data sets and transcoding tables are also functions in this group.

Reference Data Relationships

Reference Data Relationships provide functions to manage relationships between reference data sets or hierarchies of reference data. For example, there is a relationship between the reference data set of country codes and the reference data set of provinces and/or states within a country.

Reference Data Distribution

An RDM Hub must be able to distribute reference sets and transcoding tables appropriate interfaces to publish them to integration platforms such as an enterprise service bus (ESB)—one example provided through the integration engines.

Master Data Hub

As you might guess—Master Data Hub engines are the ones we care about most from a Social MDM point of view. A Master Data Hub is used to manage master data. Given that MDM is not a new discipline in the marketplace, we summarize some of the key functionalities required in the following sections. If you need more details regarding detailed MDM capabilities, we recommend you to consult [18], [28], and [29].

Master Data Repository

The Master Data Repository is usually a database server able to manage master data with OLTP-type workload patterns. The Master Data Repository stores the master data instances for the various master data domains such as customer, product, and supplier. If the Master Data Hub has a history feature enabled, the Master Data Repository also stores the history of all changes with a timestamp, who changed it, enabling subsequent point-in-time queries. Over the past several years, two implementation techniques have been used for the Master Data Repository: *physical* and *virtual*. In a physical repository, a master data record is fully materialized and maintained through the Master Data Hub. A virtual repository receives master data records from the sourcing applications used to maintain master data and persists them within the Master Data Hub. Upon request in a virtual repository, the golden master data record is derived in real time and returned to the requester. Note that the golden record is not persisted in a virtual repository implementation and the records themselves often only represent a thin slice of the master data attributes. You can find more details on the implementation styles in [21].

Social MDM adds the following new functionalities to the Master Data Repository:

- **Cultural awareness:** The data model for master data entities requires cultural awareness to be really social because in different cultures personal information might be different. For example, in some cultures, people might have a religious as well as a regular birth date, thus requiring two birth date fields. Address information has quite different structures per country, possibly requiring a country-specific attribute set for some countries.

- **Veracity capability:** As outlined in Chapter 2, for some attributes with Social MDM, we might need to manage confidence, context, and consequence scores. The data model for the Master Data Repository requires appropriate extensions.

- **Separation of external and internal master data entities and attributes:** As we discussed in previous chapters, with the rise of social media, social personas for real people are commonplace. Thus, the MDM system needs to manage a data model for internal master data entities as well as a data model for external master data entities. Depending on the implementation, the master data model can be a superset of all attributes for the internal and external master data entities, or the two models could have some overlap. In the latter case, the data model for the external entities might have some attributes for technical processing that are not used to enrich master data entities managed with the internal master data model. With Big Data functionality, social personas can be captured, becoming external master data records. However, they may not necessarily be linked immediately to internal master data records. As shown in Figure 3.10, because Social MDM is on the rise, the Master Data Repository needs to have a capability to manage internal and external master data records appropriately.

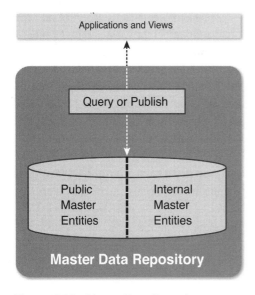

Figure 3.10   Master Data Repository—external and internal perspective

- **Federated access across external and internal master data attributes:** With the logical separation of external versus internal master data entities, the Master Data Repository now requires query and publishing capabilities either by area (internal or external) or seamlessly across the internal and external area.

- **Matching, deduplication, and unmerge of external and internal master data attributes:** While for a social persona, an external master data record might not be immediately matched to an internal master data entity, matching may occur at a later point as information continues to change. Note that matching here is not only the well-known application of deterministic or probabilistic matching algorithms to internal master data records. The "matching" between internal and external master data entities might be events—for example, a customer interacting with a support employee providing a contact method stored in a social persona record, allowing the support employee to link an external with an internal record. Additional rules for matching names, phone numbers, and so on also can be implemented as well. Deduplication between external master data records and internal master data records is not necessarily the same as deduplication amongst internal master data records. For example, deduplication may link the social persona captured as an external master data record to an internal master data record without actually merging them. Erroneous connections can be simply remedied by unlinking the records.

Master Data Loading

Whether recognized as such or not, master data exists in every enterprise and Master Data Hubs provide a better way to manage it. When a Master Data Hub is deployed, master data from existing operational applications such as customer relationship management (CRM), enterprise resource planning (ERP), human resources (HR), or eCommerce systems needs to be extracted, harmonized, and loaded to the Master Data Hub. Master Data Loading functionality is a required capability for a Master Data Hub. The demands of Social MDM lead to additional requirements for this loading capability including:

- **Improved scalability and performance:** For social personas, the number of master data entities may be substantially larger and the frequency of change higher than traditional MDM systems. For example, in the summer of 2013, Facebook reported more than 1.1 billion users (see [30]) and LinkedIn reported more than 200 million members (see [31]), and these social personas are frequently updated. Improving performance and scalability of the Master Data Loading is therefore critical.

- **Increased number of supported encodings and languages:** For a more seamless consumption of culturally aware master data, there might be a need to enhance Master Data Loading capability to support more encodings and languages.

Master Data Maintenance

Master Data Maintenance is a group of functions for CRUD processing of master data, including abilities to approve, manage, and extend master data entities.

Master Data Lifecycle

Master Data Lifecycle is a group of functions orchestrating, for example, Master Data Maintenance services, business logic services based on context, data quality services, and event management services.

Master Data Relationships

The set of functions within Master Data Relationships provide all capabilities to manage master data hierarchies and master data relationships. Examples of hierarchies are product hierarchies (such as UNSPSC, GPC code-based hierarchies, or custom product hierarchies), organization hierarchies (from third-party data sources, for example, like Dun & Bradstreet), or location hierarchies. Relationships can be bidirectional (spouse-of) or unidirectional (manager-of, father-of, and so on). Groupings (such as household) are another instance of relationship functions. As master data deployments have matured, cross-domain relationships are increasingly common (for example, customer-product, supplier-product, vendor-product, sales person-customer organization, and so on). These relationships are explicitly defined—in many cases by human beings as part of the master data authoring process.

With the rise of Social MDM, relationships are often derived or inferred based on analytics. Each internal master data entity might have linkages (a new type of relationship) to many external master data entities since a person might have multiple social personas (we all meet on Facebook, LinkedIn, Xing, and Twitter, don't we?) As the number and complexity of relationships increases, utilizing graphs to represent these inter-relationships becomes attractive and graph navigation becomes important. Social networks are essential for marketing and customer care solutions, as we discuss in Chapters 6 and 7. Lastly, Semantic MDM appears on the horizon, deriving insight from relationship networks using ontologies. We discuss this topic in more detail in Chapter 9, "Future Trends in MDM."

Master Data Distribution

An MDM Hub must be able to make changes such as new master data records or updates to existing ones available for the applications which need to receive them. Therefore, the MDM Hub must have appropriate interfaces to publish changes to integration platforms such as an enterprise service bus (ESB)—one example provided through the integration engines. The interfaces must support proven integration pattern such as Publish / Subscribe.

Deployment

At some point, any information platform needs to be installed and deployed to physical infrastructure. With the rise of appliances and cloud computing in recent years, we see the deployment capabilities shown in Figure 3.11.

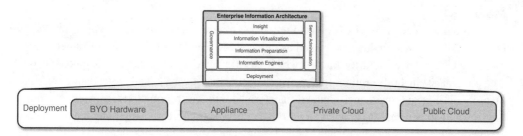

Figure 3.11   Deployment capability view

- **BYO Hardware:** Bring your own (BYO) hardware essentially means you purchase the hardware from your preferred hardware supplier (that might be different from your software supplier), and install the purchased software on it. For MDM deployments to date, this has been the most common deployment scenario.

- **Appliance:** Recently, MDM vendors have started to offer MDM appliances with MDM software preinstalled and preconfigured on hardware that they then offer as an MDM appliance.

- **Private Cloud:** This deployment style utilizes shared hardware resources for optimal utilization, simplified administration to achieve a faster deployment time, and simplify the ability to elastically grow (or shrink) capacity. Deploying an MDM solution with this model is gaining acceptance and is perhaps the second most common deployment pattern.

- **Public Cloud:** A company may purchase infrastructure from a public cloud provider and then follow a traditional MDM deployment style or MDM itself may be offered as a managed service (SaaS). While there has been interest expressed in private and public cloud scenarios, we have yet to see significant deployments.

In IT environments today, we commonly observe hybrid models of the preceding categories. For example, a Social MDM solution might be installed using the BYO hardware approach onsite that feeds other in-house applications such as eCommerce as well as public SaaS offerings like Salesforce.com.

Information Governance

IT governance is a discipline and set of processes to govern the full lifecycle of IT systems from deployment through operations all the way to the decommissioning. A subdiscipline of IT governance is *Information Governance,* sometimes known as *Data Governance.* Information governance is a well-known field, we will focus our discussion on the most essential aspects related to MDM.[15]

About a decade ago, IBM founded the Data Governance Council with approximately 50 companies from many industries as well as universities. The Data Governance Council created the Data Governance Maturity Model, which is a framework covering all relevant aspects of data governance in 11 disciplines that assists in documenting current and target data governance maturity. The Data Governance Council transformed into the Information Governance community,[16] which expanded into a much larger community. Through crowd sourcing the community evolves the Information Governance Maturity Model and shares best practices.[17]

As you can see in Figure 3.12, we focus on six areas, which are as follows:

- **Lifecycle:** Information lifecycle management must balance the legal and business drivers for retaining information as long as it is useful (or required) and then deleting information when no longer needed. Defining, enforcing, and monitoring information retention policies is the primary objective of this category. The term defensible disposal has emerged to refer to the audited deletion of information to conform to legal requirements.[18]

- **Quality:** This category has two subcategories for managing information quality on values and controlling the integrity of the information supply chain. From a Social MDM perspective, both are important. Information standardization (for example, address standardization) and information validation (for example, verification of addresses against postal databases) are commonly used functions. New requirements to support culturally-aware Social MDM have led to a growing demand for transliteration capabilities.

15. Information governance is a broad theme in its own right and has multiple angles to it that we cannot cover in this book, and there is lots of literature out there already. For example, governing information from a security perspective according to international standards such as ISO 27001 and ISO 27002 is discussed in [32]. Building a business case for information governance is discussed in depth in [33]. Big Data, a driver of new information governance requirements, is discussed in [34]. References [26] to [37] provide details on various other aspects of information governance. Reference [38] is a nice blog on the subject by Steve Sarsfield, a well-known expert in this field.

16. You and/or your company can engage in the community at www.infogovcommunity.com/.

17. For best practices, the community also has a YouTube channel. For example, Amy Pfaff from TIAA-CREF provides an introduction to information governance and the Information Governance Maturity Model at http://www.youtube.com/watch?v=8Brj1GCMZaY&feature=c4-overview-vl&list=PLD236E172F1F94865.

18. See http://www-03.ibm.com/software/products/us/en/disposalmgmt/ for a solution in this space.

Transliteration can enhance the accuracy of name matching and de-duplication—especially where different variations of the same name are used. Like many kinds of data, master data can decay over time, so the ability to proactively address decay is important. For example, an individual's email address may change over the course of several years—left unvalidated, our belief that an email address is still accurate decreases. Understanding the typical decay rate, we can pro-actively re-validate such information through normal customer interactions or by providing a self-service channel for customers to directly update their information. One way to deliver such a self-service channel is through an extension of the MDM solution to mobile platforms. Another challenge within Social MDM systems is establishing (and maintain) the confidence in algorithmically inferred or derived attributes. Because master data is required by many operational and analytical systems, information synchronization is mission critical for successful MDM implementations. Special attention must be paid to bidirectional master data synchronizations in coexistence-style deployments to avoid lost update situations through inappropriate resolution of conflicting updates. Information provenance is the ability to understand where particular values, for instance a customer record, came from. Given that relationships in Social MDM scenarios are defined by human beings in some cases and in other cases are inferred through social analytics, information provenance can be useful in developing confidence in relationships based on their source—for instance, we might have more trust in a relationship provided by some social media over others.

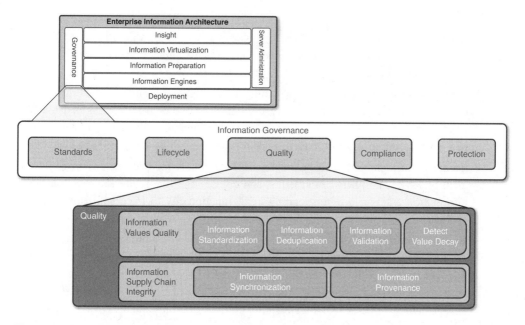

Figure 3.12   Information governance—detailed capability view

- **Compliance:** Compliance can be managed in four steps. First, you need to be able to define, update, and deactivate information policies as needed; this is known as policy administration. An information policy could be a policy indicating that address information has to be standardized. Second, you need to implement the policies—for example, a function that performs address standardization. In general, this step is known as policy implementation. Third, you need to enforce policies by executing their implementation—a process known as policy enforcement. Fourth, you need to measure the results of your executed policies—for example, how many addresses could be successfully standardized. This last step is known as policy monitoring.

- **Standards:** This category contains capabilities to capture information requirements, and to discover and identify information and information dependencies. Defining an enterprise information architecture and governing it over time is an example of the Standards category.

- **Protection:** Controlling the access to information by managing the information usage and privacy. This area is fundamental to Social MDM where privacy and regulatory requirements in many countries define how we can collect, manage, and use personal information.

Server Administration

Any deployed system—and information systems are no exception—requires administrative functionality, as illustrated in Figure 3.13 and described in the list that follows:

- **Install and Upgrade:** Capabilities in this category cover the installation of the software stack if required by the deployment model (for example, BYO hardware), software patching mechanisms, and the ability to migrate systems.

- **Configuration Management:** The ability to configure resources, the ability to turn resources on and off, and the ability to control resources from a workload management perspective are key functionalities in this category. Examples include tuning performance, adding nodes for horizontal and vertical scaling, and improving availability.

- **Security Management:** This broad area of functionality includes identity management, identity propagation between systems, and coarse- and fine-grained access controls to information assets and corresponding audit functionality to trace who accessed what and when.

- **Backup and Restore:** Again, this is another category with a broad range of functionality that includes techniques such as information mirroring, various techniques for backups (hot standby, full cold and hot backups, delta backups, incremental backups), and appropriate restore functionality. The primary purpose of all these functions is to protect against data loss in case of software and/or hardware failures and outages.

- **Problem Determination:** Problem determination starts with the review of log files, so not surprisingly, logging functionality is part of this category. Systems are expected to have various levels of traces and logs that can be turned on and off as needed. Furthermore, for certain types of problems, smart advisers either autocorrect the issue or provide tuning tips (such as for performance problems) to the user to reduce the time needed for problem resolution. A library of known solutions for a particular problem is obviously helpful for a user and included in here, too.

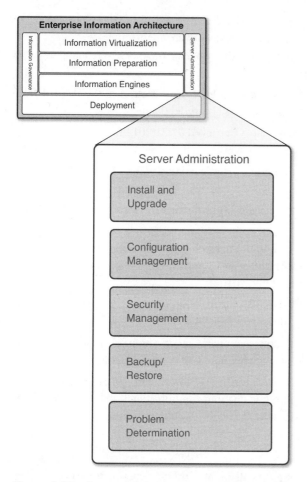

Figure 3.13   Server Administration—detailed capability view

Conclusion

In this chapter, we provided an introduction to Social MDM by introducing the functional capabilities. We explored the MDM Hub and the Reference Data Hub capabilities in more depth since they are particularly relevant for Social MDM solutions. In the next chapter, we will introduce the Social MDM Reference Architecture which provides the architectural framework that allows the user to deliver Social MDM solutions successfully.

References

[1] IEEE Computer Society, IEEE Systems, and software engineering - Architecture description. Retrieved 07/21/2014.http://www.iso.org/iso/catalogue_detail.htm?csnumber=50508.2011.

[2] DeveloperWorks. "What Is a Software Architecture?" Retrieved 07/21/2014 from http://www.ibm.com/developerworks/rational/library/feb06/eeles/.

[3] Matthe, D. "Matthes Framework Map." Retrieved 07/21/2014 from http://dirkmatthes.com/Matthes%20FrameworkMap.pdf.

[4] The Open Group. "Architecture Forum." Retrieved 06/19/2013 from http://www.opengroup.org/togaf/.

[5] Object Management Group Inc., UML 2.0 Infrastructure Specification: Document number 03-09-15. September 2003.

[6] Godinez, M., E. Hechler, K. Koenig, S. Lockwood, M. Oberhofer, and M. Schroeck. *The Art of Enterprise Information Architecture: A Systems-Based Approach for Unlocking Business Insight* (Pearson Publishing, 2010).

[7] Fryman, L., Inmon, W., O'Neil, B. *Business Metadata. Capturing Enterprise Knowledge*. Morgen Kaufmann, 2007.

[8] World Health Organization. "International Classification of Diseases (ICD)." Retrieved 07/21/2014 from http://www.who.int/classifications/icd/en/.

[9] IBM Knowledge Center. "DB2 10.5 for Linux, UNIX, and Windows: DB2 BLU." Retrieved 07/21/2014 from http://pic.dhe.ibm.com/infocenter/db2luw/v10r5/index.jsp?topic=%2Fcom.ibm.db2.luw.wn.doc%2Fdoc%2Fc0060311.html.

[10] W3C Resource Description Framework (RDF) standard. http://www.w3.org/RDF/.

[11] Knowledge Center. "DB2 10.5 for Linux, UNIX, and Windows: DB2 RDF." Retrieved 07/21/2014 from http://pic.dhe.ibm.com/infocenter/db2luw/v10r5/index.jsp?topic=%2Fcom.ibm.db2.luw.wn.doc%2Fdoc%2Fc0060311.html.

[12] SopranoDB. "Soprano: The Qt/C++ RDF Framework." Retrieved 07/21/2014 from http://soprano.sourceforge.net/.

[13] SparkleDB. "Revolutionary Database System. Big Data Problem Solved." Retrieved 07/21/2014 from http://www.sparkledb.net/.

[14] SPARQL. "SPARQL Query Language for RDF." Retrieved 07/21/2014 from http://www.w3.org/TR/rdf-sparql-query/.

[15] Hadoop. "Welcome to Apache Hadoop." Retrieved 07/21/2014 from http://hadoop.apache.org.

[16] Chisholm, M. "Master Data versus Reference Data." Retrieved 02/28/2014 from http://www.information-management.com/issues/20060401/1051002-1.html?zkPrintable=1&nopagination=1.

[17] Chisholm, M. "Reference Data Portal." Retrieved 02/28/2014 from http://www.refdataportal.com/index.cfm.

[18] Dreibelbis, A., E. Hechler, I. Milman, M. Oberhofer, P. van Run, and D. Wolfson. *Enterprise Master Data Management: An SOA Approach to Managing Core Information* (IBM Press, 2008).

[19] IBM. "InfoSphere Master Data Management Reference Data Management Hub." Retrieved 07/21/2014 http://www-03.ibm.com/software/products/us/en/infomastdata-manarefedatamanahub/.

[20] IBM. "InfoSphere MDM Reference Data Management Hub Overview." Retrieved 07/21/2014 from http://pic.dhe.ibm.com/infocenter/mih/v10r0m0/index.jsp?topic=%2Fcom.ibm.swg.im.mdmhs.rdm.nav.doc%2FRDM_Introduction.html.

[21] IBM. "Introduction to IBM InfoSphere Master Data Management Reference Data Management Hub v10." Retrieved 07/21/2014 from http://www.ibm.com/developer-works/data/library/techarticle/dm-1210mdmhubv10/.

[22] Baldwin, J., W.J. Chen, T. Dunn, M. Grasselt, S. Hussain, D. Mandelstein, I. Milman E. O'Neill, S. Pandit, R. Tamlyn, and F. Xu. "A Practical Guide to Managing Reference Data with IBM InfoSphere Master Data Management Reference Data Management Hub." *IBM Redbook,* 2013, http://www.redbooks.ibm.com/Redbooks.nsf/RedpieceAbstracts/sg248084.html.

[23] Milman, I., M. Oberhofer, S. Pandit, and Y. Zhou. "Principled Reference Data Management for Business Intelligence." *Information Quality and Governance for Business Intelligence* (J. Talburt, W. Yeoh, and Y. Zhou, Eds.). IGI Global, December 2013.

[24] IBM Knowledge Center. "DB2 10.5 for Linux, UNIX, Windows. Federation." Retrieved 07/21/2014 from http://www-01.ibm.com/support/knowledgecenter/SSEPGG_10.5.0/com.ibm.swg.im.iis.db.prod.fed.nav.doc/dochome/iiypfnav_dochome.html?lang=en.

[25] Wang, Z., Zhou, Z.: Best practices for using InfoSphere Federation Server to integrate web service data sources. Retrieved 07/21/2014 from http://www.ibm.com/developerworks/data/library/techarticle/dm-1308federation/index.html?ca=drs.

[26] IBM Knowledge Center. "DB2 10.5 for Linux, UNIX, Windows. Replication and Event Publishing" Retrieved 07/21/2014 from http://www-01.ibm.com/support/knowledgecenter/SSEPGG_10.5.0/com.ibm.swg.im.iis.db.prod.fed.nav.doc/dochome/iiypfnav_dochome.html?lang=en.

[27] IBM. "InfoSphere Watson Data Explorer." Retrieved 07/21/2014 from http://www-03.ibm.com/software/products/en/dataexplorer.

[28] Berson, A., Dubov, L. *Master Data Management and Customer Data Integration for a Global Enterprise*, McGraw-Hill, 2007.

[29] Berson, A., Dubov, L. *Master Data Management and Data Governance*, McGraw-Hill, 2010.

[30] Small Business Trends. "Facebook Keeps Growing: Now at 1.15 Billion Active Users." Retrieved 07/21/2014 from http://smallbiztrends.com/2013/07/facebook-reaches-1-billion-active-members.html.

[31] LinkedIn. "200 Million Members!" Retrieved 06/19/2013 http://blog.linkedin.com/2013/01/09/linkedin-200-million/.

[32] Calder, A., Watkins, S. *IT Governance: An International Guide to Data Security and ISO27001/ISO27002*, Editor: Ian Hallsworth, Kogan Page, 2012.

[33] Soares, S. *Selling Information Governance to the Business: Best Practices by Industry and Job Function*, McPress, 2011.

[33] Soares, S. *Big Data Governance: An Emerging Imperative*. McPress, 2013.

[34] Soares, S. *The IBM Data Governance Unified Process: Driving Business Value with IBM Software and Best Practices*, McPress, 2010.

[35] Ladley, J. *Data Governance: How to Design, Deploy and Sustain an Effective Data Governance Program*, Morgan Kaufmann, 2012.

[36] Bhansali, N. *Data Governance: Creating Value from Information Assets*, Crc Pr Inc, 2013.

[37] Sarsfield, S. *The Data Governance Imperative*, It Governance Ltd, 2009.

[38] Sarsfield, S. "Big Data is Not Just Hadoop." Retrieved 06/19/2013 from http://data-governance.blogspot.de/.

CHAPTER 4

Social MDM Reference Architecture

Reference architectures encapsulate architectural best practices harvested and harnessed from a series of implementations. In this chapter, we introduce the Social MDM Reference Architecture regarding its key capabilities based on the capability framework. The primary purpose of this chapter is to enable you to understand the relevant components, their relationships, and interactions for building MDM solutions—specifically for Social MDM use cases.

Introduction

In this chapter, we introduce the Social MDM Reference Architecture (Social MDM RA). We do this by embedding a master data management (MDM) system in the broader enterprise context of operational and analytical systems. With the rise of Big Data in information management, the architectural ecosystem for MDM systems is changing alongside the analytical systems. Social persona information, customer sentiment, etc. is analytics-derived using Big Data analytics. Thus it is not surprising that Social MDM solutions depend on new enterprise information architectures also able to deliver Big Data solutions. We will show you in the Architecture Overview how the ecosystem in which Social MDM solutions live evolved over the last few years by showing you the old and the new environment.

Using a component model comprised of a component relationship diagram providing a static perspective of the key components, as well as some component interaction diagrams providing dynamic views, we introduce the Social MDM RA on a more detailed level.

Architecture Overview

In this section, we first take a look at MDM in the application landscape for an enterprise followed by the introduction of an architecture overview. When we introduce the architecture overview, we first take a look at the ecosystem prior to the rise of Big Data. In a second step, we show how the architecture overview evolved due to the impact of Big Data.

MDM as Central Nervous System for Enterprise Data

Although many MDM implementations historically focused on operational use cases, with the rise of Social MDM, an MDM system truly becomes the central nervous system for the enterprise, as shown in Figure 4.1. It is connected to the operational landscape as well as to a broad range of analytical applications. A key observation in Figure 4.1 is that in many cases the connections are bidirectional because with Social MDM, the MDM system becomes a core essential part of the operational fabric. For example, although social media analytics might enrich a particular customer record with insights gleaned from unstructured sources such as social media, customer interaction logs from the call center, and so on, the starting point for that analysis is the customer records that define a "search scope" to the analysis. Similarly, with self-service capabilities to update their master data record exposed to the customer through various operational channels, the link between operational applications and MDM becomes more and more bidirectional where a couple of years ago many MDM systems were fed with a consolidation style architecture pattern.

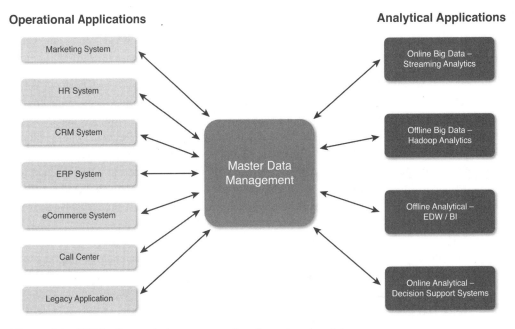

Figure 4.1   MDM—the central nervous system for enterprise data

MDM: Architecture Overview

Now that you have a better understanding of the functional scope of the discussed capabilities in the previous chapter, let's switch gears to implementation architecture. A few quick words regarding nomenclature will help to more easily convey key messages in the drawings. A *functional area* is a collection of related subsystems delivering a major IT function. A *technical capability* is a specialized type of technology performing a specific role; we introduced those relevant to us in Chapter 3. With information provisioning as an example, there are collections. In this example, it is a collection of mechanisms for locating, transforming, or aggregating information from all types of sources and repositories. A *zone* is a scope of concern describing a usage intent for a particular cross-cutting service. It has associated requirements and governance that any system in the zone must adhere to. Figure 4.2 shows iconic examples we use for these concepts in the drawings.

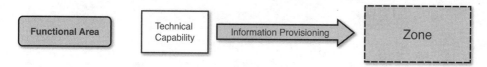

Figure 4.2   Nomenclature

To understand what is changing with Social MDM, we first need to understand common deployment architectures today, such as shown in Figure 4.3.

In Figure 4.3, you can see two types of capabilities:

- **Technical capabilities introduced in Chapter 3:** Examples include (but are not limited to) Master Data Hubs, Reference Data Hubs, and so on, which are technical capabilities introduced in the Information Engine capability layer in the category Managed Operational Data Hub. Other capabilities are grouped in functional areas; for example, the Analytic Sources Area is composed of the capabilities in the Data Server category from the Information Engine capability layer as well as some analytical functions from the Insight capability layer.

- **Technical capabilities external to the capabilities defined in Chapter 3:** These are primarily well-known IT systems such as customer relationship management (CRM) applications.

In the functional area of traditional sources on the left side in Figure 4.3 are the sources for master-data-comprised third-party data sources such as Dun & Bradstreet, as well as operational applications such as customer relationship management (CRM), enterprise resource planning (ERP), human resources (HR), supply chain management (SCM), supplier relationship management (SRM), and eCommerce. In a typical enterprise, some of these applications are packaged from vendors like SAP and Oracle, or from software as a service (SaaS) providers like Workday and Salesforce.com, or custom-built applications.

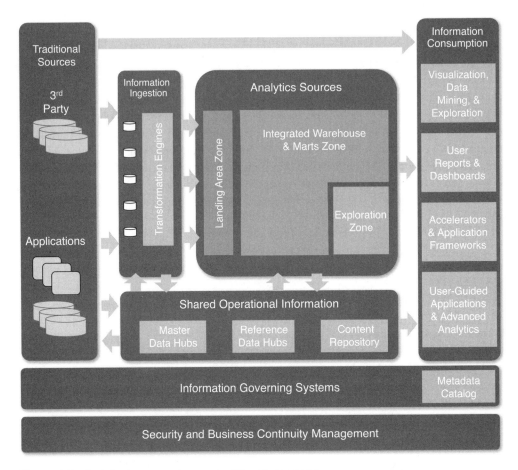

Figure 4.3   Architecture overview—a traditional viewpoint

The functional area of information ingestion has transformation engines providing, for example, ETL or CDC capabilities. Using these transformation engines master data can be moved from the sources to MDM or from MDM into the data harmonization processes feeding the analytical sources. The MDM system resides in the functional area of shared operational information systems alongside Reference Data Management and Content Management Systems. The name "Master Data Hubs" is intentionally plural for two reasons: first, commercial software vendors historically provided Master Data Management software for a single domain only, such as for a customer or product, creating the two disciplines customer data integration (CDI) and product information management (PIM). Early adopters of MDM sometimes implemented multiple MDM products for different purposes, from the same or different vendors resulting in multiple master data hubs. Today, many MDM software vendors provide multi-domain MDM software often reducing the number of distinct hubs. Multiple Master Data Hubs can also be the result of a merger and acquisition where both companies have an MDM system already. Yet another reason could be that the company adopted different MDM software solutions from different vendors to address different MDM requirements. The functional area for analytical sources is composed of the landing zone where the data harmonization for operational data stores and data warehouses located in the integrated warehouse and marts zone is done. For exploratory analytics such as pattern detection, a dedicated exploration zone exists. For the functional area of information consumption where business users consume information, the figure shows various well-known technical capabilities such as data mining and reporting. For governing the information architecture, the functional area of information governing systems provides a metadata catalog storing business technical and operational metadata, among other capabilities. The functional area of security and business continuity management provides necessary security features for controlling and auditing information access as well as features for backup and restore, high availability, disaster recovery, maintenance, and so on.

With the rise of Big Data, the implementation landscape changes to reflect the new sources and capabilities available as shown in Figure 4.4.

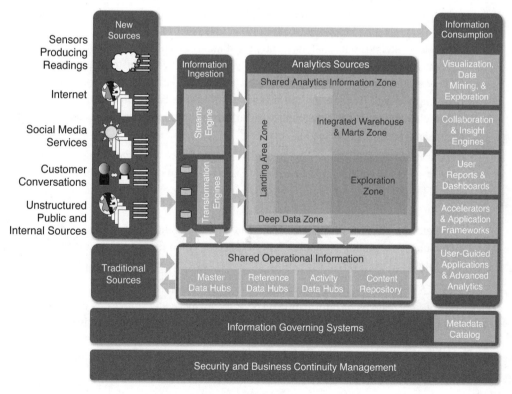

Figure 4.4 Architecture overview—impact of Big Data

Major changes in key functional areas are:

- **Data sources:** A whole new group of data sources has emerged. As internet-connected sensors and devices become more common (often called the Internet of Things), more information can be collected, integrated, and analyzed to improve operational efficiencies and quality of life across a number of areas. Examples include instrumentation for food transport ("farm to fork"), utility networks (smart water/gas/electricity networks and smart meters), and smarter homes as just three examples implementing sensors producing data at an unprecedented rate and massive volume. New kinds of unstructured content sources have also emerged including blogs and wikis. Social media sources grow at a rapid pace as well, and examples include Facebook, Twitter, LinkedIn, and Yelp.

- **Information ingestion:** A new technique known as streams processing has emerged to address new use cases where data is produced at speeds and volumes too large to actually persist all the data. A streams engine can apply real-time analytics as information is created to make timely decisions and to selectively store the most interesting information.

- **Analytical sources:** A new zone of deep analytics is added—the location of new analytical capabilities based on the MapReduce paradigm, as we will see. With a Hadoop platform to implement a Map-Reduce platform allows you to land the data, perform possibly some cleansing, do some analytics, and persist the results of the analytics which might be also moved to a DW. With such a system, you would have all historic and current data. This possibly changes the DW procedures because instead of archiving of the DW you can simply delete because the full history is still in the Hadoop platform.[1] The second major change is that the consumption of information is radically simplified, creating a true shared analytics information zone.

- **Information consumption:** New techniques of collaboration and new insight engines appear as novel technical capabilities. Examples include new matching engines to search for duplicates and nonobvious relationships, pattern mining, and natural language analytics.

- **Information governing systems:** Major functional enhancements include the extension of the metadata catalog to enable a broad class of users to find and provision the information they need from across the variety of systems and zones.

Figure 4.5 shows the architecture overview from an Social MDM perspective. Integration and analysis of new sources of information, especially social media sources, is one of the most striking changes from Figure 4.5. Another key change is the introduction of activity hubs.

---

1. More details on this topic can be found in [1].

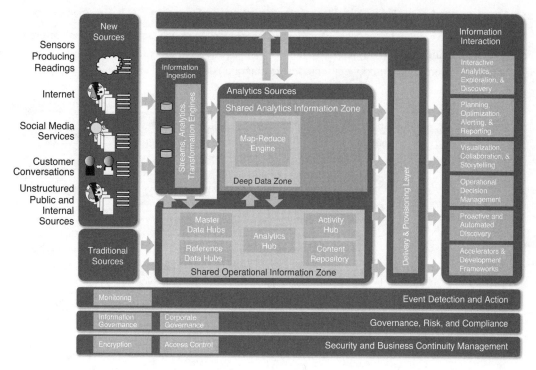

Figure 4.5   Architecture overview—focus on Social MDM

Component Model

The architecture overview in the previous section is useful to provide enterprise architects, IT managers, and business users a conceptual perspective of key capability areas for a Social MDM architecture, however, it is not detailed enough to understand how the components in this architecture interact with each other. For this, a component model is necessary.

In the following sections, we explore the Social MDM RA on a functional component level using a component relationship diagram. A component relationship diagram provides a static view of the relationships between the components. We then walk through a sample component interaction diagram to demonstrate the dynamic interaction of the components. Component interaction diagrams will be used in subsequent chapters to describe various angles of the Social MDM RA from different architectural perspectives.

Component Relationship Diagram from an Enterprise SOA Perspective

You may have read [1], which provides an enterprise Master Data Management reference architecture aligned with an SOA-based enterprise architecture blueprint.[2] Figure 4.6 shows an updated version of the component relationship diagram published in [1].

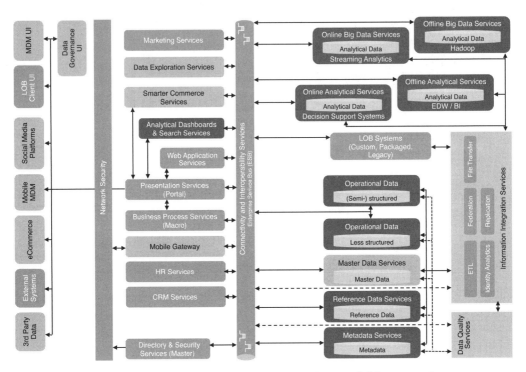

Figure 4.6   Social MDM component relationship diagram from an SOA perspective

The major differences are as follows:

- **Simplification:** Since the previous component relationship diagram was published as part of the MDM RA, roughly six years have passed. Working with many clients during this time, we found that many components have become commoditized as SOA has matured. Following are some examples:

    - The DMZ zone with a reverse proxy pattern, firewalls, and so on has been collapsed into a single network security component.

2. You probably noticed that several authors of this book coauthored the previous book, so we decided to provide you with this perspective as well as an evolution to the previous version.

- Different types of LOB systems have been summarized into a single component.

- The subcomponents of the MDM component are not explicitly shown anymore. They are well understood and common knowledge in the MDM practitioner community at this point.

- Various messaging gateway components and the interconnectivity and interoperability component have been merged into a single ESB component.

- **Changes in data domains:** At the time the previous MDM RA was created, reference data was subsumed as part of master data. With the lessons learned since then, we see it now as a separate domain with domain-specific functionality to be appropriately managed, thereby justifying a component in its own right.

- **New third-party data sources:** Over the years, we have worked with enterprises that expressed some degree of dissatisfaction with commercial third-party vendors. Examples of issues include lack of completeness, cost, and and to some extent staleness of the data. Social media sources are perceived to address some of these aspects better but at the same time with the risk of some uncertainty and fuzziness. Also, additional processing is required to make these sources usable from an MDM standpoint. For these reasons we moved this into a different component.

- **New use cases:** The expansion of banking services to support mobile devices is one of several drivers for Mobile MDM—a capability that also requires new components, which we added to the component model.

- **The impact of Big Data for analytics:** As indicated with the data domain introduction, Big Data use cases broaden the scope of analytical capabilities, which we represent with a functional processing capability set with dedicated components.

Component Relationship Diagram for Social MDM from an Information Architecture Perspective

Although the SOA-centric component relationship diagram of the MDM RA remains a very useful reference architecture, for Social MDM, we felt the urgent need for a more information-centric view. Figure 4.7 shows the Social MDM RA component relationship model from an information-centric perspective. As you will notice, most of the important components from the MDM RA remain but some components have been removed or combined to allow us to focus on Social MDM. For example, network components have been removed and others have been combined such as portal, Web, and eCommerce.

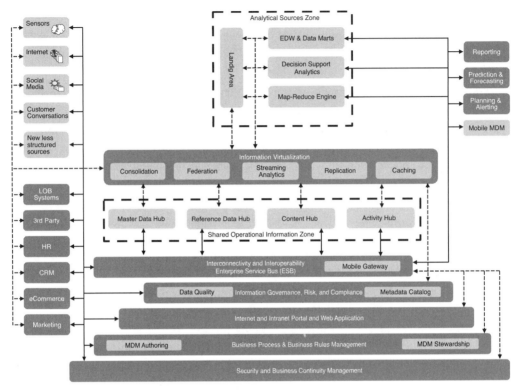

Figure 4.7   Social MDM component relationship diagram from an information architecture perspective

On the left side of the figure, you can see the key operational data sources—traditional ones like CRM, HR, and marketing systems as well as new sources like social media platforms. The Master Data Hub and the Reference Data Hub are enterprise-wide (and in some cases, cross-enterprise) shared information assets. Through the information virtualization layer and the ESB, they are connected to all relevant IT systems to provide seamless access to these critical information assets. The information virtualization layer provides technical capabilities for information access, consolidation, replication, and so on. In industries such as banking, the digital transformation brings new banking services on mobile platforms like Android or iOS for smart phones. The ESB has been extended to include a mobile gateway that exposes services to mobile platforms. A mobile gateway provides the ability to map a Web service interface to a REST service interface to make the service consumable for Android devices. Additionally, the mobile gateway provides Mobile MDM capabilities independent of the target device environment—thereby supporting native Android, iOS, or even HTML5-based applications. Within the analytical sources zone, the landing area enables data harmonization prior to analytical use in other components such as the DW and data mart. A new component is the MapReduce engine, which we will explore in depth in Chapter 5. The information in the analytical sources is consumed as analytical data through technical capabilities such as reporting, prediction and forecasting, and enterprise planning.

For a Social MDM solution to work, additional common infrastructure components are necessary. The information governance, risk, and compliance component, for example, provides capabilities for data quality (for example, address standardization services) and a metadata catalog (for example, to manage business terms for master data entities alongside logical and physical data models of the Master Data Hub). The Internet and Intranet portal and web application component delivers functionality to surface master data such as employee or intranet employee dictionary applications or customer master data self-service functionality for being able to notify an organization about address or contact detail changes. The business process management component delivers business process functionality for authoring and stewardship processes of master data. Typical master data process examples include new product introduction, hierarchy maintenance, account creation, or duplicate suspect processing. Like other IT solutions, Social MDM depends on appropriate security and business continuity infrastructure. An MDM solution usually has very demanding requirements regarding availability (after all, master data is required by many of the mission-critical operational and analytical applications) as well as security (for example, enterprises need to protect their customer master data or face reputational damage as well as possible legal consequences).

Component Interaction Diagram

Whether or not a component relationship diagram represents a good component model can be assessed by a use-case-driven validation through component interaction diagrams. In subsequent chapters, you will see a lot more component interaction diagrams for various use cases. In this section, however, we start with a basic use case in a business-to-consumer (B2C) scenario where we would like to add influencer scores to the customer master data records in the Master Data Hub. To determine influencer ratings, we need to analyze information coming from sources such as videos on YouTube, blogs, wikis, forums, posts on Facebook and Twitter, and so on. Analyzing these sources requires a broad range of analytics such as voice-to-text or video analytics on the raw data, followed by deeper analytics on topic and sentiment detection. These analytics may be implemented as a sequence of Map-Reduce jobs based on a social analytics library. The output of these jobs is written to a well-modeled social media mart where predictive analytics are deployed to determine influencer scores. In addition, the data derived from social media can also be used for the matching of social personas to customer records in the Master Data Hub. Figure 4.8 shows the end-to-end component interaction diagram for this use case.

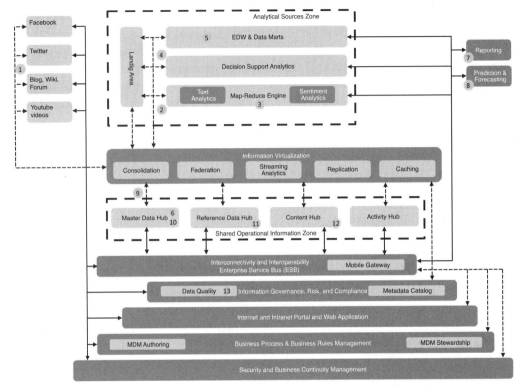

Figure 4.8   Component interaction diagram for enriching master data with influencer scores

Step 1. In this step, connectors consume data feeds from the new information sources such as Facebook and Twitter. Depending on software selection, the connectors might be part of the information virtualization component or the MapReduce engine. For monitoring ongoing marketing campaigns, events, or 1:1 customer engagement opportunities, information is accumulated frequently—usually every few minutes—for some situations, for example where we are integrating customer service with social media, we may receive updates continuously.

Step 2. In this step, the raw data is loaded into the MapReduce engine.

Step 3. Configured as a series of analytical operations, the MapReduce engine executes a broad range of analytics. Initially, "document-centric" analytics strive to identify concepts, social personas, authoring location, demographics, behavioral patterns, and sentiment. Subsequently, topic detection analytics are applied, including correlation and assignment of individual mentions of concepts to topics. Leading MapReduce engines can execute this analytical sequence in a matter of minutes.

Steps 4 and 5. After the MapReduce engine finishes, the results are moved to a social media mart. Depending on the database used for the social media mart as well as the software for the MapReduce engine, this could be as simple as a flat file produced by the MapReduce engine that gets loaded through a bulk load interface into the database. Of course, alternatively, the flat file might also be loaded with ETL software (the consolidation engine in the information virtualization component) that may also be used to simultaneously restructure and enhance the information as it is loaded.

Step 6. Using the matching capability of the Master Data Hub,[3] we can now determine which social persona might correspond to a customer record. There might be social personas with no match in the Master Data Hub or vice versa where a customer uses different social personas on different social platforms.

Step 7. The outcome of the matching task can be visualized with reports using the reporting component.

Step 8. Using predictive analytics with appropriate models and scoring functions, we can compute influencer scores.

Steps 9 and 10. The influencer scores can be moved from the social media data mart to the Master Data Hub using capabilities such as ETL (part of the consolidation functionality) from the information virtualization layer. As a result, the master data records in the Master Data Hub are enriched with the influencer scores from the social media platforms.

In addition to these core steps of the use case, there are additional options for consideration. Influencer scores might change over time from a more coarse-grained to a more fine-grained level or vice versa. Influencer categories based on lower and upper thresholds might be defined through reference values. If the influencer score analytics suggest a change in these categories, the corresponding reference value sets might require an update in the Reference Data Hub (step 11). Possible social media sources might contain additional opportunities to enrich master data beyond the influencer scores. There might be additional contact, address, or other demographic information found—that with cleansing through appropriate data quality services (13) could be added to the matched master data records as well. For example, if a match is found for a social persona, there might be pictures or documents available from the social media that could be persisted in a Content Hub (step 12) and linked as unstructured master data to the master data record in the Master Data Hub.

---

3. IBM ported the MDM matching engine to the Hadoop Map-Reduce engine. This version of the IBM MDM matching engine is known as BigMatch. If such technology is available, then the comparison of social personas using a matching engine can happen within the Map-Reduce environment. If a match is found with a feasible degree of similarity, then depending on the certainty of the match, either a link is established or the customer profile gets enriched.

Subject-Oriented Integration

With an understanding how the Social MDM Reference Architecture works, we want to now investigate how we can make master data available from a consumer standpoint. Provisioning the subset of information based on consumers' social context requires the capability to perform *subject-oriented integration* for Social MDM solutions. Let's look at some examples:

Ubiquitous Internet availability anywhere anytime on mobile devices allows people to interact with corporate IT in novel ways. The salesperson meeting a customer's contact person wants to refresh his memory on that person's current social context by doing a lookup from a mobile device in the car just a few minutes before entering a meeting at the client's site. A member of the support organization looking at a product defect reported by someone from the customer's site would like to know if that person is possibly already deeply frustrated. In this case, the support engineer would like to see if that person who opened the product defect report already posted negative statements online about the product or posted questions in forums related to the problem reported. Having that context available might affect the support engineer's style of communication with the person who opened the product defect report and may reduce the time of analyzing the problem (there is no need to explore causes and possible solutions that have been identified as not helpful by the person opening the product defect report in forum discussions). These are just two examples illustrating how different consumers in different social contexts have different perspectives on the same 360-degree complete social master data based on their role.

Before we can integrate information, we need to *understand* it first, and this also applies to subject-oriented integration. Although information integrations have been built for a long time, in many cases this has been done in an *ungoverned* way. For example, an extract-transform-load (ETL) developer might have looked at source and target models and just built an ETL program based on a mapping of source to target attributes. The semantics of each field of the source and target data models, the relationship of these models to certain business entities and functions, and user roles consuming the data on the target are not captured in many cases. For a while, an inhibiting factor was the lack of appropriate metadata software to manage business, technical, and operational metadata and data lineage; and impact analysis functionality was not part of enterprise information integration platforms. This changed in the past several years with commercial metadata management solutions now available, fully supporting the creation of enterprise glossaries where technical (for example, logical and physical data models, mappings, and data profiling rules) and operational metadata can be attached to business metadata (for example, terms and policies). With this metadata functionality available through an enterprise glossary, it's now possible to seamlessly define a *subject* composed of:

- A term describing the subject from a business perspective
- An assigned owner (for example, an information steward) who is responsible and accountable for the data asset described in the term

- Policies governing how the information asset related to the term has to be managed in terms of data quality, security, retention, privacy, and so on, and implementation rules linked to these policies used for enforcement
- Technical metadata linked to the term expressing how and where the data asset is stored, how it is related to other assets (for example, mappings), and permissible value ranges (for example, through linkage of applicable reference data tables)
- Operational metadata such as results of enforced security constraints, measured data quality, and so on

With the subject defined, it's now possible to provide a catalog for information assets in the enterprise. Various users in the enterprise looking for information assets can now use this catalog of information assets. However, on a high level, we see two very distinct use cases. First, based on requests from the business, technical users can develop the integration to deliver the necessary subject considering all constraints attached to it for the consuming users from a consumption point of view. Second, business users can browse the catalog of information assets by subject, and if state-of-the-art *self-service capabilities* provided through the enterprise information integration platform are available and enabled, they can generate the integration for the subject of interest to the desired consumption point without having IT personnel involved.

More details on this topic of subject oriented integration can be found in [2].

Conclusion

In this chapter, we provided an introduction to the Social MDM RA. We provided an architecture overview and a component model perspective, organizing the functional scope of the Social MDM RA into architectural deliverables. We demonstrated how the Social MDM RA works by using a component interaction diagram showing how it works for a specific use case. We then explained how to use the concept of subject-oriented integration to provision master data for Social MDM solutions from a consumption viewpoint.

In the next chapter, we explore software solutions which can be used to deliver the discussed components in the component model in more depth.

References

[1] Dreibelbis, A., E. Hechler, I. Milman, M. Oberhofer, P. van Run, and D. Wolfson. *Enterprise Master Data Management: An SOA Approach to Managing Core Information* (IBM Press, 2008).

[2] Chessell, M., Smith, H.: *Patterns of Information Management*. (IBM Press, 2013).

CHAPTER 5

Product Capabilities for Social MDM

Regardless of whether you are working with the Social MDM Reference Architecture or developing a concrete Next Best Action (NBA)[1] solution to improve customer care and marketing initiatives, eventually you will need to choose a combination of products for implementing the solution. IBM has a mature and growing portfolio of products that provide the capabilities for implementing the variety of solution architectures that we outline throughout the book. In this chapter, we describe key capabilities of select IBM products that underpin a social MDM endeavor.

Table 5.1 lists the key products that we will cover along with some of their primary capabilities. As described in the table, you can see that there appear to be some products that overlap in the capabilities they offer. For example, both InfoSphere Streams and InfoSphere BigInsights provide contextual insight; throughout this chapter, we will discuss these apparent overlaps and describe criteria to help in your product selection. For instance, as we focus on the particulars of this example, we find that a key distinction between these two products is that InfoSphere Streams addresses near real-time and continuous processing while InfoSphere BigInsights tends to be used for more of a request/response and batch-oriented processing—thus, selecting between them is primarily a question of understanding what styles of processing your solution needs. Further, as we look at a more sophisticated architectural pattern such as NBA, we find that deploying this pattern requires both styles of processing—and, unsurprisingly, we see both of these products used together in such a solution. Throughout this chapter, we will highlight some common integration patterns between these products.

More generally, it is important to consider that the capabilities we discussed in Chapter 3 describe the functions that we need and as we look at selecting products to implement these functions for deploying a solution pattern we need to also consider non-functional characteristics that address the needs of the solution. Finally, we should also mention that in the product discussions,

---

1. The term NBA will be explained in detail in Chapter 6 on "Social MDM and Customer Care."

we have tried to focus on the primary capabilities that would lead someone to select a given product in the context of Social MDM; many of the products offer a richer set of capabilities that are described online and elsewhere. Our intention is not to repeat detailed product characteristics, functions, and features that are well described in the existing product documentation.[2] Our focus is on the IBM Social MDM Reference Architecture and its key architectural building blocks, specifically in regards to the following aspects:

- Big Data impact on the MDM architecture
- Social MDM Component Model and Capabilities Framework
- MDM aspects of the information architecture, including information governance

However, we examine these aspects in the context of the following architectures, models, and solution areas introduced in this book:

- Social customer care reference model
- NBA solution architecture
- MDM sentiment analytics
- Influencer determination capability model
- Trustworthiness of social media—dimensions and technical capabilities
- Mobile marketing and advertisement solution
- Real-time marketing
- Viral marketing

To take these areas into consideration, we list the relevant IBM products and tools and indicate where their technical capabilities, functions, and features contribute to the themes listed here. Emphasis is given to the MDM-related product capabilities in conjunction with other key areas, such as information integration, pervasive analytics including natural language processing and text analytics, Hadoop-based infrastructures, and enterprise marketing management areas. However, we don't dive deeply into products that constitute the data persistency layer, such as Hadoop-based data storage with the Hadoop Distributed File System (HDFS), HBase, or Hive, and data warehouse aspects.

2. You can find more information about IBM InfoSphere MDM in [1].

Table 5.1 List of Products with Primary Capabilities

Product	Primary Capabilities
InfoSphere MDM	Master Data Hub
InfoSphere RDM	Reference Data Hub
InfoSphere Big Insights	Contextual Insight Discovery Insight Insight Server
IBM Watson Explorer	Exploration and Visualization
SPSS & Cognos	Descriptive Insight Discovery Insight Predictive Insight Prescriptive Insight
InfoSphere Information Server	Information Delivery Information Provisioning Information Preparation Information Governance
InfoSphere Streams	Real-Time Analytics Contextual Insight Predictive Insight
InfoSphere Guardium	Information Protection

Social Master Data Management (MDM)

Since 2003, IBM has done some significant investment in developing a comprehensive MDM set of technical capabilities that include Customer Data Integration (CDI), Product Information Management (PIM), and Reference Data Management (RDM) product offerings. The latest IBM MDM offerings[3] include both transaction-oriented MDM and collaborative authoring and workflow capabilities to handle multiple domains, implementation styles, and use cases across various industries.

In the following sections, we highlight these existing IBM MDM functions and features that are relevant in a Social MDM context:

- Master data governance and data stewardship
- Probabilistic Matching Engine (PME)

---

3. We are referring to the latest offering, which is IBM InfoSphere Master Data Management (MDM) v11.

- Social MDM matching
- InfoSphere BigInsights integration
- Watson Explorer integration

Master Data Governance and Data Stewardship

IBM InfoSphere MDM offerings contain a rich set of technical capabilities to enable simplified MDM deployments and master data governance,[4] and to support Big Data initiatives. The offerings come as a single solution to support virtual, physical, and hybrid MDM styles that allow modular implementations and upgrades to support multidomain environments including required product/service and party domains. Furthermore, there are significant enhancements to the collaboration UI to improve the user experience.

Integration with IBM InfoSphere Information Server[5] allows for comprehensive master data governance capabilities, including data quality, monitoring and dashboarding of the entire master data supply chain, and sharing of metadata to enable efficient collaboration between IT and LOB organizations. In addition, it comes with enhanced hierarchy support for reference data and a workflow dashboard for IBM MDM Collaboration Server. Additional metrics help monitor master data quality, evaluate data stewardship activities, and plan data stewardship resources.

Master data stewardship enables you to establish trusted information using robust data stewardship tools and processes such as party-suspected duplicate processing through the data stewardship UI, event management, and evergreen console. In addition, it offers prebuilt data integration and data quality capabilities.

Following are the key objectives of master data governance:

- Establish a master data governance council or board.
- Formulate master data governance imperatives, policies, and processes that establish accountability and enforcement.
- Monitor, oversee, and enforce proactive, collaborative, and effective data stewardship that is driven by the master data governance initiative.
- Implement and use tools that enable master data governance and data governance–driven stewardship, including policy administration, enforcement, remediation, and monitoring.

IBM offers a comprehensive set of products and components for master data management and governance. Figure 5.1 illustrates the pervasive and integrated capabilities of master data governance. It highlights the flow of governing master data from the initial master data discovery and analysis to the ongoing master data monitoring and dashboarding.

---

4. You can find more information on master data governance in [2], [3], and [4].
5. You can find more information on IBM InfoSphere Information Server in [5] and [6].

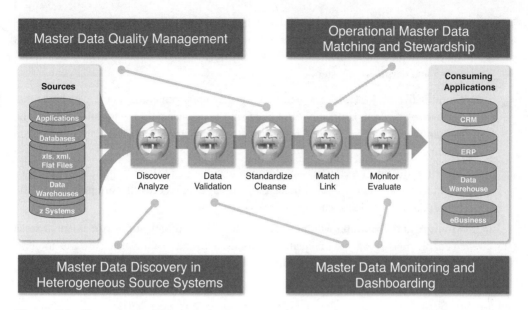

Figure 5.1   Pervasive and integrated governance of master data

Master data governance is a key concern for Social MDM because it needs to provide business owners assurances that master data is a trusted asset that is ready for use within their business processes. Specifically, with the ever-growing importance of integrating insight from company-external data sources to enrich the customer profile, for instance, consuming processes have requirements to increase the trustworthiness of derived analytical insight that the master data governance initiative must achieve. These consumption-centric master data requirements can include attribute validation requirements that are associated with the completeness of a record, specific attribute values, and code table validation. Master data governance provides the capabilities that are necessary to administer, monitor, and also enforce these requirements as policies. Using a master data governance process to enforce these policies provides the assurances to business owners that master data not only is accurate but also supports their usage requirements.

IBM Business Process Management (BPM) Express, is packaged with some versions of InfoSphere MDM for implementing this process-oriented data stewardship. This process includes policy administration, policy monitoring, and policy enforcement.

As you can see in Figure 5.1, the integrated master data governance flow is composed of the following steps. These steps have to be customized and further refined on a project basis:

1. **Discover and Analyze:** Because master data is traditionally stored and managed in a heterogeneous set of source systems, the initial step consists of discovering, analyzing, and profiling master data.

2. **Data Validation:** Master data validation is a continuing process to ensure the trustworthiness and completeness of master data throughout its lifecycle. This step contributes not only to the standardization and cleansing, but also to the ongoing master data monitoring and dashboarding step.

3. **Standardize and Cleanse:** Master data quality management is a core capability that consists of the standardization and cleansing of master data for initial load into the master data hub. It can also be used for data quality improvements of any source data system.

4. **Match and Link:** Operational master data matching and stewardship allow for ongoing master data validation and linkage of master data records that are persisted in the master data hub and also various source systems.

5. **Monitor and Evaluate:** Master data monitoring and dashboarding are essential steps to enable transparency in the quality of master data and to allow data stewards to guarantee master data quality throughout its entire lifecycle.

Most of these master data governance capabilities are deployed through IBM InfoSphere Information Server[6] product modules and components and can be deployed in conjunction with IBM MDM offerings. Information Server can be used to implement a pervasive information governance solution that goes far beyond just the master data management aspects.

We elaborate more on the Information Server capabilities later in this chapter.

Probabilistic Matching Engine (PME)

Probabilistic matching and searching are highly accurate matching and record comparison capabilities that are part of the InfoSphere MDM Probabilistic Matching Engine (PME).[7]

In a Social MDM context, the InfoSphere MDM PME plays a vital role because it provides organizations with the ability to perform party matching and suspected duplicate processing using a sophisticated and configurable scoring algorithm. The InfoSphere MDM PME is a library that can be used to perform probabilistic matching and comparison on record data. Probabilistic matching algorithms calculate scores based on weights associated with values for specific attributes and are used across all attributes configured for comparison. This method of matching takes into consideration the frequency of data occurrence. The algorithm calculates one composite weight that is a result of a probabilistic calculation of match and no-match weights for individually compared fields. The InfoSphere MDM PME generates matching scores based on its probabilistic scoring system. Then InfoSphere MDM takes the score and uses it to determine survivorship and decide what suspect duplicate processing actions must be completed.

6. For more information on using the IBM InfoSphere Information Server for information governance purposes, see [7].

7. You can find more detailed information on the IBM InfoSphere MDM Probabilistic Matching Engine (PME) in [1].

The InfoSphere MDM PME as part of the MDM Standard and Advanced editions employs a set of indices that are optimized for matching party records, specifically persons or organizations. These indices are a part of the InfoSphere MDM PME and must be kept synchronized with the InfoSphere MDM data. Each time party data, such as a person's address or a business's phone number, changes in InfoSphere MDM, the InfoSphere MDM PME indices must be updated so that matching can be performed against the latest party data. The data contained in the InfoSphere MDM PME indices is almost the same data set that is used to determine whether suspect duplicate processing must be performed. Consequently, the same mechanism that is used to detect changes to data for suspected duplicate processing is also used to detect changes in the data for the InfoSphere MDM PME indices.

In the Social MDM context, party records may be derived from data sources, where the level of trust is somewhat reduced, compared to traditional MDM environments. This represents a new dimension of the InfoSphere MDM PME to play an essential role in gaining and maintaining trust in the master data records.

Determining when to carry out suspected duplicate processing is driven by changes to critical party data. For this reason, it is important to identify when changes to critical party data occur.

With the InfoSphere MDM Probabilistic Matching Engine, the process for identifying critical data changes is as follows:

1. The InfoSphere MDM PME examines any business objects that took part in the transaction to determine if there were changes to any critical party data that is specified in the CRITICALDATAELEMENT table.

2. If any changes to critical party data are identified, the InfoSphere MDM PME updates its indices accordingly.

3. The InfoSphere MDM Probabilistic Matching Engine carries out suspected duplicate processing activities for the party whose data has changed.

The CRITICALDATAELEMENT table defines the data elements that constitute the critical party data that is monitored to determine whether to synchronize the InfoSphere MDM PME indices or perform suspected duplicate processing.

The architecture of the InfoSphere MDM PME within an InfoSphere MDM solution consists of a suite of adapters and converters that enable communication between InfoSphere MDM core components and the InfoSphere MDM PME. The constituent components of the InfoSphere MDM PME are illustrated in Figure 5.2.

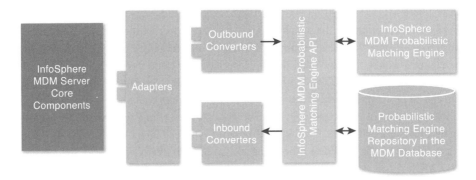

Figure 5.2   IBM InfoSphere MDM Probabilistic Matching Engine (PME) architecture

- **Outbound converters:** Convert business objects into InfoSphere MDM PME records and pass those records to InfoSphere MDM PME for matching.

- **Inbound converters:** Convert InfoSphere MDM PME results into business objects and return them to InfoSphere MDM core components for further processing or displaying to users.

We now take a closer look at the InfoSphere MDM Probabilistic Matching Engine for InfoSphere BigInsights.[8]

Social MDM Matching

Although the InfoSphere MDM Probabilistic Matching Engine for InfoSphere BigInsights is technically part of InfoSphere MDM, it is deployed as an InfoSphere BigInsights[9] application to derive, compare, and link large volumes of records, using HBase tables as a nonrelational data store. We refer to this capability informally as *Social MDM matching*, *Big Data matching*, or simply *Big Match*.

With the InfoSphere MDM PME engine for BigInsights, you can efficiently derive and enrich master data, compare members, resolve members into entities, and do probabilistic searches. By executing the PME algorithm, the linking process determines whether to create linkages between records that the PME considers to be the same member. This BigInsights application can either run automatically while data is loaded into the underlying HBase tables or as batch processes after the data-loading process.

As we discuss further in subsequent chapters of this book, social media data, transaction records, telephone call detail records (CDR) and other telephone network related Probe data,

8. For more information on the IBM InfoSphere MDM Probabilistic Matching Engine (PME) for Info-
   Sphere BigInsights, see [1].

9. You can find more information on IBM InfoSphere BigInsights in [8].

and multichannel interactions including call-center transcripts or log data will be used to better understand and even predict customer behavior and product or service usage patterns and to derive customer micro segmentation. In other words, the InfoSphere MDM PME for BigInsights provides a key capability for Social MDM to perform matching on a vast amount of data from heterogeneous data sources. It does this by leveraging the Hadoop-based InfoSphere BigInsights processing platform.

The Big Data match uses only a limited portion of the InfoSphere MDM capabilities. Specifically, it uses the InfoSphere MDM Workbench to create a PME configuration that will then be exported for use within InfoSphere BigInsights. The chief component of the PME configuration is one or more MDM algorithms. In the realm of IBM InfoSphere MDM, an algorithm is a step-by-step procedure that compares and scores the similarities and differences of member attributes. As part of a process called *derivation,* the algorithm standardizes and buckets the data. The algorithm then defines a comparison process, which yields a numerical score. That score indicates the likelihood that two records refer to the same member. As a final step, called entity linkage, the process specifies whether to create linkages between records that the algorithm considers to be the same member. The matching process can be used to generate review tasks for potential linkages that don't surpass a certain threshold of certainty. The Big Data matching capability does not generate tasks. Potential linkages that do not meet the threshold are simply not linked together as entities.

Figure 5.3 illustrates a use case that leverages the PME for InfoSphere BigInsights to significantly improve confidence in social media–derived profiles and sentiment scoring by mapping them with customer records exported from InfoSphere MDM. As you can see, social MDM matching is mainly processing and linking two data sets:

- Customer profiles and sentiment scoring that is derived from internal company websites and customer interaction (such as call center transcripts and email)
- Party data that is exported from an InfoSphere MDM system

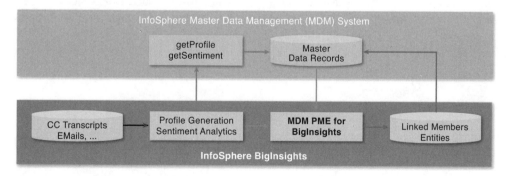

Figure 5.3 Social MDM matching

Through Social MDM matching, the relevance and trustworthiness of the customer profiles and sentiment scoring can be improved by linking this information to golden party records from the MDM system—for example, trusted customer names, addresses, and demographics data. As a result, MDM can now seamlessly show the customer records and their related social personas, as shown in Figure 5.4.

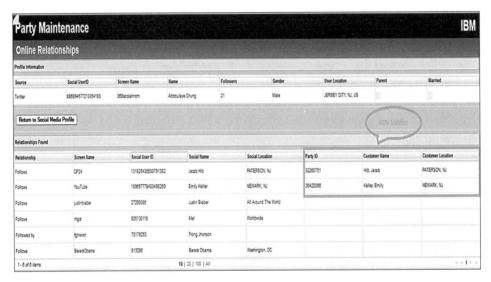

Figure 5.4   Big Match results linked to customer records in MDM

InfoSphere BigInsights Architecture

InfoSphere BigInsights from IBM is more than MapReduce and Hadoop. IBM has taken those basic building blocks and extended and integrated them into a broader, extensible ecosystem anchored by IBM InfoSphere BigInsights. Figure 5.5 illustrates the high-level BigInsights architecture.

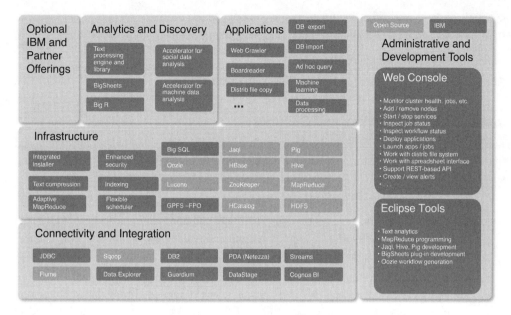

Figure 5.5   IBM InfoSphere BigInsights architecture overview

Logically, BigInsights is organized into five layered capabilities:

- **Connectivity, Integration, and Security:** These tools tie the platform into non–Big Data source and target systems.

- **Infrastructure:** This is the core of the BigInsights offering. It includes the data storage mechanisms for BigData, different interfaces for applications to access Big Data, and additional platform enhancements such as improved security and an integrated installer.

- **Analytics and Discovery:** These tools deliver insight from the data collected at the infrastructure level. There are some specific tools for different types of data (social media, machine logs) and some tools for end users to generate their own insight (BigSheets).

- **Applications:** BigInsights includes some sample applications to address common deployment scenarios—importing and exporting data, extracting data from the Web, monitoring, and so on. We do not cover these items in this chapter.

- **Administrative and Development Tools:** BigInsights delivers a web console for managing the BigInsights environment in a single tool and also adds in a set of Eclipse plug-ins for development in the different languages and interfaces used for BigInsights. We do not cover these items in this chapter.

The entire platform is extensible through consuming APIs (and in some cases, command-line interfaces) at the infrastructure level, as well as adding on to other plug points. As we review the details of these categories, we focus on the components we deem the most relevant to Social MDM. In addition, we will elaborate on the following important integration aspects:

- InfoSphere MDM and BigInsights
- IBM Watson Explorer and BigInsights and Streams

Connectivity, Integration, and Security

The first piece of any Big Data environment involves actually connecting to sources of data and bringing the data into the environment. For BigInsights, we break this down into three general areas:

- **Connectivity:** These components host the data used to extend the reach of BigInsights from the Hadoop file systems to other traditional and nontraditional sources: SQL, data warehouses, unstructured data sources, and streaming data. We do not cover the connectivity components in this overview because they are pretty standard.

- **Integration:** This is another way of delivering data to and from BigInsights. Traditionally, extract-transform-load (ETL) is a major piece of any enterprise data architecture. With Big Data, the roles are the same, but the integration changes to accommodate BigInsights as a source and target, and optionally, MapReduce as a transformation engine.

- **Security:** Logically, security is a cross-cutting component that should be across the entire stack (like management and monitoring). However, the BigInsights architecture prefers to represent this as a part of the integration and connectivity layer, so we adopt their style with a minimum of protest. Security in this layer addresses policy about access to the underlying data in the traditional and BigInsights repositories, and is extended to the BigInsights platform to protect the MapReduce infrastructure.

BigInsights supports both the open source tools for loading data into the BigInsights system (Sqoop and Flume) and IBM's enterprise class ETL product (IBM InfoSphere Information Server). Sqoop and Flume[10] are relatively simple integration engines that move data into HDFS, as shown in Figure 5.6.

Sqoop (an Apache project whose name is derived from the combination of "SQL" and "Hadoop") simply runs import jobs using its own JDBC connector to access and read data from standard relational repositories and then load that data into Hadoop/Hive/HBase (as CSV files for Hadoop). Sqoop can also run the inverse process (export) by reading serialized data from the BigInsights environments; it then populates that into tables on the RDBMS side using the JDBC driver. Sqoop reads the metadata structure from the relational tables to properly handle data moving between the RDBMS and the BigInsights repository.

---

10. For more information on Sqoop and Flume, see [9] and [10] respectively.

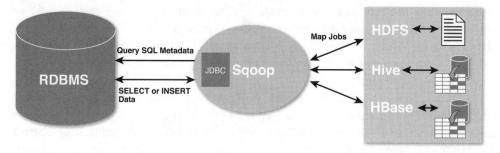

Figure 5.6 Sqoop overview

Flume is another Apache project with a clever name; a flume is a channel that redirects water, often used to move logs or provide hydroelectric power. The log movement is a clear hint as to the purpose of Flume—primarily to move streams of log data from external systems into the BigInsights repositories for long-term storage and analysis. Figure 5.7 illustrates the Flume architecture.

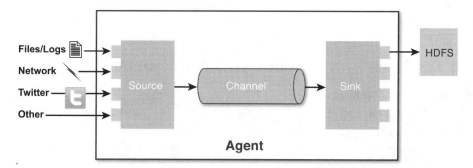

Figure 5.7 Flume overview

Flume follows a variation of the standard producer–consumer pattern.[11] Sources produce data; they can do this by grabbing files or listening on a port for events (an individual data element) to be sent to them. Channels receive the data, transform it if needed, and then store it and deliver it to the consumers (sinks). The combination of source, channel, and sink runs within a single agent. Typical sources are log4j, syslog, Avro, and JMS (Java Messaging Service). A typical channel would be a file system, and HDFS is a standard sink. Flume flows can be chained together (wiring a sink to a source) and can be scaled out horizontally for performance.

Sqoop and Flume are useful for moving data into and out of environments that are primarily Hadoop. But enterprises move data between a wide variety of structured and unstructured

11. You can find more information on the standard consumer–producer pattern in [11].

repositories, using different transformations. Ideally, we would have a single engine with an integrated toolkit that can move data between all these repositories to service the full range of enterprise data movement. That is exactly what the DataStage component of IBM InfoSphere Information Server[12] does; it is an enterprise class system for high-volume ETL across a wide variety of structured and unstructured sources and targets, with a graphical palette for designing data integration using a data flow model. Furthermore, DataStage is well integrated with automated information discovery and data quality tools that are part of Information Server to improve the overall governance of data being moved into (and out of) BigInsights. Keeping track of the flow of information both within and to/from Hadoop environments is critical to understanding the dependencies between the systems and is a key factor in providing confidence that the information delivered into Hadoop is appropriate for analytical processing. Governance of the information flow is a key reason that many customers choose to use Information Server with Big Insights to address their data movement, cleansing and transformation needs.

DataStage has both connectors (to read and write data) and transformers for changing the data to fit what is needed for downstream systems. For BigInsights, DataStage has both extended the connectors to communicate with BigInsights repositories and modified the transformers to build JAQL operators that can be deployed directly against MapReduce to enhance performance of data integration jobs. This dramatically simplifies the integration and transformation process, as shown in Figure 5.8.

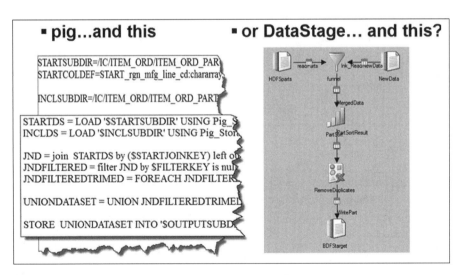

Figure 5.8   Using DataStage for BigInsights integration

12. We present the key concepts of the IBM InfoSphere Information Server later in this chapter.

BigInsights shares a set of security concerns with classic RDBMS and data warehouses:

- What type of data is in the system?

- Is that data sensitive?

- Who can access the data, and who is accessing it? Are enterprise policies being enforced? Is there proof that these policies are being followed?

- Who is making changes to the system?

The volume, variety, and velocity of processing data in a Hadoop-based engine introduces a new and challenging dimension to data security. IBM InfoSphere Guardium[13] addresses that challenge by extending its standard infrastructure for monitoring and auditing to a BigInsights (and generic Big Data) environment, as shown in Figure 5.9.

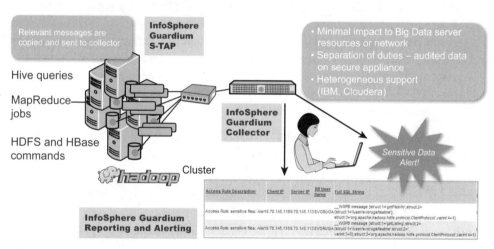

Figure 5.9   IBM InfoSphere Guardium overview

IBM InfoSphere Guardium uses a lightweight agent (S-TAP) to intercept traffic to the Hadoop based data repositories (HDFS, Hive, HBase, and others) and then routes a copy of that traffic to a Guardium controller. The controller then audits requests against security policies, generating alerts when policies are violated (such as unauthorized attempts to access sensitive data). It then stores the access requests to generate compliance reports. Guardium has specific extensions for a BigInsights environment, such as support for non-SQL requests (like those of HDFS, HBase, and Hive). Guardium can also monitor MapReduce jobs (what job was run, which operations, what permissions were needed, and so on) and HDFS commands to see who is operating on the data outside a database perspective.

---

13. You can find more information on Guardium in [12].

Infrastructure

The infrastructure layer is the core of the BigInsights environment. In this section, we cover a key subset of those components found in Figure 5.4, the underlying storage systems, and the parallel distributed data-handling components.

The underlying storage systems contain the HDFS and GPFS file systems:

- **HDFS (Hadoop Distributed File System):** This special-purpose distributed file system (with its own API and command-line utilities) is used to store the data consumed and created by BigInsights. It is scalable (with clusters) and deals with failure through replication.

- **GPFS[14] (General Parallel File System):** GPFS is IBM's high-performance file system; it was developed as a SAN file system in the 1990s for high-performance applications such as BlueGene and Watson, but was later altered to be a more general-purpose parallel file system. IBM extended GPFS with File Placement Option (FPO) to allow the movement of MapReduce jobs to the same node where the data runs (achieving the same core capability of HDFS). GPFS-FPO shares the same advantages as HDFS but offers additional benefits in the form of standardized POSIX file system semantics. Using standard file system interfaces allows non-Hadoop applications to access files and enables standard backup and restore regimes to work with Big Data.

The parallel distributed data-handling components consist of MapReduce and Adaptive MapReduce:

- **MapReduce[15]:** This is the baseline core of Hadoop—a parallel execution framework that takes distributed data, maps that data into sets of key-value pairs, and then uses a second set of jobs to reduce the data into a result set based on the desired outcome. Examples are entity linking, sort, log correlation, sentiment analysis, and so on.

- **Adaptive MapReduce:** Previously called Platform Symphony, Adaptive MapReduce introduces an alternative runtime for MapReduce jobs that can provide significant benefits for some workloads, such as those with smaller jobs. Figure 5.10 calls out the key benefits. The C and C++ implementation improves latency and reduces time in memory management. The coordination layer (akin to JobTracker) uses an efficient event-driven model rather than polling. Data is serialized in the OMG Common Data Representation (CDR) format, which is more compact (and hence introduces less latency) than the formats used in standard MapReduce.

Some additional components make up the BigInsights ecosystem[16] and simplify use of MapReduce:

14. You can find more information on GPFS in [13].
15. For more information on MapReduce, see [14].
16. For more information on Pig, Hive, Jaql, HBase, and BigSQL, see [15], [16], [17], [18], and [19].

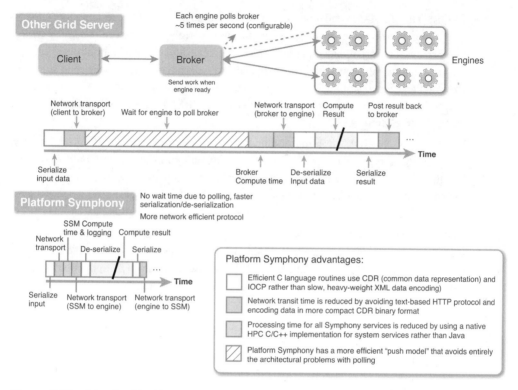

Figure 5.10 Adaptive MapReduce overview

- **Pig:** This simple system has its own language (PigLatin, another joke from the open source community) on top of MapReduce that creates an almost SQL-like layer on top of MapReduce. Pig splits a job into three parts:

  - **Load:** This part tells the Pig program what files will be used.

  - **Transform:** Pig can perform this simple set of operations on data, very much in the MapReduce paradigm: FILTER (eliminate data), GROUP (aggregate data), UNION (merge data), SPLIT (partition data), and so on.

  - **Store:** Both intermediate and final results (using STORE) can be dumped back into the repository.

- **Hive:** This component consists of a set of external interfaces (command line, client), a query language (a derivative of SQL called Hive Query Language, or HQL), and a service layer that converts HQL into MapReduce jobs. Unlike relational languages, Hive is best suited for sequential table scans and read-only activity, limiting its utility.

- **JAQL:** This IBM-donated component acts as a JavaScript Object Notation (JSON) query language on top of Hadoop. There is a nice correlation between the JSON string-value representation of data and the MapReduce key-value representation of data. JAQL creates another SQL type of layer primarily to manipulate JSON data files stored in BigInsights using a parallel, extensible framework to handle large amounts of data and to interact with other JSON providers and consumers (REST-based applications of JSON databases like MongoDB).

- **HBase:** This "NoSQL" column-oriented database runs on top of HDFS and GPFS. It doesn't have typed data, transactions, triggers, and so on that you would find in an RDBMS, but instead uses tables that represent column key-value pairs that can be joined together. The general access language is Java (or REST) and is best used for very large-scale (millions of rows) applications that need quick record access and update.

- **BigSQL:** This component offers a standards compatible SQL-based approach to updating, querying, and managing data within BigInsights. Developers are given a JDBC/ODBC interface to the data, while administrators use familiar DDL to manipulate databases and tables. Figure 5.11 shows the features of BigSQL version 3.

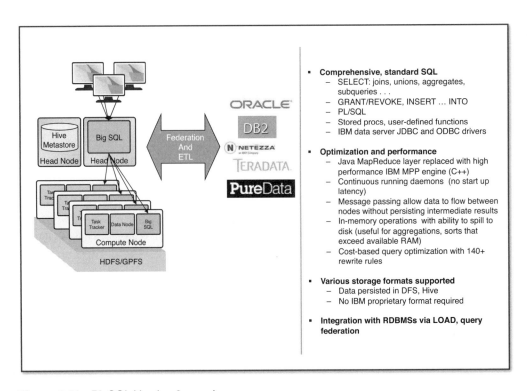

Figure 5.11   BigSQL Version 3 overview

With BigSQL version 3, developers get the benefits of a comprehensive and familiar SQL engine (including out of the box JDBC/ODBC drivers, standard syntax and data types, powerful query optimization and more) layered alongside the parallel processing model of Hadoop—with access to the files already in HDFS and GPFS. In addition to the ability to leverage traditional data movement technologies (such as IBM InfoSphere DataStage) to exchange information between BigInsights and other data sources, BigSQL also has the ability to directly federate data in external relational databases. In other words, a SQL query sent to BigInsights can reference both local information and information stored in existing databases, returning a combined result set. This can be particularly powerful when the majority of the information already resides within BigInsights and we want to combine this data with (for example) current operational results from an existing relational database.

Other supporting infrastructure components are available, such as Oozie and Zookeeper,[17] to help coordinate and manage the Big Data infrastructure:

- **Oozie:** A distributed workflow and job-coordination system that chains together different types of Big Data jobs (MapReduce, Java, Pig, and so on) in a graph to create an ordered set of tasks (where the input of one task may require the output of another one).

- **Zookeeper:** A standard service that maintains the status and synchronization of common objects needed in a BigInsights cluster, including configuration information, name space data, and group services. Applications can leverage Zookeeper for process coordination by using a shared hierarchical namespace (like a file system) called *znodes* to generate and consume events.

Analytics and Discovery

We've spent a lot of time describing the capabilities of BigInsights. In this section, we examine how to use those capabilities for business value. Following is the scope of analytics provided by InfoSphere BigInsights. In conjunction with the existing trusted master data records in InfoSphere MDM, this can be used for analyzing structured and nontraditional data to enable a truly 360-degree customer-centric enterprise.

- **Social Data Analytics Accelerator:** This set of end-to-end applications extracts relevant information from tweets, boards, and blogs and then builds social profiles of users based on specific use cases and industries.

- **Text Analytics:** InfoSphere BigInsights Text Analytics is a powerful system for extracting structured information from unstructured and semi structured text.

- **Analyzing data with BigSheets:** You can use BigSheets in the IBM InfoSphere BigInsights Console to analyze your business intelligence data.

---

17. You can find more information on Oozie and Zookeeper in [20] and [21], respectively.

- **Analyzing data with IBM InfoSphere BigInsights Big R:** You can use IBM Info-Sphere BigInsights Big R to access, manipulate, visualize, and analyze data on the Info-Sphere BigInsights server.

The Social Data Analytics Accelerator[18] is a prebuilt tool to take in feeds from social media and extract concepts relevant for lead generation (discovering potential purchasers of a product) and Brand Management (what different demographics are saying about a product) across a variety of industries. Figure 5.12 illustrates the Social Data Analytics Accelerator and the list that follows describes its components.

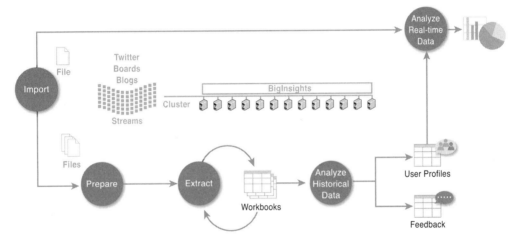

Figure 5.12 Overview of IBM BigInsights Social Data Analytics Accelerator

- **Import:** The accelerator uses the Gnip[19] Decahose, PowerTrack, and Replay tools to import requested Twitter data, and BoardReader to import blog (and newsgroup and forum) data into the BigInsights environment.
- **Extract:** These components are the first part of the analysis phase, looking at the imported data to extract different types of insight based on configurable rules. The extraction puts the data into CSV format for downstream consumption and also matches the users and sentiments found in the social media stream to already-known users (for example, those known by MDM).
- **Feedback:** This component is composed of buzz (general amount of interest), sentiment, and polarity (is an opinion expressed? if so, is it positive or negative?), intent (whether

---

18. For more information on the Social Data Analytics Accelerator, see [22].

19. For more information on Gnip, see [23].

or not someone wants to buy a product), and ownership (does someone own a product?). Some additional feedback can be customized on a per industry basis.

- **User profiles:** Generally, these are all the things you can find in a master data management profile along with social media–specific data: gender, marital status, name, location, occupation, and influence.

- **Historical analysis:** The resulting data can be viewed in BigSheets or in a set of interactive charts on the BigInsights Console, as well as indexed into Data Explorer for a 360-degree view of the extracted social data.

- **Real-time analysis:** Instead of using offline analytics, we can pipe real-time data from Gnip into InfoSphere Streams, and the same extraction and analysis for lead generation and brand management can be done in real time.

The Social Data Analytics Accelerator described in the preceding paragraphs depends on the *extractors* that pull meaning out of the unstructured and semi structured text found in tweets, blogs, emails, and so on. Extracting elements of text, classifying those elements (such as name, address, telephone number, and product) into standardized and structured data, associating those elements both with each other and across entities (*entity extraction* and *entity resolution*), and allowing search and understanding of the extracted elements in multiple languages are complex and powerful capabilities of the Text Analytics Toolkit delivered with the BigInsights platform. Figure 5.13 illustrates a simple example of what Text Analytics can extract.

In this example, a simple paragraph of structured text has been broken down into individual relevant elements, each of which is then classified into specific domains of structured data elements (name, position, company, city, state/province, and country). This structured data is now easily consumed for analysis and, in particular, can be linked to master data about the named individuals. The text analytics capabilities of BigInsights comes from a well-established IBM Research project called System T[20] and is exposed to developers through a specialized language known as Annotation Query Language (AQL) for creating extractors.

AQL is similar in nature to SQL, but it also supports regular expressions for pattern discovery along with some additional context that can be added to rules to more accurately classify data (for example, to help distinguish a fax number from a cell phone number, look for "fax" or "contact me" in adjacent text). AQL can be invoked from BigSheets, JAQL, or Java, and extractor modules (text analytic modules [TAM]) can be built using the Eclipse tools provided with BigInsights.

A number of multilingual prebuilt extractors come with BigInsights, including Person, Organization, Location, Address, City, DateTime, EmailAddress, NotesEmailAddress, PhoneNumber, and State. Note that some of the prebuilt extractors are actually first-class entities that contain a set of elements (Person has first name, middle name, last name, full name). Many of

---

20. You can find more information on text analytics in [24].

these entities are either master data (Person, Organization, Location) or can be linked to master data during analysis.

Eberhard Hechler is an Executive Architect with IBM in Boeblingen, Germany.
Ivan Milman is a Senior Technical Staff Member with IBM in Austin, Texas.
Martin Oberhofer is an Executive Architect with IBM in Boeblingen, Germany.
Scott Schumacher is a Distinguished Engineer with IBM in Los Angeles, California.
Dan Wolfson is a Distinguished Engineer with IBM in Austin, Texas.

Original Source Text

Extracted with
AQL and Classified

Name	Position	Company	City	State/Province	Country
Eberhard Hechler	Executive Architect	IBM	Boeblingen		Germany
Ivan Milman	Senior Technical Staff Member	IBM	Austin	Texas	
Martin Oberhofer	Executive Architect	IBM	Boeblingen		Germany
Scott Schumacher	Distinguished Engineer	IBM	Los Angeles	California	
Dan Wolfson	Distinguished Engineer	IBM	Austin	Texas	

Figure 5.13   Text Analytics example

For Social MDM, we are trying to improve the behavior of the business based on what we know about our customers and products, and what we can learn from social sources. Within the business community, the standard tools for looking at data are spreadsheets and charts, and these days, more sophisticated visualization (tag clouds and connected clouds). BigSheets fills the need for this form of visualization and manipulation of BigData without exposing the complexities of MapReduce to the business user.

BigSheets is a web-based tool that uses the paradigm of workbook, sheets, and visualizations to layer spreadsheet-type capabilities on BigData. Figure 5.14 provides an example of this.

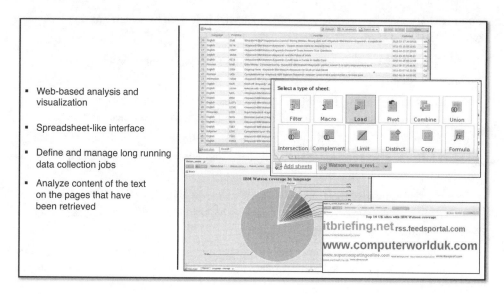

Figure 5.14   BigSheets example

In this example, a workbook has been created (similar to spreadsheet workbooks) from social media, website, and blog feeds searching for the term "IBM Watson." Subsets of the data in the workbook can be put into individual sheets, based on selection criteria (combine sheets, pivot on a column, apply functions, and so on). Then those sheets can be visualized using different charting mechanisms such as charts (bar charts, pie charts, and time-series), clouds (tag clouds and bubble clouds), and maps (heat maps and geographic maps). Workbooks can be created from files in BigInsights repositories (HDFS, GPFS), Amazon S3 or HTTP, applications (like the BoardReader Application), or through views on existing data (using JAQL or BigSQL, for example). Visualizations can be persisted on the console.

InfoSphere MDM and BigInsights Integration

InfoSphere MDM is designed to handle Big Data volumes in real time and to link a variety of data including social media and other unstructured content to master records. It thus enables and supports Big Data initiatives and Social MDM. The integration of MDM with InfoSphere BigInsights[21] goes above and beyond the Big Match capability; it enables Social MDM by augmenting and operationalizing customer insight that is derived from vast social media analytics—for example, sentiment scores of customer products and services, topic-based influencer ranking, and viral marketing scores for individual subscribers.

---

21. Although we are highlighting the integration between MDM and InfoSphere BigInsights, there are additional Big Data integration points, such as the integration of MDM with IBM Watson Explorer and InfoSphere Streams, which we address in subsequent sections of this chapter.

Following are some key value points of Social MDM, derived by integrating Big Data analytics with MDM-based customer centricity:

- Leverage pervasive operational customer insight for consistent cross-channel subscriber communication.

- Launch improved mobile marketing and advertisement campaigns by choosing adequate latency and relevant geospatial knowledge with Big Data–derived insight.

- Use Social MDM and workflow integration for viral marketing; generate and leverage social influencer score, past acceptance score, and other measures (for example, social network profile–related scores).

- Execute real-time next best action (NBA) scenarios with Social MDM–enabled customer interaction; augment with pervasive exploration and visualization across entire internal and external data source landscape.

- Leverage Social MDM customer data integration system to communicate consistently via social media; use trusted and complete master data for social media–based customer interaction.

As you have seen already in this chapter, with its pervasive analytics capabilities on text and unstructured data in general, InfoSphere BigInsights enables the discovery of linkages between unstructured data and relevant master data entities.

With this rich set of analytical capabilities in InfoSphere BigInsights, business insight that is hidden in large volumes of a diverse range of data can be discovered and analyzed. This data—including log records, clickstreams, social media data, news feeds, email, electronic sensor output, and even some transactional data such as Telco CDR and Probe data—is often ignored or discarded because it's too impractical or difficult to process using traditional means. With the integration of InfoSphere BigInsights with InfoSphere MDM, it links master data entities that are managed and maintained in InfoSphere MDM with additional information and insight derived from unstructured data, for instance, from social networking sites.

IBM Watson Explorer Integration with BigInsights and Streams

The IBM Watson Explorer complements InfoSphere BigInsights and InfoSphere Streams in exploring master data in a broader Big Data context. This platform for navigating and filtering large amounts of data in nearly any format offers a visual dashboard that joins master data about an individual with that person's detailed transaction history from emails, social media, packaged applications, and more.

IBM Watson Explorer lets users specify existing master data records and puts these records into a broader perspective. With master data as the starting point, IBM Watson Explorer can also place real-time activity streams into context for analysis. Intelligence, law enforcement, and fraud analysts need to leverage all relevant pieces of information to connect the dots and make well-informed decisions instantly. IBM Watson Explorer works from known master data to give intelligence agencies a unified view of all their information sources to deliver visibility, transparency, and insight.

IBM Watson Explorer[22] addresses these challenges by delivering, exploring, and visualizing information from heterogeneous data sources—internal and external—in a form that is usable for LOB personnel. IBM Watson Explorer provides indexing and integration capabilities across all data sources—structured and unstructured—in place, which means that data doesn't have to be moved. It also supports the existing security model of each repository so users can't see information that would not be accessible to them if they were directly logged in to the target systems.

For external systems such as web-based information sources or systems, direct indexing is not required. Instead, federated access is provided by querying the target systems to integrate results at query time. The resulting rich discovery and navigation capabilities provide easy access to vast information with features such as dynamic categorization and rich end-user applications that deliver information in context to users based on their role and responsibilities.

In a Social MDM context, customer service agents can view information from multiple sources in a single view, enabling them to assist customers more efficiently. This allows dynamic integration, exploration, and visualization of a true 360-degree customer profile. With IBM Watson Explorer, customer data is much more accessible and can be visualized in a social context and analyzed to expose new revenue opportunities. Risk is reduced because otherwise-hidden information is exposed; compliance is improved with better access to information. Security is enhanced by enabling corporate security officers and investigators to view information across multiple sources.

Trusted Information Integration

Social MDM relies significantly on services that are provided by a trusted information integration layer. We provided an overview of these capabilities in Chapter 3, "Capability Framework for Social MDM," but also in other chapters such as the ones on customer care, marketing, and mobile MDM.

We complement the architectural and additional aspects of Social MDM by providing a high-level overview of the following three products. The emphasis is on the integration of some of the capabilities in these products to deliver a pervasive, trusted information integration layer:

- **IBM InfoSphere Information Server:** We limit our presentation to describing the purpose and role of the various Information Server product modules and components in the Social MDM context.

---

22. Information on IBM Watson Explorer (previously known as IBM InfoSphere Data Explorer) can be found in [25], [26], and [27].

- **IBM InfoSphere BigInsights:** The purpose of including IBM InfoSphere BigInsights is to highlight its Apache Hadoop MapReduce-based information integration and processing capabilities, especially in conjunction with key components of the Information Server, specifically InfoSphere DataStage.

- **IBM InfoSphere Streams:** We concentrate on real-time processing and analytics of incoming streaming data to augment the information integration capabilities of the Information Server. Again, we emphasize the integration of InfoSphere Streams with InfoSphere DataStage.

Besides providing a high-level product overview, we intend to illustrate the integration and coexistence of all three offerings as they provide a holistic and pervasive set of trusted information integration capabilities for Social MDM.

Instead of repeating pure product functions and features in this chapter, we provide links to IBM product information centers and product documentation.

InfoSphere Information Server

In a Big Data and Social MDM context, customers need to successfully and flexibly integrate data anywhere it resides, with sources ranging from mainframe to Big Data, while applying governance and data quality best practices. IBM InfoSphere Information Server V11.3[23] delivers information integration capabilities that an organization can use to succeed as the volume of data and sources grows with accelerating speed and complexity. Because IBM developed InfoSphere Information Server with a focus on agile integration, business-driven governance, and sustainable data quality, organizations gain the responsive yet sophisticated information integration capabilities necessary to thrive in today's exceedingly information-rich environment.

With the end-to-end information integration capabilities of InfoSphere Information Server, companies are able to better understand, cleanse, monitor, transform, and deliver their data, as well as collaborate to bridge the gap between business and IT. The "anywhere integration" capabilities of InfoSphere Information Server help firms ensure that the information that drives their business and strategic initiatives—from Big Data and point-of-impact analytics to Social MDM and data warehousing—is trusted, consistent, and governed.

---

23. You can find more information on IBM InfoSphere Information Server in [5], and new features and changes for IBM InfoSphere Information Server 11.3 in [28].

The capabilities of InfoSphere Information Server V11.3 are available in four essential packages[24] that help firms target key information challenges, as depicted in Figure 5.15.

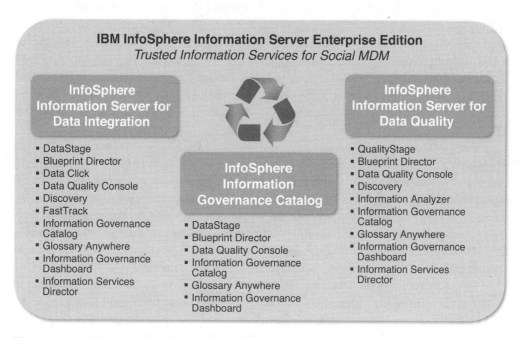

Figure 5.15   IBM InfoSphere Information Server v11.3

- **InfoSphere Information Server for Data Integration:** Transform data in any style and deliver it to any system, supporting faster time-to-value and reduced risk for IT.

- **InfoSphere Information Server for Data Quality:** Establish and manage high-quality data, turning a deluge of data into trusted information.

- **InfoSphere Information Governance Catalog:** Understand data and foster collaboration between IT and line-of-business teams to narrow the communication gap and create business-driven information integration. Helps users find relevant data.

- **InfoSphere Information Server Enterprise Edition:** Gain the capabilities of all three individual packages in one comprehensive package so firms can start information integration efforts in one area and then be ready to expand when needed to further optimize results.

---

24. You can find more information on all IBM InfoSphere Information Server packages in [29].

InfoSphere DataStage Balanced Optimization for Hadoop

InfoSphere Information Server V11.3 includes new capabilities that organizations need in order to integrate and address the extreme volume, variety, velocity, and veracity of Big Data from existing but also new and emerging data sources. Building on IBM's existing InfoSphere Big Insights, Cloudera, and Hortonworks-certified HDFS support, InfoSphere Information Server V11.3 includes Balanced Optimization for Hadoop.[25] Extending the HDFS features in Info-Sphere Information Server V9.1, the Balanced Optimization features of InfoSphere DataStage[26] can be used to push sets of data integration processing and related data I/O into a Hadoop cluster. InfoSphere DataStage adds integration with Oozie workflows, as well as real-time integration with InfoSphere Streams.

For job designs that use connectors or the InfoSphere Big Data File Stage (BDFS)[27] to read or write data from data sources, Balanced Optimization can be used to provide greater control over the job execution. The job is designed as usual, and then Balanced Optimization is used to redesign the job automatically to stated preferences. This redesign process can maximize performance by minimizing the amount of input and output performed, and by balancing the processing against source, intermediate, and target environments. Balanced Optimization enables you to take advantage of the power of the databases without becoming an expert in SQL and Hadoop clusters without becoming an expert in a MapReduce language, such as JAQL.

When a data integration job includes a Big Data source, InfoSphere Information Server pushes the processing to the data. Using the same common set of InfoSphere DataStage stages and links to build the data integration logic, developers may now choose to run the entire logic, or only portions of that logic, for instance, as a Jaql MapReduce job that will execute directly on the Hadoop platform. When the sources and targets of the integration task are Hadoop data stores, this approach will yield significant performance gains, as well as savings in network resource consumption.

Figure 5.16 illustrates the InfoSphere Information Server Balanced Optimizer for Hadoop (Hadoop ETL). In addition to the Balanced Optimization for Hadoop, new connectors are available for download on IBM developerWorks. These connectors plug into InfoSphere DataStage and QualityStage and operate just like any other stage. This includes features to exploit specific data sources, such as Mongo, Cassandra, HBase, Avro, Hive, JMS, and more.

---

25. For more information on the Balanced Optimization for Hadoop, see [30] and [31].

26. For more information on InfoSphere DataStage Balanced Optimization, see [32].

27. For more information on the InfoSphere Big Data File Stage (BDFS), see [5], [6], and [33].

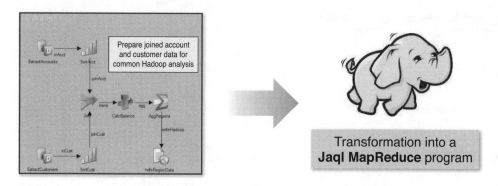

Figure 5.16   InfoSphere Information Server Balanced Optimizer for Hadoop

Real-Time Data Processing

IBM InfoSphere Streams[28] provides an effective execution platform, as well as developer tools, for extracting insights from real-time data streams—before data is saved into databases. Using Streams, organizations can perform advanced real-time analytics and trend prediction, helping improve business insights and accelerate responses to critical events. InfoSphere Streams processes huge volumes and varieties of data from diverse sources while achieving extremely low latency, enabling decision makers to extract relevant information for timely analysis. Streams radically extends the state of the art in information processing by helping organizations to:

- Respond in real time to events and changing requirements and adapt rapidly to changing data forms and types

- Analyze data continuously at rates that are orders of magnitude greater than existing systems, and deliver real-time cognitive computing functions to learn patterns and predict outcomes

- Manage high availability, heterogeneity, and distribution for the stream paradigm, and provide security and confidentiality for shared information

InfoSphere Streams provides required real-time data processing and analytics in the Social MDM context. For Social MDM implementations that focus on real-time analytical processing, IBM offers direct data flow integration between InfoSphere Information Server and InfoSphere Streams to combine the power and reach of both platforms. With this feature, organizations can use standard data integration conventions to gather information from across the enterprise and pass that information to the real-time analytical processes. Similarly, when InfoSphere Streams finds records of insight, that data can now be passed directly to a running data-integration job and made available to data stores or applications across the information landscape, using the full depth and breadth of InfoSphere Information Server connectivity, as illustrated in Figure 5.17.

28. You can find more information on IBM InfoSphere Streams in [34].

IBM InfoSphere DataStage Job

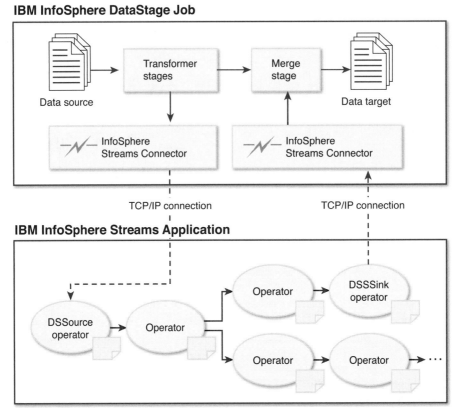

Figure 5.17   InfoSphere DataStage and InfoSphere Streams integration

When data from the InfoSphere DataStage jobs is sent to InfoSphere Streams, InfoSphere Streams can perform near real-time analytic processing (RTAP) in parallel to the data being loaded into a warehouse or being made available to the Social MDM system by InfoSphere DataStage. Alternatively, when data from InfoSphere Streams is sent to InfoSphere DataStage, the InfoSphere Streams job performs RTAP processing and then forwards the data to InfoSphere DataStage to enrich, transform, and store the details for archival and lineage purposes.

Following are some DataStage and Streams integration scenarios:

- An enterprise may want to send data from DataStage to Streams to perform near RTAP on the data stream. When data from the DataStage flow is sent to Streams, Streams can perform RTAP in parallel to master data being updated.

- Alternatively, an enterprise may want to send data from Streams to DataStage. A typical use case might be processing Telco CDR records: the Streams job performs RTAP processing and then forwards the CDR records to Data Stage to enrich, transform, and store the mediated CDRs for archival and lineage purposes.

• A Streams application may require a data source that is not provided by Streams but has a first-class connector in DataStage (for example, Oracle).

Figure 5.17 illustrates the operators and commands that facilitate integration between IBM InfoSphere Streams and IBM InfoSphere DataStage,[29] where the solid and dashed arrows represent the data flow and network connections, respectively.

Pervasive Analytics Capabilities

As we discuss further in subsequent chapters of this book, Social MDM relies significantly on obtaining analytical insight from a vast amount of structured and non-structured data made available from a heterogeneous source data landscape. These pervasive analytical capabilities enrich, for instance, the customer profile and deliver true 360-degree customer insight. They are provided by a variety of IBM products that address traditional descriptive and predictive analytical insight, but also prescriptive and ever-growing cognitive analytical requirements.

Figure 5.18 illustrates the various levels and the evolution from descriptive to predictive and prescriptive to cognitive analytics. It lists the key characteristics and technical capabilities of each phase or analytics domain. Naturally, there are several possible analytics journeys and entry points. Clients will not always need to have a mature prescriptive analytics platform in place to launch a cognitive analytics initiative.

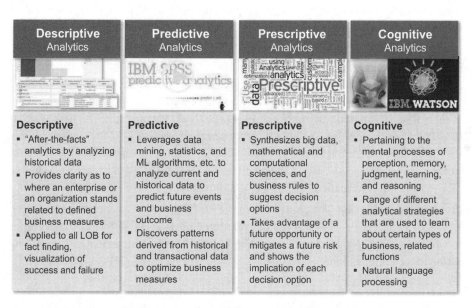

Descriptive Analytics	Predictive Analytics	Prescriptive Analytics	Cognitive Analytics
Descriptive	**Predictive**	**Prescriptive**	**Cognitive**
▪ "After-the-facts" analytics by analyzing historical data ▪ Provides clarity as to where an enterprise or an organization stands related to defined business measures ▪ Applied to all LOB for fact finding, visualization of success and failure	▪ Leverages data mining, statistics, and ML algorithms, etc. to analyze current and historical data to predict future events and business outcome ▪ Discovers patterns derived from historical and transactional data to optimize business measures	▪ Synthesizes big data, mathematical and computational sciences, and business rules to suggest decision options ▪ Takes advantage of a future opportunity or mitigates a future risk and shows the implication of each decision option	▪ Pertaining to the mental processes of perception, memory, judgment, learning, and reasoning ▪ Range of different analytical strategies that are used to learn about certain types of business, related functions ▪ Natural language processing

Figure 5.18   Pervasive analytics capabilities

29. You can find more information on the integration between IBM InfoSphere Streams and IBM InfoSphere DataStage in [35] and [36].

We define cognitive systems as those systems that can navigate the complexities of human language and understanding, ingest and process vast amounts of structured and unstructured data, generate and evaluate countless possibilities, and scale in proportion to the task. These systems apply human-like characteristics to conveying and manipulating ideas that, when combined with the inherent strengths of digital computing, can solve problems with higher accuracy, more resilience, and on a massive scale.

The reality of analytics-related use case scenarios is that clients may have requirements on the entire continuum of analytics. The focus may be on descriptive analytics with the need to implement all corresponding technical capabilities, but also analytical requirements from the remaining three analytics domains, including cognitive analytics. For instance, some clients may have a rather mature descriptive analytics platform and require natural language processing (NLP) capabilities for a sentiment analytics project. This can then be used to derive to brand sentiment and affinity analytical insight, without necessarily implementing a sophisticated predictive analytics platform.

The following list is a high-level mapping of IBM's products and tools to the four domains of analytics. This list, however, is not complete; it simply illustrates the product and tool scope of IBM:

- **Descriptive Analytics:** This is mainly delivered through IBM Cognos Business Intelligence[30] software, which provides for reports, dashboards, analysis, collaboration, and scorecarding to help support the way people think and work when they are trying to understand business performance.

- **Predictive Analytics:** The two primary products that provide predictive analytics is the IBM SPSS[31] family of products. SPSS provides both the tooling and the runtime for data collection, statistics and modeling, social media and predictive analytics for Big Data, and analytical decision management. SPSS offers a choice about where to execute many of their analytic algorithms—they can be executed standalone, in a database such as IBM PureData System for Analytics[32] (powered by Netezza technology), in InfoSphere streams or InfoSphere DataStage. In other words, we can perform many of the analytics where it makes the most sense—either close to where the data already is (such as within a database) or as information is collected or moved.

- **Prescriptive Analytics:** The ability to suggest decision options—one of the key capabilities of prescriptive analytics—is delivered via IBM Unica software.[33] IBM Unica software provides, for instance, cross-channel marketing optimization and marketing performance optimization.

30. For more information on IBM Cognos Business Intelligence (BI) software, see [37] and [38].
31. For more information on IBM SPSS software, see [39].
32. For more information on IBM PureData for Analytics, see [40].
33. For more information on IBM Unica software, see [41].

- **Cognitive Analytics:** In addition to InfoSphere BigInsights and InfoSphere Streams, IBM Watson pertains to the mental processes of perception, memory, judgment, learning, and reasoning and provides NLP capabilities. IBM Watson[34] is a cognitive technology that processes information more like a human than a computer—by understanding natural language, generating hypotheses based on evidence, and learning as it goes.

References

[1] IBM. "IBM InfoSphere MDM Version 11 Information Center." Retrieved 03/2014 from http://pic.dhe.ibm.com/infocenter/mdm/v11r0/index.jsp.

[2] IBM Software Solution Brief. "Master Data Governance: Strengthen Your Master Data Management Program with Trusted Data and Continuous Data Quality Improvement." Retrieved 12/2012 from http://www-03.ibm.com/software/products/en/infomastdatamanaenteedit/.

[3] Ballard, C., T. Anderson, L. Dubov, A. Eastman, J. Limburn, J., and U. Ramakrishnan. "Aligning MDM and BPM for Master Data Governance, Stewardship, and Enterprise Processes." IBM Redbooks. Retrieved 03/2013 from http://www.redbooks.ibm.com/redbooks/pdfs/sg248059.pdf.

[4] IBM Technical White Paper. "IBM InfoSphere Master Data Management V11 Standard Edition: Functional Overview." Retrieved 07/2013 from http://public.dhe.ibm.com/common/ssi/ecm/en/imw14624usen/IMW14624USEN.PDF.

[5] IBM. "IBM InfoSphere Information Server Version 9.1 Information Center." Retrieved 03/2014 from http://pic.dhe.ibm.com/infocenter/iisinfsv/v9r1/index.jsp.

[6] IBM. "IBM InfoSphere Information Server Version 9.1 product documentation." Retrieved 03/2014 from http://www-01.ibm.com/support/docview.wss?uid=swg27035772.

[7] Ballard, C., M. Bhide, H. Kache, B. Kitzberger, B. Porst, Y.H. Sheng, and H. C. Smith. "IBM Information Server: Integration and Governance for Emerging Data Warehouse Demands." IBM Redbooks. Retrieved 07/2013 from http://www.redbooks.ibm.com/redbooks/pdfs/sg248126.pdf.

[8] IBM. "IBM InfoSphere BigInsights Version 2.1.2 documentation." Retrieved 03/2014 from http://www-01.ibm.com/support/knowledgecenter/#!/SSPT3X_2.1.2/com.ibm.swg.im.infosphere.biginsights.welcome.doc/doc/welcome.html?cp=SSPT3X.

[9] The Apache Software Foundation. "Apache Sqoop." Retrieved 04/2014 from http://sqoop.apache.org/.

---

34. You can find more information on IBM Watson technology and solutions in [42].

[10] IBM. "What Is Flume?" Retrieved 04/2014 from http://www-01.ibm.com/software/data/infosphere/hadoop/flume/.

[11] Gamma, E., R. Helm, R. Johnson, and J. Vlissides. *Design Patterns: Elements of Reusable Object-Oriented Software* (Upper Saddle River, NJ: Addison Wesley, 1994).

[12] IBM. "IBM InfoSphere Guardium." Retrieved 04/2014 from http://www.ibm.com/developerworks/data/library/techarticle/dm-1210bigdatasecurity/index.html.

[13] Woodle, A., "What Can GPFS on Hadoop Do for You." Retrieved 04/2014 from http://www.datanami.com/datanami/2014-02-18/what_can_gpfs_on_hadoop_do_for_you_.html.

[14] MacLean, D., "A Very Brief Introduction to MapReduce." Retrieved 04/2014 from http://hci.stanford.edu/courses/cs448g/a2/files/map_reduce_tutorial.pdf.

[15] IBM. "What Is Pig?" Retrieved 04/2014 from http://www-01.ibm.com/software/data/infosphere/hadoop/pig.

[16] IBM. "What Is Hive?" Retrieved 04/2014 from http://www-01.ibm.com/software/data/infosphere/hadoop/hive.

[17] IBM. "What Is Jaql?" Retrieved 04/2014 from http://www-01.ibm.com/software/data/infosphere/hadoop/jaql.

[18] Apache Habse. "Welcome to Apache HBase." Retrieved 04/2014 from https://hbase.apache.org.

[19] Saracco, C.M., and U. Jain., "What's the Big Deal about Big SQL?" IBM developerWorks. Retrieved 07/2014 from http://www.ibm.com/developerworks/library/bd-bigsql/index.html.

[20] IBM. "What Is Oozie?" Retrieved 04/2014 from http://www-01.ibm.com/software/data/infosphere/hadoop/oozie/.

[21] IBM. "What Is ZooKeeper?" Retrieved 04/2014 from http://www-01.ibm.com/software/data/infosphere/hadoop/zookeeper/.

[22] IBM. "IBM Knowledge Center. IBM Accelerator for Social Data Analytics." Retrieved 04/2014 from http://www-01.ibm.com/support/knowledgecenter/SSPT3X_2.1.1/com.ibm.swg.im.infosphere.bigdata.sda.doc/doc/acc_sda.html.

[23] GNIP. "GNIP Products." Retrieved 04/2014 from http://gnip.com/products/.

[24] Saracco, C.M., G. Robinson, and V. Bommireddipalli., "Analyze Text from Social Media Sites with InfoSphere BigInsights." IBM developerWorks. Retrieved 05/2013 from http://www.ibm.com/developerworks/library/bd-socialmediabiginsights/index.html?ca=drs-.

[25] IBM. "IBM Watson Explorer." Retrieved 04/2014 from http://www.ibmbigdata-hub.com/tag/1552.

[26] IBM. "IBM InfoSphere Data Explorer." Retrieved 04/2014 from http://www-03. ibm.com/software/products/en/dataexplorer/.

[27] IBM. "IBM InfoSphere Data Explorer Version 9 Information Center." Retrieved 04/2014 from http://pic.dhe.ibm.com/infocenter/dataexpl/v9r0/index.jsp.

[28] IBM. "New Features and Changes for InfoSphere Information Server 9.1.2." Retrieved 04/2014 from http://www-01.ibm.com/support/docview. wss?uid=swg27038752.

[29] IBM. "IBM InfoSphere Information Server packages." Retrieved 04/2014 from http://www-03.ibm.com/software/products/en/infoinfoserventeedit/.

[30] IBM. "IBM InfoSphere DataStage and QualityStage Version 9 Release 1, Parallel Job Developer's Guide." Retrieved 04/2014 from http://publibfp.boulder.ibm.com/ epubs/pdf/c1938270.pdf, SC19-3827-.

[31] Lella, R., "Optimizing BDFS Jobs Using InfoSphere DataStage Balanced Optimization." IBM developerWorks. Retrieved 02/2014 from http://www.ibm.com/ developerworks/data/library/techarticle/dm-1402optimizebdfs/dm-1402optimizebdfs-pdf.pdf.

[32] IBM. "IBM InfoSphere Information Server Version 9.1.2 Information Center. Introduction to IBM InfoSphere DataStage Balanced Optimization." Retrieved 04/2014 from http://pic.dhe.ibm.com/infocenter/iisinfsv/v9r1/index.jsp?topic=%2Fcom.ibm. swg.im.iis.ds.parjob.dev.doc%2Ftopics%2Fintroductiontobalancedoptimization.html.

[33] IBM. "IBM InfoSphere Big Data File Stage (BDFS)." Retrieved 04/2014 from http://www-01.ibm.com/support/docview.wss?uid=swg21515617.

[34] IBM. "IBM InfoSphere Streams Version 3.2 Information Center." Retrieved 04/2014 from http://pic.dhe.ibm.com/infocenter/streams/v3r2/index. jsp?topic=%2Fcom.ibm.swg.im.infosphere.streams.dev.doc%2Fdoc%2Ftut-container. html .

[35] IBM. "InfoSphere Streams Version 3.2 Information Center. IBM InfoSphere DataStage Integration Toolkit." Retrieved 04/2014 from http://pic.dhe.ibm.com/ infocenter/streams/v3r2/index.jsp?topic=%2Fcom.ibm.swg.im.infosphere.streams. datastage-toolkit.doc%2Fdoc%2Fds-container.html.

[36] Ballard, C., O. Brandt, B. Devaraju, D. Farrell, K. Foster, C. Howard, P. Nicholls, A. Pasricha, R. Rea, N. Schulz, T. Shimada, J. Thorson, S. Tucker, and R. Uleman. "IBM InfoSphere Streams—Accelerating Deployments with Analytic Accelerators." Retrieved 02/2014 from http://www.redbooks.ibm.com/redbooks/pdfs/sg248139.pdf, IBM Redbooks, SG24-8139-00.

[37] IBM. "Cognos Business Intelligence." Retrieved 04/2014 from http://www-03. ibm.com/software/products/en/business-intelligence/.

[38] IBM. "IBM Cognos Business Intelligence 10.2.0 Information Center." Retrieved 04/2014 from http://pic.dhe.ibm.com/infocenter/cbi/v10r2m0/index.jsp?topic=%2Fcom.ibm.swg.ba.cognos.cbi.doc%2Fwelcome.html.

[39] IBM. "IBM SPSS." Retrieved 04/2014 from http://www-01.ibm.com/software/analytics/spss/.

[40] IBM. "IBM PureData System for Analytics." Retrieved 04/2014 from http://www-01.ibm.com/software/data/puredata/analytics/.

[41] IBM. "Unica Software Is Now Part of IBM." Retrieved 04/2014 from http://www-01.ibm.com/software/info/unica/.

[42] IBM. "What Is Watson?" Retrieved 04/2014 from http://www.ibm.com/smarterplanet/us/en/ibmwatson/.

CHAPTER 6

Social MDM and Customer Care

Improving customer care is a top priority for leading CMOs, who are trying to understand individuals as well as markets.[1] Enterprises today are extending their customer care systems by integrating social media programs. The value of MDM to improve customer care is not new. MDM has been used for years to build, maintain, and leverage an enterprise-wide "single version of the truth" of customer data for the purpose of enhancing the customer experience. The novel aspect comes through additional insight that is derived, for instance, from social media that complements the existing knowledge of your customer base.

Additional customer insight is also derived from analytics of data related to the many ways customers interact with the business, such as call centers including interactive voice response (IVR), company websites and Facebook sites, emails and chats, customer touch points, and so forth. Even transactional data that contains social media–related pieces will be incorporated to gain additional insight.

Customer care is a central mission of many MDM systems. Through improving customer care, organizations hope to maintain customer satisfaction, manage customer retention, and attract new customers. Social MDM extends your ability to improve customer experience by leveraging social media and social relationships to better understand the behavior, needs, and wants of individuals and groups.

Throughout this chapter, we provide an industry perspective on social customer care and also address the enriched analytical insight gained across all sources of data.

Gauging Social Media Data

In our engagements with customers, we often need to address the relevance of the analytical insight that is derived from social media data. Customers' social media–based profiles and other insights may not necessarily be related to the nature of the company's business. Depending on the source data, some social media analytics will remain at an aggregation level, where market

1. You can find the IBM 2011 CMO Study in [1].

133

trends, the "public opinion," or sentiment about a company and its brands, products, and services cannot be linked to an individual customer; and it doesn't necessarily have to be to an individual customer.

Customer care can still be improved even if the linkage to a specific customer cannot be deduced from social media analytics. Of course, if a Facebook, Twitter, or YouTube contribution can be linked to a specific customer, the relevance for improving customer care for that particular customer and members of his or her social network and interest group(s) is significantly higher.

Following are some questions that are addressed in this chapter:

- What do *customer care, customer experience,* and *customer centricity* mean, and do these terms relate to each other?

- What is changing in customer behavior and their expectations that motivate enterprises, strengthening their customer-centric business model even more?

- How can we analyze and influence the impact of social media on the customer perception regarding enterprise-relevant business metrics?

- What is the relationship of social MDM to DW and CRM systems from a customer care perspective?

- How can we characterize the changing nature and new aspects of customer care in the context of social media?

- What are the current and emerging customer-centric models, such as cliques, social networks, and interest groups?

This chapter provides insight into the changing characteristics of customer-centric business models and the determination of next best action (NBA) for a specific customer in a given situation. It furthermore examines the trustworthiness of social media for customer care and underpins key messages through some basic examples.

This chapter also discusses the following key themes that will enrich your customer insight:

- **Sentiment analysis:** For instance, how are my products and services viewed by my customers, competitors, analysts, and my employees?

- **Topic-based influencer determination:** Do particular individuals strongly influence the opinions and behaviors of other customers?

- **Social network:** How are my customers interconnected with each other—for instance, families, cliques, circle of friends, clubs, and communities?

Although many social attributes are generally interesting, they are often augmented by industry-specific characteristics. In the telecommunications industry, for instance, the influence of a churned subscriber on the churn propensity for other subscribers is a strong characteristic in that industry.

Customer Centricity

Customer care and insight are part of a long-established discipline within many businesses and are well recognized for their paramount importance to the business.[2] In the following sections, we highlight the ever-increasing importance of a customer care and insight business model that is influenced by the shift toward *social* customer centricity.

In addition, we introduce a high-level customer care reference model that underpins the vital role of social MDM in this context. Last but not least, we highlight the improved customer lifetime view (in a separate section) that constitutes a key-value add within the shift toward social customer centricity.

Moving Toward Social Customer Centricity

When we are moving toward social customer centricity, what is the role of MDM in contributing to and enriching a customer-centric care model? If customer interaction is based on individual and effectively isolated channels, where each channel uses customer profiling information based on its own system, this will certainly result in poor customer experience. As we highlighted in Chapter 1, "Introduction to Social MDM," MDM can significantly improve the trustworthiness, completeness, and accuracy of subscriber information enterprise-wide. This is mainly due to the cross-channel capabilities of MDM. Social media augments the MDM customer profile.

Social media represents yet another channel by itself that allows an enterprise to effectively communicate to an individual party or a party group. With regard to the customer base, an MDM customer data integration system with its complete and accurate knowledge about the customer base should be leveraged in communicating consistently via social media. Later in this chapter, we explore this topic further. An MDM system that manages other master data domains, such as the product and services domains, will also enable a mature social media–based customer engagement model. That is, trusted and complete master data is made available for social media–based customer interaction.

On the other hand, social media represents a wealth of source data that can be used to gain deeper insight into the subscriber base, the social network and communities, the sentiment about products and services, and hot topics that are relevant for an enterprise, to list just a few examples. It is essential to understand how insight derived from social media influences and enriches the customer profile persisted in the MDM system. Social media analytical insight not only should be consumed by, for instance, a marketing campaign management system or a real-time service delivery platform, but also should be captured by an MDM system to improve the relevance, breadth, and depth of master data domains for the benefit of improving the customer-centric business model.

To illustrate how social media–derived insight improves the relevance of MDM operational aspects and how downstream systems can consume and benefit from that information, we need a customer care reference model, which we illustrate in the following section.

---

2. You can find more information on customer care in [2], [3], and [4].

Social Customer Care Reference Model

Let's look at the key components of a social customer care reference model, the role of an MDM system, and the benefit of social media–derived insight in that customer care reference model. Figure 6.1 presents a high-level depiction of the MDM system as a key component within this social media–centric customer care model. Furthermore, it depicts the role of the MDM system as a consuming system to leverage social media–derived insight to enrich the single view of the customer profile.

This model encompasses offline, online, and real-time capabilities. Although reports and dashboards may describe periodic or current behavior, supporting automated responses to current customer needs often requires real-time capabilities. For instance, depending on the use case scenario, a social customer care model needs to allow for adequate customer care actions in real time. That is, the analytical insight as well as the customer engagement and interaction need to be executed in real time.

Figure 6.1 illustrates the social customer care reference model, the key components of which are described in the list that follows.

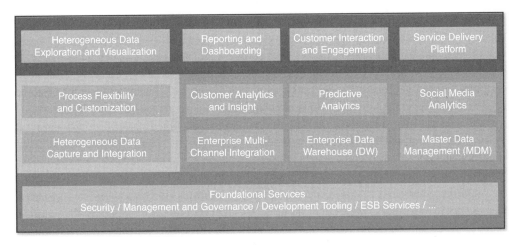

Figure 6.1 Social customer care reference model

- **Foundational Services:** This component provides ESB services for the communication and interaction of application and system software components in an SOA architecture, such as Service Registry and Repository (SRR) services, service management and invocation services, and the external services gateway.
- **Heterogeneous Data Capture and Integration:** Above and beyond the traditional information integration capabilities, this component needs to provide access to the heterogeneous social media data that resides in social networking websites (such as

Facebook, Twitter, and LinkedIn), blog websites (such as WordPress.com, Blog.com, and Flickr.com), newsgroups[3], and forums[4], but also nonstructured operational data (for example, telco CDRs[5], energy and utility smart meter data, and financial services feeds in real time). It may also (temporarily) store social media data. This component constitutes essential capabilities for the *social* customer care reference model.

- **Process Flexibility and Customization:** Existing processes have to be rapidly customized and continuously optimized according to new business requirements. The required process flexibility needs to orchestrate and assemble customer care services and new customer-centric offerings.

- **Enterprise-wide Multichannel Integration:** Any customer interaction needs to represent a consistent customer experience across multiple channels, including social media channels. Information, offerings, and campaigns need to be consistently managed across multiple channels. Customer communication preferences also need to be taken into consideration. Channel preferences need to be understood in the action context and the customer interaction content. Social media networks, such as Facebook or Twitter, may serve as a channel to respond to customer complaints or negative sentiments regarding a product or service.

- **Master Data Management (MDM):** This component ensures a single view of core information, such as parties (customers, supplier, employees, households, and so on), products and services, and accounts. It provides required services as outlined in Chapter 1. MDM also provides services to other components in the reference model, such as the analytics components. In addition, MDM is a consumer of the analytics components, meaning that customer profiles are enriched through insight derived by social media analytics (such as influencer scores), and product or service information is enriched through sentiment information.

- **Customer Analytics and Insight:** This component is composed of analytical capabilities to provide insight into the customer base. This includes customer needs, preferences, money-spending behavior, and insight into other activities that are related to the business of the enterprise and beyond. This component tightly interacts with the "predictive analytics" and "social media analytics" components.

---

3. You can find some examples of newsgroups in [5].
4. You can find some examples of forums in [6].
5. Telco call detail records (CDRs) contain details on every telecommunication transaction (call, SMS, data usage). A CDR for a particular phone call might include the phone numbers of both the calling and receiving parties, the start time, and duration of that call, and so on.

- **Predictive Analytics:** Business optimization is strongly related to predictive capabilities, where the scope addresses prediction of marketing campaign response rates, acceptance of a next best offer for a particular customer, churn prediction, acceptance, and responsiveness to a new product or service.

- **Social Media Analytics:** This component represents one of the key components of the reference model, which aims for insight that is derived from social media data sources, such as social networking and blog websites, newsgroups, and forums. The insight relates to customers and public sentiments and perceptions on enterprises and institutions, products and services, elections, and social themes.

- **Heterogeneous Data Exploration and Visualization:** Specifically in regards to the massive amount of social media data, the visualization, and the early exploration of data are key capabilities to be provided by this component. This serves the purpose to decide on what data to focus on prior to executing costly data transformation and preparation jobs as part of a comprehensive information supply chain. Executing data exploration at the social data source level and linking this together with data from other sources (for example, CRM systems, MDM system, billing systems) to visualize it in context constitute a paradigm shift in the social customer care reference model.

- **Reporting and Dashboarding:** This component provides the "standard" reporting and dashboarding capabilities that you are most likely familiar with from existing DW environments. However, it also needs to provide this capability on platforms other than the traditional DW system—for instance, on a Hadoop platform, such as IBM InfoSphere BigInsights.

- **Customer Integration and Engagement:** This component ensures that the loop is closed back to the customer. In other words, this component should be viewed as part of the "systems of engagement and interaction"[6] concept that transforms the analytical insight into an adequate interaction with the customer. This component ensures the delivery of an adequate response back to the customer, including the use of social media as a channel.

- **Service Delivery Platform:** Analytical insight needs to result in a new service or update of an existing service. The service delivery platform goes beyond a simple response back to the customer; it transforms insight into a suitable action or service for a customer or a defined customer segment. This could be a marketing campaign to improve the sentiment of a newly launched product or service.

Figure 6.2 depicts the role of the MDM system within social customer care.

---

6. For more information on IBM Systems of Interaction, see [7].

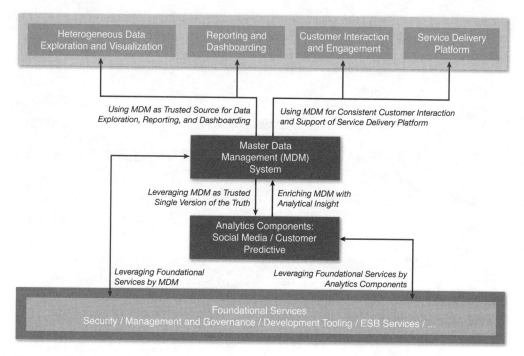

Figure 6.2   Role of MDM system within social customer care environment

As illustrated in Figure 6.2, the MDM system plays a vital role as a trusted source of core information for data exploration and visualization, but also for "traditional" reporting and dashboarding purposes. Furthermore, the MDM system will be leveraged to enable consistent customer interaction and engagement experience to feed trusted master data into the service delivery platform.

A key interaction also is illustrated—namely, the one between the MDM system and the various analytics components. On one hand, the MDM system serves as a trusted source of master data for a wide variety of analytical tasks. On the other hand, the analytical insight that is derived from the analytics components is used to enrich the MDM system. For instance, the customer profile within the MDM system can be significantly enriched by insight derived from social media analytics.

The foundational services will be leveraged by both the MDM system and the analytical components.

Figure 6.3 highlights the role of MDM within social customer care in the context of the Social MDM Reference Architecture, which has been introduced in Chapter 3. The key components, such as the MDM system itself, the analytics components, the foundational services, and the top layer for visualization, reporting, customer interaction, and the service delivery platform are highlighted in the context of the Social MDM Reference Architecture.

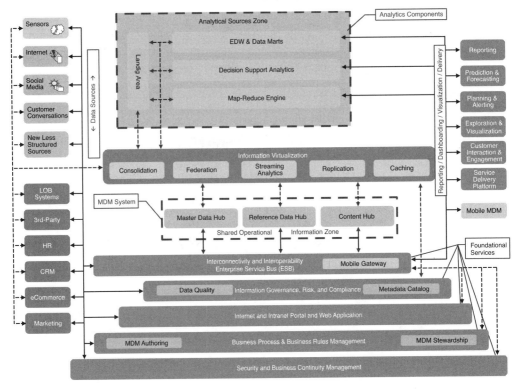

Figure 6.3   Social customer care in the context of the Social MDM RA

As you have seen in this section, using social media as a channel for customer interaction raises interesting challenges for traditional customer care and CRM solutions. The social customer care reference model needs to be underpinned with a strategy and architecture that includes processes and technologies.[7]

Customer Lifetime View

Customers' behavior and expectations, their interests, and communication preferences will change over time. Subsequently, the customer lifetime view needs to be architected to manage customer relationships as a means for extracting the greatest value from customers over the lifetime of the relationship.

7. For a fairly detailed and comprehensive review of the Social CRM topics, see [8]. You can find a high-level IBM point of view on Social CRM in [9] and [10].

This process includes the following aspects:

- Understanding and honoring customer preferences and interests in communications, including social media as a channel to communicate with customers as well as understanding customers' preferences

- Defining and understanding the customer lifecycle (for example, unknown, prospect, customer, former customer) and how it is influenced through social media

- Managing customer relationships across their career—as customers change jobs and affiliations—and using social media as a means to improve customer care

As a new channel through which enterprises and institutions can engage their customers, social media, including Facebook, YouTube, Google, and Twitter, represents a significant shift in the customer interaction and engagement model. The traditional customer lifetime view was primarily managed through sales and conventional marketing strategies. Social consumers, however, act very different, which requires an adjustment of the customer lifetime model.

Advanced and predictive analytics on social media data are obviously key capabilities to address the aforementioned aspects. Analytics, of course, always played a key role in understanding the behavior, preferences, buying patterns, and sentiment of customers. The novel aspect is the improved and new insight that can be derived from social media, how this enriches the customer profile stored in the MDM system (and other core information as well), and—most importantly—how this insight can be leveraged to positively influence the customer lifetime view.

Figure 6.4 provides a high-level depiction of the breadth of social media analytics influencing the customer lifetime view.

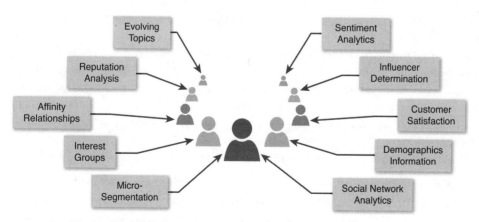

Figure 6.4   Social media analytics influencing the customer lifetime view

In subsequent sections, we elaborate on some of these areas, such as sentiment, buzz, influencer determination, interest groups, and social networks.

Next Best Action (NBA)

Next best action (NBA) is a paradigm that is widely used in marketing, customer care, and business decision making. In the context of customer care, NBA takes into consideration all possible actions and aims to determine the best one for a particular customer. This best action could be a concrete offer, service, or promotion for a specific customer. IBM has developed quite a comprehensive NBA solution and value proposition that is composed of architecture patterns and IBM product underpinnings.[8]

In this section, we review NBA in the context of social media and customer care by answering the following questions:

- How does social media and analytical insight derived from social media augment NBA customer care models?

- What is a sample NBA solution architecture overview diagram for customer care that leverages social media?

- What are the role and value of MDM in NBA scenarios, and what does the NBA solution architecture look like?

- Are there industry-specific aspects to be taken into consideration, and what does a "typical" industry-specific NBA solution look like?

- What are the key technology components, products, and tools that comprise an NBA solution?

Being able to determine the next best action for a particular customer is obviously dependent on rich and relevant analytical insight. Analyzing social media can significantly improve the NBA decision-making process; it can yield more meaningful and relevant actions for a specific customer.

Some social media that is used as a data source to derive insight can be directly linked to a particular customer. Other insight is derived from anonymous contributions to social networking sites, which is nevertheless relevant for a subscriber subset. Obviously, today's enterprises have access to a more pervasive set of source information that is used for the NBA decision-making process, such as behavioral and transactional data (which includes money-spending patterns). Here, we are limiting our view to social media as a data source.

Following are a few examples regarding insight that can be derived from social media:

- Opinions and sentiments (including complaints), perceived value (for example, regarding a service or product), preferences and interests, affinity relationships, and so on

- Social networks and communities, relationships and microsegments (including household and clubs), topic-based influencers, group leaders and followers, and so on

---

8. You can find details about IBM's NBA solution and value proposition in [11] and [12].

Some of this NBA-related analytical insight is also highly relevant for capture in the MDM system, such as cliques, preferences, interests, and preferences.

NBA Technology Components

In this section, we elaborate on the key technical capabilities and technology components that are required to gain analytical insight into the customer base. Table 6.1 lists these required capabilities and components, which can then be easily mapped to products and tools. The four architecture layers are used in the next section, where we provide a high-level NBA solution architecture overview diagram.

Table 6.1   NBA Technology Components

Architecture Layer	Technical Capabilities / Technology Components
Real-Time Data Integration and Transformation Layer	Social media data access, ETL with data quality, metadata management, real-time data transformation, federation of heterogeneous data sources including social media, contextual exploration, and selection of social media data
Data Persistency Layer	Hadoop storage platform (e.g., HDFS), data warehousing, Master Data Management, in-memory DB capabilities
Next Best Action (NBA) and Customer Interaction Layer	NBA definition and management capabilities, customer engagement and interaction capabilities, business rules management, NBA-relevant (real-time) event detection from social media (but also from operational systems)
BI & Predictive Analytics Layer	Social media analytics, integration with DW systems, advanced predictive analytics on social media data, reporting, dashboarding, contextual visualization of social media content

The structure and scope of the four architecture layers in Table 6.1 have been derived from a real customer project with a communications service provider (CSP) in Asia Pacific. Next, we take this one step further by describing these capabilities in the context of an NBA solution architecture.

NBA Solution Architecture

Figure 6.5 depicts an NBA solution architecture overview diagram (AOD) with key required components that are likewise derived from the same CSP implementation project in Asia Pacific.

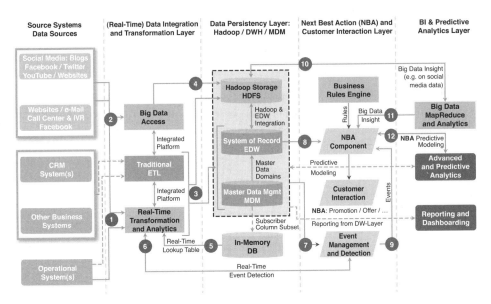

Figure 6.5   NBA solution architecture overview diagram (AOD)

Although it provides a high-level abstraction of the actual architecture, the figure illustrates the key NBA components.

Source systems and data sources can be roughly grouped into four categories:

- **Operational systems:** Banking transaction systems, telco network switches, and probe devices, for instance, provide a wealth of data that can be analyzed to derive money-spending and call patterns. Telco probe devices capture network-level protocol data that includes—depending on the probe and network device configuration—social media–related data, such as URL, domain, and Internet search terms.

- **Internal social media:** Other social media data can be captured through emails from customers, call-center and IVR logs, and logs from websites that an enterprise or government institution maintains, including Facebook sites.

- **External social media:** This is data coming from blogs, Facebook, Twitter, YouTube, external websites, and the like.

- **Business systems:** Even traditional business systems, such as CRM, ERP, and billing systems, are used as key data sources.

Now we walk you through this NBA solution architecture by describing just the key components.

The key NBA solution architecture components shown in Figure 6.5 are as follows:

- **Big Data Access:** This component provides access to social media data. It can also be used in conjunction with real-transformation engines and traditional ETL components.

- **Real-Time Transformation and Analytics:** This component allows real-time capture of incoming data streams in any format, including nonstructured format, such as video streams, voice data, continuous financial and news feeds, and telco network data.

- **Hadoop Storage:** This component can be the Hadoop Distributed File System (HDFS) or IBM's General Parallel File System—File Placement Optimizer (GPFS FPO)[9] storage system to store huge amounts of nonstructured social media but also other data.

- **In-Memory DB:** This component is used in conjunction with real-time transformation and the analytics module for high-speed access of data stored in memory (for lookup purposes).

- **NBA Component:** This key module is used to manage the NBA portfolio that is available to an enterprise, such as an offer, service, or promotion.

- **Event Management and Detection:** This component allows the definition, management, and detection of NBA-relevant events that can be detected in real time through the real-time transformation and analytics component but also through triggers that are defined in the data warehouse.

- **Customer Interaction:** This component ensures the appropriate engagement and interaction with a particular customer, using the most appropriate channel.

- **Big Data MapReduce and Analytics:** This essential component provides visualization and advanced text analytics on nonstructured and social media data.

- **Advanced and Predictive Analytics:** This component is used to develop predictive models that can be deployed on a variety of different platforms (for example, on the real-time analytics platform via Predictive Model Markup Language, or PMML, compliancy).

Following is a brief description of some of the component interaction flow:[10]

> **Flow 1.** Data that feeds into the real-time transformation and analytics component can come directly from social media networking sites (internal and external), as well as from operational systems.

> **Flow 2.** Social media data is made available via the Big Data access component. The data integration layer enables data flows between the various components within the layer. For instance, data feeds can be made available from the real-time transformation and analytics component to the Big Data access component. Depending on the use case attributes (such as ultra low latency) and the data transformation requirements (such as complex transformation), social media data can also be processed in combination with the "traditional" ETL component.

---

9. For more information on GPFS-FPO, see [13] and [14].

10. The list numbers correspond to the numbers in Figure 6.5.

Flow 3. Once processed, the social media data flows into the data persistency layer and is made available to the MDM and EDW components. Core information (such as subscriber information) should be made available to the EDW component via the MDM layer.

Flow 4. Social media data from internal or external sources is made available to the Hadoop storage component for further processing and analytics. Through the data integration layer, data from additional source systems, other than social media sites, can also be made available to the Hadoop platform for further analysis.

Flow 5. The real-time transformation and analytics component accesses the in-memory DB component for ultra-fast lookup of, for instance, a customer ID and to enable NBA decision making in real time.

Flow 6. The event management and detection component defines and manages events and also acts on analytical insight that is derived in real time via the real-time transformation and analytics component.

Flow 7. Likewise, the event management and detection component also defines and manages events that can be detected, for instance, via triggers or other conditions captured in the EDW.

Flow 8. The NBA component accesses data from the data persistency layer for definition and management of next best actions. This data mainly comes from the EDW but could likewise be provisioned from the Hadoop storage and MDM components. The data flow is likely to be implemented in such a way that analytical insight derived via the Hadoop layer is made available in the EDW component to be used for NBA management purposes via the EDW component.

Flow 9. Events are routed to the NBA component for appropriate action for a particular customer. Identical events that have been detected may result in a different NBA for different customers, depending on other information and circumstances that are managed in the NBA component. The final NBA for a particular customer may be based on additional data stored in the MDM system that relates to the segment of a customer, its churn propensity score, personal interest, and other attributes.

Flow 10. The Big Data MapReduce and analytics component analyzes social media (and other) data on the Hadoop layer. This involves, for instance, execution of state-of-the art text analytics capabilities on any kind of social media data. Through the Hadoop and EDW integration capabilities, text analytics can be executed in combination with data that resides on the EDW.

Flow 11. Insight from the Big Data MapReduce and analytics component is made available to the NBA component. This insight augments the insight derived from the traditional EDW layer and works in concert with real-time analytical insight.

Flow 12. Advanced and predictive analytical insight influences the NBA decision-making process. For instance, depending on the projected acceptance level in regards to an offer, this is made available to one customer but perhaps not to another one.

As we mentioned previously, IBM has successfully implemented this NBA solution at a CSP in Asia Pacific. The NBA solution architecture was underpinned with IBM's Big Data and software product portfolio.

Sentiment Analytics

Sentiment analytics relates to the application of text analytics, natural language processing (NLP), and computational linguistics to determine the contextual classification of a given text or parts within a text into positive, negative, or neutral.

Furthermore, sentiment analytics aims to go beyond the pure classification or polarity of a given text; it tries to capture emotions and moods, attitudes and opinions, and even the perception and appreciation of, for instance, a new product, service, or offering.[11]

Scope of Sentiment Analytics

The ever-increasing importance of sentiment analytics is associated with the significant growth of social media and its relevance in almost every business domain. Obviously, sentiment analytics has a huge impact in optimizing customer care. Prior to discussing solution capabilities, we briefly address the following questions:

- How do we define the scope of sentiment analytics and opinion mining?
- What are the business drivers for sentiment analytics, and how does social media change the overall landscape?
- What is the role of MDM in delivering sentiment analytics, and how can sentiment analytics in conjunction with MDM improve customer care?

Opinions, attitudes, and emotions are subjective in nature and complement the actualities and matters of fact. As such, the range of application for sentiment analytics goes far beyond the scope of customer care. It is used in political elections and other social events (such as sports), in life sciences and health care, as well as in social and behavioral sciences. Following are some business drivers regarding sentiment analytics for customer care:[12]

- Improve brands, reputation, products, offerings, services, and service delivery consistently across different channels.
- Deepen the customer relationship and social engagement to improve customer experience, satisfaction, and loyalty.

---

11. For more information on sentiment analytics, see [15] and [16].
12. For more information on business drivers, see [17] and [18].

- Understand the buzz related to a particular theme, evolving topics within a business application area, affinity and relationship among topics and themes, and opinions and other aspects of sentiment to gain deeper and more relevant insight into existing customers and prospects.

- Respond to and resolve real customer issues before they develop into major problems, and identify trends versus one-of-a-kind issues.

- Gain relevant sentiment analytical insight as input into the NBA decision-making process in order to personalize offers and services that resonate with a particular customer.

- Understand customers in new markets and their specific cultural and geographical attributes to develop and evolve products and solutions from direct social media analysis.

On one side, the role of MDM for sentiment analytics is to provide consistent and complete party and customer records where applicable. Apart from that, sentiment analytical insight can enrich the customer and product record in the MDM system. It is possible to link news articles, Facebook postings, and tweets to an "author" and possibly even to a customer. However, discussion forums and contributions to blogs may very well be anonymous.

Nevertheless, even if social media sources (such as postings and tweets) may not be directly linked to a particular customer, sentiment analytics can still enrich the core information that is managed in the MDM system.

Solution Capabilities

IBM has developed a Social Media Analytics solution that provides sentiment analytics.[13] It can segment your audience across geography, demographics, influencers, recommenders, detractors, users, and prospective users. It enables you to measure social media activities, behaviors and sentiment, affinity relationships, and evolving topics; plus, it allows you to discover the affinities, associations, and causes that drive them.

The IBM Social Media Analytics solution analyzes data from publically available Internet data sources, such as Twitter and Facebook, blogs and newsgroups, publications, and analyst reports. It is based on IBM InfoSphere BigInsight.[14]

MDM and Sentiment Analytics Scenario

Figure 6.6 provides a high-level illustration of a possible "MDM-sentiment analytics" co-existence scenario.

As you can see in Figure 6.6, this analytics scenario is composed of three major components: (1) the MDM system, (2) the Enterprise DW system, and (3) the sentiment analytics component.

---

13. You can find more information on the IBM Social Media Analytics solution in [19].

14. For more information on IBM InfoSphere BigInsights, see [20].

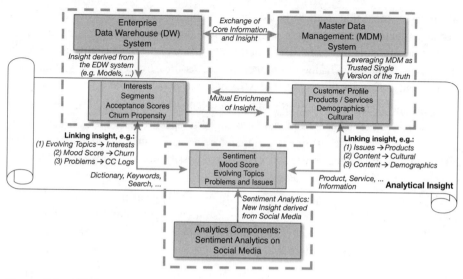

Figure 6.6 MDM-sentiment analytics scenario

The MDM system contains a pervasive customer profile and information regarding products, services, and other core information. It may also contain demographics information about customers, such as age, gender, income, and address. The Enterprise DW system allows further insight, such as customer segmentation, acceptance scores for offers and services, and churn propensity scores. As you saw earlier in this chapter, there is a mutual enrichment of insight that occurs between the MDM and DW systems. In other words, core information is provisioned to the DW system to develop models, customer segmentation, and so on. Likewise, the MDM system is enriched by leveraging insight that is derived from the DW system.

The sentiment analytics component derives insight regarding the sentiments and opinions, mood scores, evolving topics, problems, and issues that are related to products and services.

As we stated previously, some social media sources are difficult if not impossible to assign unambiguously to a particular customer. However, by artfully linking the various analytical insights from these three components, we can very well establish a relevant mapping of "anonymous" sentiment analytics to individual customers or at least a customer segment.

Following are just a few mapping examples (illustrated in Figure 6.6):

- Problems and issues can be mapped to specific products or services, which can be mapped to a specific customer or set of customers.

- The social media content—certain terms, phrases, and keywords—that serves as input to the sentiment analytics component can be interpreted in a cultural and demographic context. This may allow issues and problems, important themes, and evolving topics to be linked to a certain age group or gender, or even a geographical location.

- Attributes or input that leads to mood scores, emotions, and feelings can be linked to customers with a certain churn propensity score. For instance, if a price increase for a product or service is discussed very emotionally in social media, this will influence the churn model and may change the propensity scores for certain customers, which will consequently influence the input to the NBA decision-making process.

- Problems and issues can be linked to data that is collected from various customer touch points (such as call centers) and can be mapped to specific customers. Concerns and comments from specific customers can therefore be newly interpreted and given much higher implications in the context of concrete and possibly very negative sentiments and emotions derived from social media.

- Evolving topics and frequency of themes, discussed in social media, can be linked to known interests and preferences of known customers. Again, this has an influence on the NBA decision-making process and can support the adjustments of products, services, and offerings for specific customers.

From this list, it should be obvious that even anonymous social media contributions can still be analyzed, interpreted, and applied in the context of a specific customer or set of customers.

Social Influencer Determination

Individuals are influencing each other every day; they always have. In this section, we focus on two aspects of social influencer determination: first and foremost, how does social media change this influencer paradigm, and what does influencing in the social media context really mean? And second, how do we describe the role and co-existence of social influencer determination with the MDM customer profile and other core information? In pursuing this, we view influencer determination more from a technical perspective, meaning to describe technical capabilities (text analytics, solution capabilities) and not deal with the social and psychological phenomena.[15]

Following are just two examples of what is meant by "social influencing":

- **Responding and following:** When you share an opinion, emotional statement, or an observation on social media and others follow you and respond to your postings, this influence can be measured by an influencer or follower score.[16]

- **Topic-based influencer:** The impact of your social media postings can be measured in regards to a specific topic—for example, politics, fashion, or a particular sport. This means we can calculate a topic-based influencer weight, for instance, within a defined cluster.

15. You can find more information on social influence from a psychological perspective in [21] and [22].

16. Klout (http://klout.com/home) is a prominent website and mobile app that applies social media analytics to rank the social influence of its users via a score, which is a numerical value between 1 and 100.

Solution Capabilities

In this section, we elaborate on topic-based influencer determination and address the following aspects:

- Key technical capabilities and concepts, solution components that are required to determine topic-based influencers
- Data sources to determine influencers and the relevance of insight for the customer care model
- Topic-based influencers and MDM profile enrichment with an additional set of customer profile attributes derived from influencer determination

Influencer determination not only is relevant for customer care of a particular customer and as input for the NBA decision-making process but also serves as input to other application areas, such as viral marketing. We come back to this application scenario in Chapter 7, "Social MDM and Marketing."

The role of the MDM system in influencer determination scenarios is similar to the other scenarios discussed in this chapter (such as sentiment analytics). In other words, the MDM system is used as a trusted single version of the truth for customer data and other core information.

Figure 6.7 is a high-level depiction of the key analytics capabilities that comprise a topic-based influencer determination solution. This solution can be integrated into a broader social media analytics and customer care infrastructure or deployed as an SaaS model. In this depiction, we focus more on the social media analytics capabilities and less on MDM, the Enterprise DW, and foundational or presentation services.

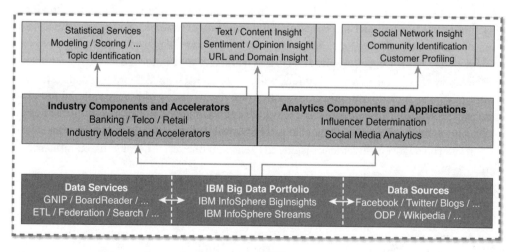

Figure 6.7   Influencer determination capability model

The influencer determination capability model consists of the following three layers:

- **Foundational Capabilities Layer:** The IBM Big Data portfolio provides foundational capabilities. These are Hadoop-based and real-time social media processing and analytics-related products and tools. They include data services, (such as GNIP[17] and BoardReader[18]) but also information integration services (such as ETL, heterogeneous data federation, and search).

- **Analytics and Industry Layer:** This layer is composed of applications, accelerators, and tools that provide capabilities to gain analytical insight. This also includes tools to develop and further customize industry-specific assets and components, such as data models and mining models.

- **Insight and Discovery Layer:** This is an abstraction of the analytical discovery and insight required for influencer determination. It includes basic insight into the social network dynamics and topic identification of a defined customer segment. It is a representation of the analytical insight derived from social media text, content, URL and domain addresses, and includes analytical modeling and statistical services for calculation of topic weights, influencer scores, and so forth.

Key Concepts and Methodology

In this section, we elaborate on the key concepts and methodology of influencer determination, which can only be done without describing the mathematical and probabilistic equations. Figure 6.8 presents a high-level depiction of the methodology.

The methodology takes chosen terms (such as politics, fashion, sports, lifestyle-related terms) and, using social media as a base, documents and relates the probability distribution of those terms, documents, and the terms within documents between a pair of two social media users A→B to all users A, B, ..., K in a defined circle. This is done for all such pairs in the defined circle: A→B, A→C, A→D, ..., A→K. The direction of influence is derived from basic interpretation of social media contributions within the circle (such as following and responding to postings). The topic-based influence (such as politics, sports, fashion) is then measured via Kullback–Leibler (KL) divergence[19] over all terms for all pairs in a given circle. This allows us to measure a term-based probabilistic divergence between all pairs and the circle that these pairs are part of. The degree of divergence is directly related to the term- or topic-based influence for a given term.

17. GNIP (http://gnip.com/) provides a social media API to aggregate data from social media websites. It can be leveraged from within IBM InfoSphere BigInsights.

18. BoardReader (http://boardreader.com/) searches for, locates, and displays information from social media websites. IBM InfoSphere BigInsights ships the BoardReader application.

19. Kullback-Leibler divergence. https://en.wikipedia.org/wiki/Kullback%E2%80%93Leibler_divergence (accessed July 29, 2013).

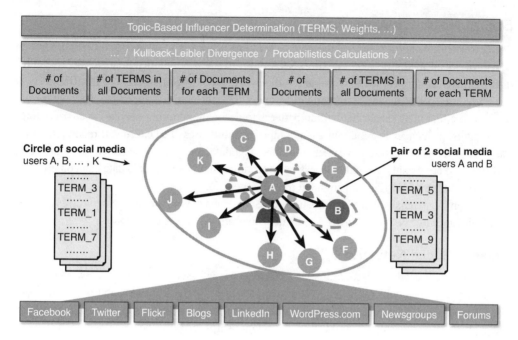

Figure 6.8 Influencer determination concepts

Let's have a closer step-by-step look at the methodology:

1. *Determine* the circle (A, B, ..., K) with the customer pairs and relationships A→B, A→C, ..., A→K, using postings, SNA insight, and so on.

2. *Choose* social media data sources, company-internal data sources (for example, emails, call-center transcripts, and Facebook sites).

3. *Identify* relevant content or documents and topics within chosen documents.

4. *Prepare* statistical measures, such as total number of terms or topics in the circle and the customer pairs, the term distribution in all documents within the pairs and the cluster for each term, and document distribution within the pairs and the cluster for each term.

5. *Calculate* probabilistic divergence between probability distribution of those measures between a pair and the circle. Do this for all pairs, using Kullback–Leibler (KL) divergence.

6. *Identify* terms or topics related to the strongest influence on KL divergence over all pairs with all terms or topics.

7. *Determine* topic-based influencer in the chosen circle.

Social Network Analytics

Social Network Analytics (SNA) has been a field in research for a few decades. Long before the advent of social media networking sites, SNA enjoyed great popularity in sociology, psychology, politics, economics, health care, and biology, and is very prominent in industries such as travel and transportation and telecommunications. CSPs, for instance, have long been interested in understanding their subscriber calling patterns to derive networking insight for churn prediction models, influencer insight, and even competitive analytics. The call detail records (CDRs) that every CSP is collecting have been exploited as a data source to depict social networks and perform predictive analytics and business optimization tasks. Social media data can complement the CDR-based SNA insight and augment the NBA decision process.

Given the extensive list of publications on SNA,[20] we devote the following sections purely to the relevance of SNA for improved NBA decisions and customer care models.

Types of Social Networks

The most widely used representation of social networks is based on graph (or network) theory, in which a graph has two components: nodes and edges. In social networks, nodes typically represent parties (such as people, citizens, customers or subscribers, users, suppliers, organizations, and groups), and edges represent interactions, relationships, or flows between parties. Networks can be simple, directed, or weighted; they can have certain structures that are related to the connectivity and other metrics.

Because we are focusing on social MDM and customer care, we limit our discussion to social networks and the role of MDM in that context and what is changing in leveraging social network insight for downstream systems. Furthermore, we describe the types of social networks we are dealing with and why they are relevant. Table 6.2 contains a high-level depiction of the most important types of social networks, such as clique, neighborhood, star, friendship, special complete graphs, and dense communities.

---

20. You can find more information on Social Network Analytics in [23], [24], and [25].

Table 6.2 Types of Social Networks

Graph Type	Description
Clique Graph 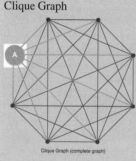 Clique Graph (complete graph)	A clique is a maximum complete connected subgraph (all pairs of nodes are adjacent). Party A is connected to everyone else in the clique, which could be a club, union, professional society, and so forth, where everyone knows and communicates with everyone else. Of course, this is a theoretical representation of the clique. We depicted a high degree of "cliquishness" in the figure on the left; in real life, there may well be some communication or relational gaps between two or even several parties (nodes). The edges represent the interaction between the parties within the clique. Weights, directions, influence, and other metrics need to be added to characterize the graph and determine the importance of clique members. Customer care is significantly improved by mapping insight from clique members to other parties, for instance, for cross- and up-sell, understanding group leaders and followers. Brand and product loyalty can be managed much more effectively.
Neighborhood Graph 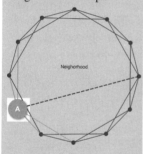 Neighborhood	In real life, people interact with their neighbors and a few "distant" people (dashed line). Such a neighborhood graph is depicted in the figure on the left. It represents a relatively ordered but larger world. Social media has shifted this picture: it is represented—in graph terms—as a relatively unstructured (we could even say chaotic) but small world; this is true in business and in private life. The importance of the neighborhood concept still holds true today. In the customer care context, this means to represent the party network as a neighborhood model. The nature and degree of the business-relevant interactions shape the social network and influence customer care. In telcos, for instance, diffusion analysis relates the distance of subscribers (CDR and social media based) to the churn influence model and enables NBA decisions to target specific subscribers to prevent churn.
Star Graph $K_{1,m}$ 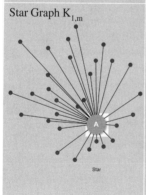 Star	The star graph represents a special case of a complete bipartite graph,[21] where party A is connected to all other parties. The star graph is an important type in regards to customer care, regardless of the direction of influence and communication: although there is no connection between any two parties in the graph (other than A), party A has the greatest impact on all other parties. Examples are politicians, industry leaders, celebrities, and pop stars; but also representatives of customer touch points (such as call-center agents) and sales representatives, who have a strong influence on other parties. This latter example represents a unique opportunity for customer care models. For instance, this can provide unique insight into special campaigns of a competitor, who is proactively reaching out or has a strong social influence on a subset of your own customers, which will influence your NBA decision process.

21. A complete bipartite graph is denoted as $K_{n,m}$, where every party in the first set is connected to every party in the second set. The star graph $K_{1,m}$ is a special case of a complete bipartite graph, where the first set consists of "only" one member A.

Friendship Graph

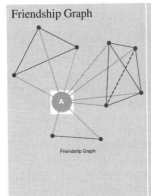

Friendship Graph

The friendship model on the left is a simple abstraction. In real life, circles of friendships can be more complex with more interaction points than just a single one as illustrated by party A. In the customer care context, friendship models are interesting, because they allow the identification of similar hobbies and interests, preferences and lifestyles, opinions and attitudes among them. The reason we separate cliques from friendships is the identification of A (in the figure on the left) playing a much more important role as a connection point bridge between different circles of friends. The determination of customers playing a social connection role depends on the analysis of the network with weights, directional influence, and other characteristics of the graph edges.[22] This strongly relates to the industry and the business model. To understand whether a network graph represents circles of friends that are schematically connected by a bridge A depends on knowledge in regards to the content and the nature of the interaction. For instance, just because a tweet triggers many posts or a Facebook user has hundreds of friends doesn't suggest this social network is a friendship graph. After a friendship graph is developed among customers (and potential customers), the knowledge about connection points is most interesting and highly relevant for customer care models.

Dense Communities Graph

The graph density is a measure of how close the graph is to complete, where all customers are connected to each other. This type of network graph is naturally associated with social media networking activity. And rightly so, in social media networking sites, communities are defined through the density measure of their graph representation. These communities are often depicted as groups, where the connection between groups may be very sparse (as depicted in the figure on the left through party or customer A). The perception of what is dense depends on the business model and the use case scenarios. Cliques, for instance, are complete communities. CSPs invested in CDR-derived social network graphs long before the rise of social media as a new data source. Despite the fact that the number of subscribers and CDRs is huge, the CDR-derived dense community graphs (derived from calling patterns) are somewhat lucid. Use of smart phones and tablets has generated a wealth of application usage data that with social media data will lead to significantly *larger* dense communities. In the context of customer care, dense communities represent the first step toward increased customer insight, enriching the MDM subscriber profile, and having a strong impact on the NBA decision process. The specific action depends on the detailed understanding and reasoning behind density of the community.

22. For more information on friendship networks and their social aspects, and the direction and pattern of unreciprocated friendships, see [26].

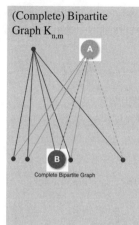

(Complete) Bipartite Graph K$_{n,m}$

Complete Bipartite Graph

Bipartite and complete bipartite graphs represent interesting models of social network structures. If we look at SNA analytics today, we typically depict the social network with one type of node (such as customers, subscribers, employees, and citizens), where the edges represent the interaction and relationship between nodes. Bipartite graphs suggest a different view of social networks. Following are some customer care relevant examples:

a. The first set are customers, and the second set are documents or information on a set of defined topics, terms, or themes. The edges represent a sentiment, a tweet, a blog, or whether the user posts a document or consumes content. This allows determination of interests, preferences, and lifestyle details that enrich the MDM customer profile and enables a more relevant and targeted customer care model.

b. The first set are customers, and the second set are products, services, or offerings (of the company or competitors). The edges relate social media content, consumption, and interaction between customers and the products, services, and offerings. This allows determination of problems, sentiment and buzz, competitive insight, and perception that enriches the MDM customer and product profiles and positively impacts the customer care model.

Bipartite graphs can also be used to infer and analyze trust in social networks, which will enrich the MDM customer profile.[23]

Similar to our discussion on sentiment analytics, the role of MDM is to provide consistent and complete party and customer records where applicable. Apart from that, SNA-derived insight can enrich the customer and product record in the MDM system.

Insight Derived from Social Networks

In this section, we briefly summarize the insight derived from social networks and its relevance for customer care. Given the different types of social networks, the insight is related to the following areas:

- The nature of the interaction and interconnectedness of your customers, including families and households, circle of friends, clubs, and communities

- Group insight and analysis that can be performed, such as leader determination, diffusion analysis, behavioral and influential prediction on the customer base

23. You can find more information on using bipartite graphs for trust inference models in [27].

- Additional insight gained from the relationship of two customers, as opposed to the knowledge of each individual customer (In the previous section on topic-based influencers, we discussed one such additional insight.)

Following are some examples of using SNA insight within the customer care context:

- Gain insight for microgroups, such as families, households, and clubs
- Predict churn accurately for an individual subscriber, such as for CSPs
- Make more appropriate NBA offers (more adequate, less pushy)
- Make more targeted marketing campaigns
- Understand relevance of NBA in the context of communities (for example, cliques)

Trustworthiness of Social Media for Customer Care

Information trustworthiness of social media sites is steadily gaining popularity in research.[24] With MDM becoming more "social," a key challenge is the trustworthiness and the linkage of the analytical insight from social media with the "traditional" customer knowledge captured in MDM and—to some degree—in the DW. This relates to the identity of a Facebook or Twitter user, which may not be known or at least not sufficiently trusted. Matching names from publically accessible social media sites with data in an MDM system may be rather challenging. But the challenge is broader than just addressing the identity issues and increasing confidence in the party credentials: systems need to be able to assess information trustworthiness in social media, and tools have to be able to provide capabilities for human beings to assess the relevance of social media data sources for a particular business scenario. This relates to the data sources themselves, identities, contributions, and postings.

In previous sections, we elaborated on the possible enrichment of the "single version of the truth" of customer master data through the analytical insight of social media. However, we should also look at MDM as a means to leverage social media more effectively and to eliminate or at least reduce "social media noise" from what's relevant.

---

24. You can find more details on information trustworthiness in social media including discourse and definitions of trust and trustworthiness in [28], [29], and [30].

In this section, we address the following questions:

- How should we adequately deal with and improve the trustworthiness and the linkage of the analytical insight from social media with the "traditional" customer knowledge captured in the MDM system and—to some degree—in the DW system?
- How can customer care be improved for individual customers, even if the linkage to a specific customer cannot be deduced in all cases from social media analytics?
- How can we ensure high relevance of social media–derived insight to augment the MDM profile?

How can MDM be used to leverage social media more effectively and to eliminate or at least reduce "social media noise" from relevant information?

As illustrated in Figure 6.9, we approach the challenge of information trustworthiness in social media along the following dimensions:

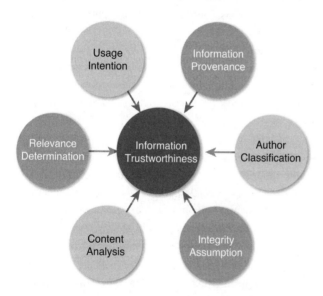

Figure 6.9 Dimensions of trustworthiness of social media

- **Information Provenance:** The authenticity and traceability of the data source play an essential role. Information provenance begins with the identification of the original source of information or some attributes of the information record. It also includes trusted knowledge regarding subsequent modifications of the information source: who changed what, when, and why. It is related to providing contextual evidence of the originality and authenticity of social media. Data lineage, information governance, data access, and authentication are considered aspects of information provenance.

- **Author Classification:** The reputation, name recognition, and even relationship of an author to the consumer are aspects that influence the information trustworthiness. To classify or categorize an author as a genuine and trusted contributor greatly contributes to the perception of a blog, tweet, opinion, and so on. We need to mention that author classification is—in a certain way—a very subjective undertaking. With regard to parties that are represented in the MDM system, author classification and trustworthiness can be captured as well and adjusted over time.

- **Integrity Assumptions:** Some social media sites are commonly associated with a certain level of trustworthiness. This can be related, for instance, to certain blogs or wikis that consumers trust because there is evidence gained by using, acting, and validating the content over time. Other social media sites—for instance, Wikipedia—may be more trusted than others. Again, there is a certain degree of subjectivity to the integrity assumption of social media sources.

- **Content Analysis:** The trustworthiness of social media is significantly related to the analytics capabilities that can be applied to its content. This would entail complicated semantic analyses on heterogeneous social media data driven by a large knowledge base. It includes advanced contextual analytics, indexing, and searching capabilities on completely nonstructured information, such as text, video streams, and even images. As we mentioned in the previous sections of this chapter, the content does not always have to be related to individual customers or parties in order to derive meaning and to increase the trustworthiness of social media.

- **Relevance Determination:** The relevance of social media, blogs, and postings can vary significantly given the context of a given business scenario. Tools need to be able to support business users in determining the relevance of social media in the context of a set of use case scenarios. This includes contextual visualization, exploration, and federation capabilities. These capabilities should also allow the business users to focus on relevant social media content in executing further actions.

- **Usage Intention:** The trustworthiness of social media depends on the business process and the usage intention. Sentiment analytics–related scenarios, for instance, can be characterized by a certain statistically relevant interpretation of many—even millions—of postings, tweets, and so on, which can be derived rather accurately even if the trustworthiness of an individual posting may be somewhat questionable. On the other hand, the opinion of a specific customer, employee, or analyst on a certain subject imposes a different view on the social media sources.

To determine the overall trustworthiness of a particular social media data source, we can assign the weights to individual dimensions that are determined by the relevance of that dimension to the business scenario that needs to be implemented.

If B represents a specific business scenario, S represents a social media data source (such as a single or even a set of tweets), $T_i(S)$ represents the trustworthiness of the data source S in regards to the ith dimension, and $w_i(B,S)$ represents the weight or relevance of that source S in the context of the business scenario B in regards to the ith dimension, then the overall trustworthiness $T(B,S)$ of data source S for the business scenario B is:

$$T(B,S) = \sum_{i=1}^{6} w_i(B) \cdot T_i(S), \text{ where } \sum_{i=1}^{6} w_i(B) = 1.$$

This basic representation allows the trustworthiness of the social media data sources to be estimated along the different dimensions and in the context of a particular business scenario. Of course, this model can be further customized by adding additional dimensions that may be highly relevant for a particular use case scenario.

Table 6.3 describes in high-level terms the technical capabilities that are required by the various dimensions of trustworthiness of social media. Some of the technical capabilities are required by several dimensions.

Table 6.3   Technical Capabilities to Address Trustworthiness of Social Media

Dimensions	Technical Capabilities
Information Provenance	Information governance, source data discovery and access, data security and data access, information integration with metadata management including data lineage, authentication, ...
Author Classification	MDM with single-view-of party, identity verification and authentication, identity mapping and matching, relationship determination, party segmentation, ...
Integrity Assumptions	Website classification and segmentation techniques, ...
Content Analysis	Text analytics and mining techniques, indexing techniques, searching and analytics on heterogeneous and nonstructured data sources, ...
Relevance Determination	Business-relevant visualization, contextual exploration of social media data, federation techniques of nonstructured data, indexing techniques, information integration, ...
Usage Intention	Business process management, use case management, ...

References

[1] IBM CMO Study. "From Stretched to Strengthened: Insights from the Global, Chief Marketing Officer Study." IBM Institute for Business Value, October 2011. http://www.ibm.com/cmostudy.

[2] Cook, S. *Customer Care Excellence: How to Create an Effective Customer Focus.* (Kogan Page Publishers, 2010).

[3] Wellington, P. *Effective Customer Care.* (Kogan Page Publishers, 2010).

[4] Margulies, E. *Social Engagement for Customer Care. A Practitioner's Guide to Driving Loyalty on the Social Web.* (Sterling Press, 2013).

[5] Usenet.net Newsgroups. http://www.usenet.net/.

[6] Open Directory Project. http://forums.dmoz.org/; Flyertalk, http://www.flyertalk.com/; IBM InfoSphere BigInsights Forum, https://www.ibm.com/developerworks/community/forums/html/forum?id=11111111-0000-0000-0000-000000002409.

[7] IBM. "Systems of Interaction." Retrieved 10/13/2013. http://www-01.ibm.com/software/solutions/systems-of-interaction/.

[8] Greenberg, P. *CRM at the Speed of Light: Social CRM Strategies, Tools, and Techniques for Engaging Your Customers.* (McGraw-Hill Companies, 2009).

[9] Heller Baird, C., and G. Parasnis. "From Social Media to Social CRM. What Customers Want. The First in a Two-Part Series." IBM Institute for Business Value. http://www-935.ibm.com/services/us/gbs/thoughtleadership/ibv-social-crm-whitepaper.html, February 2011.

[10] Heller Baird, C., and G. Parasnis. "From Social Media to Social CRM. Reinventing the Customer Relationship. The Second in a Two-Part Series." IBM Institute for Business Value, June 2011. http://www-935.ibm.com/services/us/gbs/thoughtleadership/ibv-social-crm-whitepaper.html.

[11] Chessel, M., and D. Pugh. "Smarter Analytics: Driving Customer Interactions with the IBM Next Best Action Solution." Redguides for Business Leaders, IBM Redbooks, REDP-4888-00, October 2012. http://www.redbooks.ibm.com/redpapers/pdfs/redp4888.pdf.

[12] IBM Global Services. "IBM Signature Solution—Next Best Action." IBM Smarter Analytics Solution Brief, April 2012. http://public.dhe.ibm.com/common/ssi/ecm/en/gbs03126usen/GBS03126USEN.PDF.

[13] IBM. "InfoSphere BigInsights. Bringing the Power of Hadoop to the Enterprise." Retrieved July 2013 from http://www-01.ibm.com/software/data/infosphere/biginsights/whats_new.html.

[14] IBM. "IBM United States Software Announcement 213-205. IBM InfoSphere BigInsights Enterprise Edition V2.1 Delivers Enterprise Hadoop Capabilities." May 2013. http://www-01.ibm.com/common/ssi/rep_ca/5/897/ENUS213-205/ENUS213-205.PDF.

[15] Pang, B., and L. Lee. *Opinion Mining and Sentiment Analysis (Foundations and Trends(r) in Information Retrieval).* (Now Publishers Inc., 2008).

[16] Liu, B. *Sentiment Analysis and Opinion Mining. Synthesis Lectures on Human Language Technologies.* (Morgan & Claypool Publishers, 2012).

[17] IBM. "Social Business Analytics. Gaining Business Value from Social Media." February 2013. http://public.dhe.ibm.com/common/ssi/ecm/en/ytw03279usen/YTW03279USEN.PDF.

[18] IBM. "Social Media Analytics: Making Customer Insights Actionable." March 2013. http://public.dhe.ibm.com/common/ssi/ecm/en/ytw03168usen/YTW03168USEN. PDF.

[19] IBM. "Social Media Analytics. Unlock the Value of Customer Sentiment in Social Media." Retrieved 07/27/2013 from http://www-01.ibm.com/software/analytics/solutions/customer-analytics/social-media-analytics/products.html.

[20] IBM. "IBM InfoSphere BigInsights V2.1. Bringing the Power of Hadoop to the Enterprise." Retrieved 07/27/2013 from http://www.ibm.com/software/data/infosphere/biginsights.

[21] Gass, R. H., and J. S. Seiter. *Persuasion. Social Influence and Compliance Gaining,* 4th ed. (Pearson, 2010).

[22] Kenrick, D. T., N. J. Goldstein, and S. L. Braver. *Six Degrees of Social Influence: Science, Application, and the Psychology of Robert Cialdini.* (Oxford University Press, 2012).

[23] Aggarwal, C. C. (Ed.). *Social Network Data Analytics.* (Springer, 2011).

[24] Prell, C. *Social Network Analysis: History, Theory, and Methodology.* (SAGE Publications, 2011).

[25] Ting, I.H., and T.P. Hong. *Social Network Mining, Analysis, and Research Trends: Techniques and Applications.* (IGI Global Snippet, 2012).

[26] Ball, B., and M. E. J. Newman. "Friendship Networks and Social Status." Cornell University Library, Retrieved 08/03/2013 from http://arxiv.org/pdf/1205.6822v1.pdf.

[27] O'Doherty, D., S. Jouili, and P. Van Roy, "Towards Trust Inference from Bipartite Social Networks." DBSocial '12 Proceedings of the 2nd ACM SIGMOD Workshop on Databases and Social Networks, 2012. Retrieved 08/03/2013. http://www.info.ucl.ac.be/~pvr/DBSocial2012_may01.pdf.

[28] ten Kate, S. "Trustworthiness within Social Networking Sites: A Study on the Intersection of HCI and Sociology." Master's thesis. Business Studies, Faculty of Economics and Business at the University of Amsterdam, February 2009. www.stephantenkate.nl/thesis.

[29] Moturu, S. T., and H. Liu. "Quantifying the Trustworthiness of Social Media Content." Journal of Distributed and Parallel Databases, vol. 29, issue 3 (June 2011): 239–260

[30] Kittur, A., B. Suh, and E. H. Chi. "Can You Ever Trust a Wiki? Impacting Perceived Trustworthiness in Wikipedia." 2008. ISBN-13: 978-1-6055-8007-04, http://kittur.org/files/Kittur_2008_CSCW_TrustWiki.pdf.

CHAPTER 7

Social MDM and Marketing

Marketing aims to reach the right people with the right message to influence their attitudes and actions. It is an art and a science. Well-developed patterns, processes, and technologies acquire and segment target marketing groups, tailor communications to these groups in the hopes of achieving a goal, and then measure the outcomes.

Today, many organizations have sophisticated marketing approaches that combine sales, customer, and product data for analysis and reporting, using the amassed data to design and execute marketing campaigns and analyzing their outcomes. This approach works well, but can it work better? Organizations are exploring new forms of analytics and Social MDM in the belief that it can. The key is to leverage more sources of information to better understand people as individuals. This chapter explores how.

Marketing in the era of social media offers both challenges as well as opportunities. It is incorrect to view social media as only a new kind of communications channel. Use of social media is primarily for sharing and interacting with friends and family, not with corporations and organizations. Research has shown[1] that for companies to effectively communicate via social media, customers need to believe the communication is for their own benefit—and that there needs to be transparency and authenticity in the communication. A key factor in successfully using social media for interacting with customers is to more deeply understand the customers, their interests, and their behaviors.[2] Social media sites such as Twitter, Facebook, and LinkedIn are also rich sources of information about people, products, and their relationships that are available (in accordance with the users' privacy settings) to be shared and analyzed.

Information from social media can be invaluable to marketing in many ways—from developing prospect lists to better understanding consumer behaviors and interests. These insights promise more relevant and targeted marketing campaigns, better products, and even improved placement of retail outlets.

---

1. You can find more information on social media and social CRM in [1] and [2].
2. For more detailed information, refer to http://www.newzsocial.com/tag/personalized-marketing (accessed April 25, 2014).

The rest of this chapter discusses how Social MDM can enable and enhance digital marketing initiatives. As we explore a range of topics from social media marketing to mobile and viral marketing, it is useful to keep in mind some key questions:

- How do we select people to communicate with?
- How do we craft relevant messages and offers?
- How can we make these messages and offers effective?

These questions help us to focus on the outcomes that we are trying to produce through the use of Social MDM.

Social Media Marketing and the Role of MDM

In the past few years, marketing techniques have been extended in two dimensions. As Figure 7.1 shows, traditional marketing focused on delivering messages in a wave of communications on a periodic basis to cohorts of people. These cohorts are derived through analytical marketing segmentation techniques where it is common to use data-mining algorithms to identify groups of people with similar characteristics. Ongoing trends of social media, of mobile computing, and the ever-increasing sophistication of analytics are enabling digital marketing techniques that can provide more dynamic "in-the-moment" offers tailored to an individual's situation and preferences. Figure 7.1 illustrates this new landscape.

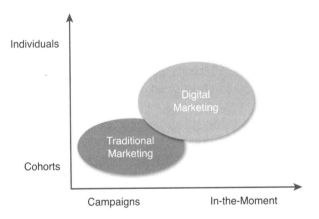

Figure 7.1   A simplified marketing landscape

The emerging trend of marketing to the individual has been named *B2I (Business to Individual)* or sometimes *personalized marketing*. For example, organizations are moving to send offers to cell phones of registered individuals as they shop. A good example of this emerging technology is Apple's iBeacons,[3] which track customer location within a store in support of a more interactive shopping experience. Digital marketing techniques are evolving rapidly to take advantage of these emerging technologies.

3. For more information, refer to http://en.wikipedia.org/wiki/IBeacon (accessed April 25, 2014).

Social MDM is a hub for all kinds of information about people, organizations, and products; it extends traditional notions of MDM with additional information from external systems and, in particular, from social media and other digital interaction data.

Social media is potentially a rich source of information that, with the right kinds of analytics (and skill), can reveal information about life events, customer and product sentiment, customer relationships, and more. Linking identities in social media with those maintained in Social MDM can augment our understanding of customers and products through different forms of social media and behavioral analytics, as illustrated in Figure 7.2. We extend traditional MDM systems with this additional insight to better serve, communicate, retain, and enhance our customer relationships.

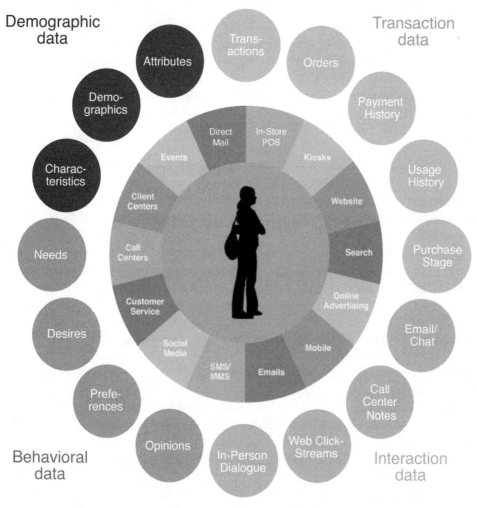

Figure 7.2   Understanding the individual

MDM serves both as an aggregation point and gateway to many kinds of information, including the following:

- **Identities:** The different accounts and identities for individuals
- **Demographic:** Information about individuals, their interests, and interaction preferences
- **Transaction:** The detailed transactions that individuals perform
- **Interaction:** Conversations across different types of communications including email, customer service calls, and web clickstreams
- **Behavioral:** Information about individual interests, social media sentiment, and expressed needs

A Social MDM implementation typically would contain the demographic and well-defined elements of the behavioral data, and it maintains references to correlated transaction and inter- action data. An MDM system can therefore be a single entry point to finding and retrieving a complete view of individuals and provide valuable insights that improve our ability to effectively communicate with them. It can also subset this single view into the personas that reflect their work, family, and leisure profiles. This notion of personalized marketing is also closely related to the idea of providing personalized customer care, as discussed in Chapter 6, "Social MDM and Customer Care." In both situations, we want to use all the information that we have available to better serve the customer.

MDM systems are sometimes confused with customer relationship management (CRM) systems because both usually contain customer information. However, where CRM systems focus on the process of managing prospects to customers, MDM systems focus on developing as complete and accurate a view as possible over the information that it manages—not only in support of CRM but wherever authoritative information is needed. A mature MDM deployment contains information about customers, the accounts that they hold, and the products within those accounts—with rich detail for each and relationships between these domains. Such an MDM sys- tem would typically integrate with other operational and analytical systems to provide authorita- tive data where it is needed and to coordinate the updating and management of the information as part of broader business processes. MDM and CRM systems are often deployed together in an integrated manner where CRM systems are sources of existing customer information as well as recipients of cleansed and integrated customer information. CRM systems are thus enhanced by the quality and completeness of information from MDM.

From a marketing perspective, MDM systems are core to managing customer profile and behavioral information that can influence how, when, and what offers we make to customers. Campaign management systems are applications for planning, executing, and evaluating a mar- keting campaign. Social MDM systems can enhance campaign management effectiveness by dif- ferentiating between prospects and customers and providing deeper information when available.

With the rise of social media, marketing organizations have been striving to further refine and improve both their understanding of their customers and the most effective and engaging ways in which to communicate with them. Social media offers not just a new set of channels for communications, but additional information about customers and the ability to expand marketing from traditional outbound communications to more of an ongoing conversation. Both of these characteristics can improve customer engagement by supporting relevant and interactive conversations. Extending Master Data Management with social information and analysis improves our ability to understand and interact with customers as individuals, to personalize their experience, and to interact with customers as they request.

Social Media–Enabled Marketing Campaigns

Social media-enabled marketing campaigns are among the most exciting and fastest-growing marketing disciplines. In this section, we elaborate on various flavors of marketing, such as personalized, social media, mobile, contextual, and viral marketing. The following three dimensions of social media–enabled marketing campaigns are used consistently to describe these various marketing flavors:

- Latency (time sensitivity)
- Activity, behavior, and analytical insight
- Geospatial knowledge (where something is located or happening)

Their relevance to marketing is as follows:

- **Latency:** This is the time sensitivity of providing mobile marketing campaigns, for instance, in real-time. Depending on the use-case scenario, mobile marketing has to be executed with low latency, meaning in real-time or "right-time." Examples are campaigns that are location sensitive, where consumers need to receive a message within a certain time window for the message to be relevant and the consumer to act on it. Other examples are real-time top-up campaigns for pre-paid SIM cards, which require real-time knowledge of the balance and other business metrics of a subscriber or set of subscribers—for example, likelihood of top-up acceptance, past top-up pattern in a defined period of time, and incentives or acceptance criteria that may influence the subscriber's decision.

  With the ever-increasing importance of social media networks, the impact on brand reputation and consumer sentiments can potentially be noticed rather rapidly and widely. Mobile campaigns with the goal to react to those phenomena need to be executed with low latency, either targeting specific consumers or even a larger consumer segment. There are quite a number of scenarios where real-time mobile marketing campaigns play a vital role.

- **Activity, behavior, and analytical insight:** This key dimension is related to analytical knowledge of parties, such as customers or consumers, potential customers, citizens, and other stakeholders. This analytical insight should be related to the interests and hobbies, preferences in using products or services, demographic information (for example, age, gender, and income), and other business metrics—for instance, the churn propensity score of a telco subscriber or the microsegment or social network that a party belongs to. Obviously, social media data and transactional data, such as money-spending behavior and credit card usage patterns, and calling and data usage patterns of telco subscribers will serve as a base for gaining this insight. The MDM system will play an essential role in provisioning party knowledge to mobile marketing engines.

The knowledge, however, goes beyond the party itself. In mobile marketing, content and messages need to be delivered in a device-dependent fashion. That is, the content and messages need to be device-aware, meaning that a consumer using a smart phone may expect the content differently than a user of a tablet or laptop. For communication service providers (CSPs), even the linkage of operator network and subscriber knowledge is essential. For instance, a telco operator may launch a mobile marketing campaign that relates network occurrences (for example, outages, performance degradation, or dropped calls) to specific subscribers. We could even consider the degree and relevance of analytical insight to be directly related to whether a mobile marketing campaign is targeted for just a few "well-known" customers or whether it is directed to hundreds or thousands of "anonymous" parties.

- **Geospatial:** Location awareness is certainly another key aspect in target mobile marketing campaigns. We dive into locality-aware marketing later in this chapter and therefore provide only a basic overview of the different techniques available today. In doing so, we focus on the accurateness of the geospatial aspects. Global positioning system (GPS) and Assisted-GPS (A-GPS) are key technologies to determine the location of an end-user device.[4] Today, most devices are still not equipped with GPS technology, nor have most telco network operators invested in the rather expensive A-GPS network technology. In the years to come, this will most likely change, as end-user devices will increasingly come with GPS capability and telco network operators will upgrade their networks with A-GPS technology. For the time being, the geospatial aspect of mobile marketing may therefore rely on network-based positioning technology.[5] Given the space available in this chapter, we can only list the available key techniques, without discussing at length the pros and cons related to performance and positioning accuracy.

The cell ID of a mobile network base station and measurement of the signal strength are key network-based measures in determining end-user device location. To improve location accuracy, the geospatial tool is often complemented with UE-assisted techniques

---

4. In the telco industry, these end-user devices are called user equipment (UE). We use this term occasionally in the remainder of this chapter.

5. You can find more information on network-based positioning, GPS, and mobile communication systems in [3], [4], and [5].

that depend on the network (for example, GSM/GPRS, UMTS, LTE). Further accuracy can be achieved with the multilateration technique based on measuring the Time Difference of Arrival (TDOA) of signals from several network base stations to the end-user device. The best accuracy will be achieved with A-GPS, which is network-based and UE-assisted and, therefore, delivers significantly better performance and accuracy, compared to UE-based GPS.

Figure 7.3 depicts these three key dimensions.

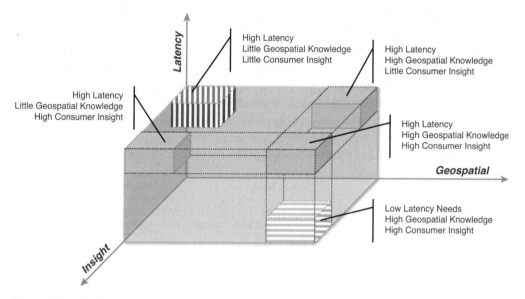

Figure 7.3 Mobile marketing dimensions

The left upper area in Figure 7.3 with the horizontal pattern represents the largest spread of mobile marketing activities because neither analytical insight nor geospatial knowledge is available. In addition, technical capabilities are limited in regards to delivering low-latency marketing campaigns. In other words, there are no or limited real-time capabilities.

The right lower area with the vertical pattern represents a desirable space to be in, because this is characterized by sufficiently deep analytical insight of the customer that is derived from social media data and other data sources. This is complemented with geospatial knowledge, meaning adequate location accuracy of a mobile user. In addition, low-latency (meaning real-time) capabilities will allow instantaneous mobile marketing message delivery to the "right" customer or rather small set of customers.

Contextual Marketing: Location and Time

In the ongoing quest to improve relevance and effectiveness of marketing, a number of approaches have emerged to take advantage of the latest technology trends. In this section, we explore two such trends—real-time marketing and locality-aware marketing—and how they are coming together to provide a context for interactions; we can call this *contextual marketing*. This area is rapidly evolving because it seems both the technology and the understanding of how to effectively use the technology are changing weekly.

The goal of real-time marketing is to provide timely, relevant, and useful offers and information to consumers. More specifically, the focus of real-time marketing that we discuss here is how to seamlessly interact with consumers based on their current activity, profile, and behavior.

You likely have encountered at least one form of real-time marketing, although you may not have realized it at the time. Here is a common situation. Say an individual named Paulo is interested in buying a new, efficient car. Using his browser, he searches for car reviews and starts reading them. As he continues to browse, he is presented with ads and offers related to the search terms he is using and the content that he is reading. He finds some of these ads interesting and clicks on them for more information. So how does this work?

As Paulo browses, marketing tools recognize Paulo and piece together that Paulo is interested in fuel-efficient cars. Based on Paulo's known profile and his current activity, his experience can be personalized with dynamically selected offers, recommendations, and other content.

There are many other forms of real-time marketing, from personalized offers printed on sales receipts as a consumer completes a purchase to offers sent to a smart phone when customers arrive at a store. Increasingly, the focus is not only on improving the responsiveness and blending marketing with other transactions, but also considering the situational context. Physical location is perhaps the most important aspect of situational context, but when we look at this issue more broadly, it is also useful to understand the current activity. For example, if we want to use location to trigger offers, then isn't it important for our system to understand the difference between someone walking past a store and driving past? It may be a disservice to send unsolicited text messages while someone is driving; however, they may be of interest if someone is shopping and strolling.

More and more systems are collecting and aggregating more kinds of data, and using this information for marketing and sales is often among the first use cases that people come up with to exploit this new information. Perhaps one of the fastest-growing and most exciting areas is around what is called "connected car." The pervasiveness of cellular communications, coupled with the decreasing costs in computers, means that it is increasingly economical for cars to be Internet connected. This capability can be useful for passengers who want to use the Internet while being driven, but auto manufacturers are also looking at how this connectivity can be safely leveraged for commercial purposes ranging from understanding consumer movement patterns to delivering preferential search results if someone is looking for a restaurant on the car's navigation system.

Customer privacy is, of course, a key concern, and work is underway to both evaluate the safety ramifications as well as provide consumers the ability to decline participation.[6]

Another important trend is the emergence of technology that supports the tracking of individuals within a store or other enclosed structure where GPS technology is insufficient. Apple's iBeacons are one example of a technology that allows the location of individuals (or rather their mobile devices) to within a foot. iBeacon-enabled applications on the device allow offers and information to be delivered to the individuals based on their proximity to different products or their exhibited shopping behavior. Of course, iBeacons can also be used in many other ways; for example, they allow museums to provide information about exhibits as visitors approach.

Social media also plays an important role in this contextual computing. Services such as Twitter allow people to share more information as it happens. Did viewers like or dislike a movie they just watched? Was the checkout line long at a particular store because of a sale? Is there a bargain to be had? This element of social media is closely tied to time and location of the person sending the tweet, and the location of those following will determine how relevant the communication is to them at that time.

Contextual marketing ties back to Social MDM in a number of ways. First, MDM is a key place where information about consumers' behavior, interests, and interaction preferences comes together and can thus support software such as IBM's Enterprise Market Management Suite in the design, management, and execution of contextually relevant offers and support. As a source of personal and demographic information, MDM can help us to understand that the location information we receive represents an individual's home or office. As a hub of personal profile information, MDM systems hold the keys that let us dynamically reach out and find the most current information from other operational systems such as the call center or CRM applications.

In summary, combining location, context, and updates to social media with individuals' profiles and interests results in a powerful combination of information that can be used by marketing to improve the timing and relevance of offers, to better understand consumer behavior, and ultimately, provide a more integrated, virtual reality kind of experience to individuals as they navigate through their everyday lives.

Social Media Marketing

In this section, we provide a definition of what social media marketing is and what it is not. This includes describing the difference between social media marketing and social marketing. While elaborating on the term *social media marketing*, we furthermore address the following aspects:

- Describing the role of social media platforms and networks for social media marketing and how this has improved the relevance and responsiveness of marketing campaigns

- Specifying key solution capabilities and components and the role of MDM for social media marketing campaigns

6. For more detailed information, refer to http://www.futureofprivacy.org/connectedcars/ (accessed April 25, 2014).

- Highlighting analytical insight derived from social media as key input for social media marketing programs

Unfortunately, the terms *social media marketing* and *social marketing* are often used interchangeably, neglecting the differences.

Hereinafter, we would like to clarify these terms:

- **Social media marketing**[7]: This term usually refers to the process of gaining website traffic or attention through social media sites.[8] Social media marketing programs predominantly have a commercial goal in mind—namely, to use social media to create a social media presence and to establish a relationship to parties (for example, customers and potential new customers) for a specific business purpose. Social media networks are used to persuade content consumers and parties in general to spread an enterprise marketing message, even adding content—hopefully positive content—and essentially using authority, authenticity, and the reputation of social media networking members in doing so. Social media marketing is about leveraging social media network members to positively participate, enrich, and underpin an enterprise marketing program or message.

  Another key point of social media marketing is the inclusion of social media analytics in shaping and executing a marketing program. In other words, similar to customer care, social media marketing programs will greatly benefit from the significantly increased insight and feedback that can be derived from social media analytics. Social media marketing can be seen as a progression of commercial marketing, which also has its primary goal in increasing revenue and number of customers, improving brand awareness and identity, and influencing enterprise reputation and customer behavior and needs. The goal of commercial marketing, as with retail marketing, is primarily business and profit-oriented.

- **Social marketing**[9]: This term surfaced in the early 1970s, long before the rise of the World Wide Web (WWW) and social media networks. It is usually referred to as a marketing discipline to influence consumers and the public in general, not necessarily in regards to a commercial interest, but to promote a certain behavior and attitude that will benefit an individual, a community, and even the society as a whole. According to the Social Marketing Institute, "social marketing is the planning and implementation of programs designed to bring about social change using concepts from commercial marketing."[10] Examples of social marketing are marketing campaigns to protect the environment or to promote a healthy lifestyle and diet. In recent years, social media platforms and networks have become a key enabler to these campaigns.

---

7. You can find more information on social media marketing in [6], [7], and [8].
8. Wikipedia. "Social Media Marketing." Retrieved 10/10/2013 from http://en.wikipedia.org/wiki/Social_media_marketing.
9. You can find more information on social marketing in [9] and [10].
10. Social Marketing Institute. "Social Marketing." Retrieved 10/10/2013 from http://www.social-marketing.org/sm.html.

Table 7.1 illustrates the relation of these two marketing terms.

Table 7.1 Marketing Terms Defined

Aspects and Characteristics	Marketing Terms	
	Social Media Marketing	Social Marketing
Origin	With the advent of the WWW and social media networks	In the beginning of the 1970s
Social media	Key originating and enabling aspect	Recent enrichment
Commercial interest	YES, business-oriented (revenue, reputation, brand...)	NO, nonprofit oriented
Target audience	Parties, such as consumers, new and existing customers, subscribers, and so on	Consumers, individuals, citizens, communities, public/society in general
Goal	Enterprise/business benefit; for example, profit increase	Societal improvements; for example, healthy lifestyle

Similar to the role of social media for customer care, social media marketing will benefit from the analytical insight that can be derived from social media. Analytical insight portrays key input for social media marketing programs, supporting campaigns in making them more relevant and successful. That is, social media analytics is a key solution capability to understand the behavior of a large number of consumers, the perception of a product or service, and the public opinion and sentiment on specific themes. Thus, from a solution capability perspective, social media marketing requires not only a marketing management engine and software components that can shape the social media presence of enterprises and their products and services, but also analytical components that derive insight from social media networks to determine and shape a social media marketing campaign.

IBM has a social media marketing solution that turns social insights into action by creating dialogues, building advocacy, and improving loyalty.[11] As we described in the section "Social Media Marketing and the Role of MDM" earlier in this chapter, the MDM system plays a vital role as a trusted source of core information and can be leveraged to enable consistent customer interaction and engagement experience to feed trusted master data into the social media marketing management engine.

Finally, we should also consider the impact of social media on the management of product master data. Master data around products and services manages information about product classification, descriptions, and attributes. Although much of the focus of this book has been around a comprehensive view of individuals, we also can apply similar techniques to understanding

---

11. You can find more information on IBM's Social Media Marketing Solution in [11].

individual products—and their relationship with customers—through analytics on social media. Combining structured data managed by a Social MDM system with insight derived from social media allows us to improve our understanding of product preferences, product recommendations, and product planning.

Mobile Marketing

Mobile marketing is probably one of the fastest-growing marketing disciplines. Often incorrectly viewed as using the Internet on mobile devices for marketing purposes, mobile marketing has its own characteristics and unique opportunities. The Mobile Marketing Association[12] defines mobile marketing as "... a set of practices that enables organizations to communicate and engage with their audience in an interactive and relevant manner through and with any mobile device or network."

In this section, we develop an understanding of mobile marketing by identifying its unique characteristics. Quite a number of excellent mobile marketing publications[13] elaborate comprehensively on this topic. We would like to provide complementary aspects by focusing on the following questions:

- What is the scope, and how do we define mobile marketing? What are the key trends, characteristics, and dimensions (for example, latency, geospatial)?

- What mobile marketing-specific challenges exist regarding content-related mobile platform-specific optimizations?

- What are the most important technical capabilities to implement mobile marketing, and what is the role of MDM for mobile marketing campaigns?

- What is the role of analytics of social media data and parties (for example, customers, consumers, citizens) for mobile marketing?

We underpin our messages with an example from a communication service provider (CSP) implementing an "improved mobile advertisement solution," derived from a CSP customer project in Asia Pacific.

Quite a number of additional issues and even legal aspects are usually associated with mobile marketing, and we do not elaborate on them in this book. They include privacy issues (especially related to using geospatial knowledge of a subscriber), personal consent that should be carefully taken into consideration regarding any mobile marketing campaign, and push-and-pull concepts regarding the initiation of the communication—just to mention a few.

12. Mobile Marketing Association, http://www.mmaglobal.com/news/mma-updates-definition-mobile-marketing (accessed August 11, 2013).
13. You can find more information on mobile marketing in [12], [13], and [14].

Figure 7.4 depicts a high-level mobile marketing and advertisement solution that lists the key components and the various data sources. It not only leverages the social media data sources that come from Facebook, Twitter, Wikipedia, ODP,[14] IMDb,[15] and other social media sites, but also analyzes data sources that come from the CSP network, such as various call detail records (CDRs) (data usage, voice, SMS), probe device data, and other behavioral data. In collaborative business models where a CSP has a business partnership with another vertical, such as a retail chain or a financial services organization, additional customer data and transactional data sources may be leveraged for the mobile marketing campaign solution. Geospatial information is available through the CSP network system and the user equipment. If GPS data is available through the UE, or if the CSP provides A-GPS capabilities, improved location accuracy is provided.

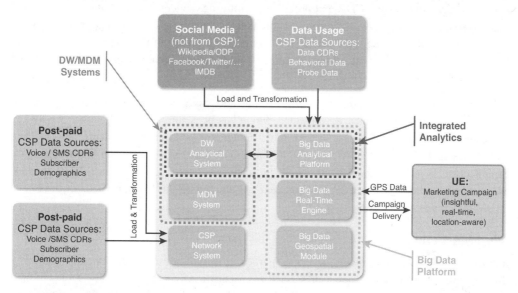

Figure 7.4 Mobile marketing and advertisement solution

Following are the key components of the mobile marketing and advertisement solution that intersect in some areas:

- **Integrated analytics component:** Is composed of a Big Data analytics platform that provides, for instance, text analytics on (semi-)structured data (such as social media data) and a traditional data warehouse system that contains further analytical capabilities including predictive analytics.

- **Hadoop platform:** Is composed of analytics capabilities (as described in the preceding

14. Open Directory Project (ODP), http://www.dmoz.org/ (accessed August 15, 2013).

15. Internet Movie Database (IMDb), http://www.imdb.com/ (accessed August 15, 2013).

paragraph), a Big Data real-time engine that provides real-time processing of social media and CSP network data, and a Big Data geospatial module. Depending on the need to implement the mobile marketing dimensions, some of the capabilities may be obsolete (for instance, the Big Data real-time engine).

- **DW/MDM systems:** Is an integrated component that ensures a single view of core information through the MDM subcomponent (such as customers, subscribers, products, and services) in conjunction with deep analytics through the data warehouse subcomponent. The interaction between the MDM and data warehouse systems was described in Chapter 6.

- **CSP network system:** Is an integral part of the telco operational support system (OSS), which contains the CDR and probe data-capturing devices, the mediation systems, and so on. The CSP network, in conjunction with the UE, also allows the determination of the UE location (using the different techniques as described in the preceding paragraphs). We are assuming that subscriber and customer data is already stored in the MDM and data warehouse systems.

Figure 7.5 illustrates this mobile marketing and advertisement solution in the context of the Social MDM Reference Architecture, which has been introduced in Chapter 3. The key components, such as the Big Data platform, the integrated analytics components, and the Data Warehouse and MDM system itself are highlighted in the context of the Social MDM Reference Architecture. In addition, the various data sources, such as post- and pre-paid CSP data sources, social media and data usage CSP data sources are depicted on the left upper side of the Social MDM Reference Architecture.

Viral Marketing

For our purposes, *viral marketing* refers to marketing techniques to disseminate information—for example, about a new product or service from person to person especially via social networks—creating a potentially exponential growth in the visibility and impact of the information. In a more generic way, viral marketing can be seen as techniques to disseminate a message from instance to instance (for example, a website) via electronic means.[16] In the past, this was known as "word of mouth" marketing.

Say you have a large existing customer base (for example, tens of millions) or a fairly large social network with a high number of potential customers. In this case, choosing 1% or only 0.1% or even less of your existing or potential customers to quickly and efficiently reach the entire or chosen segment of the customer base can make a significant difference in the cost and effectiveness of the entire marketing campaign.

16. You can find more information on viral marketing in [15], [16], and [17].

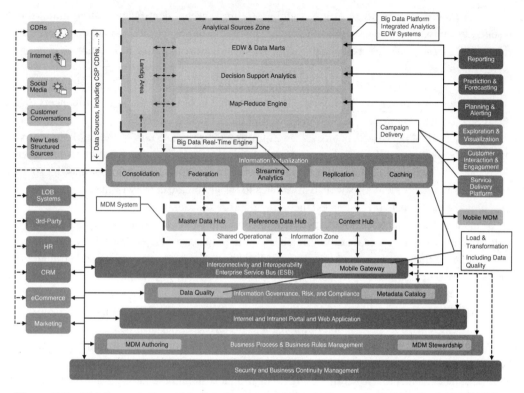

Figure 7.5   Mobile marketing and advertisement solution in the context of the Social MDM RA

In this section, we elaborate on viral marketing by:

- Explaining what viral marketing means and how it relates to other themes, such as topic-based influencer determination

- Describing the methodology of viral marketing with its key attributes and characteristics, where our focus is on how to gain the analytical insight to choose, for instance, a representative subset of customers for viral marketing purposes

- Elaborating on the relationship to graph theory and the identification of customers for viral marketing purposes

- Highlighting the solution capabilities and the role of MDM for viral marketing campaigns

- Providing references to IBM products, tools, and assets

For viral marketing to be efficient and cost-effective, the identification of an initial representative subset in a social network is vital. This initial target set of customers and websites (instances in general) should be done in such a way that the spread of the information or message is maximized.

One relevant factor in this context is the social influencer score of an individual within a social network, for instance—specifically the determination of the topic-based influencers. We discussed this concept in the previous chapter. But the influencer score by itself isn't sufficient. Another factor is the past acceptances score, meaning the response rate of the marketing campaign, such as the degree of acceptance of an individual customer to past product offers. Obviously, an understanding of the social network profile of an individual customer and the social network structure is essential as well. This relates to insight on the density of the social network, groupings of subscribers (or instances) including microsegmentation, and so on.

Insight that is related to the knowledge of products purchased and services subscribed is indeed another key factor in determining an initial target subscriber set. Especially the linkage of the social influencer score and insight regarding the social network profiles and structure to the products purchased or services subscribed to are effective means to launch successful viral marketing campaigns.

Another dimension in influencing the success of the viral marketing campaign is deep customer insight regarding sentiments, opinions, and preferences, but also demographics, such as age, gender, and income. The MDM system—a key component of the viral marketing campaign solution—should deliver most of this customer insight. Finally, it is essential to understand the most efficient channel to "go viral" through. For instance, should the message spread via online forums, social networks (for example, MySpace, Facebook), or blogs? Should an SMS be sent, or is email the right approach?

To summarize, we have identified the following factors to drive viral marketing campaigns. The required analytical insight needs to concentrate on these factors and their relationship. Figure 7.6 illustrates these influencing factors:

- Social influencer score
- Past acceptances score
- Social network profile and structure
- Products and services insight
- Deep customer insight
- Efficient channel

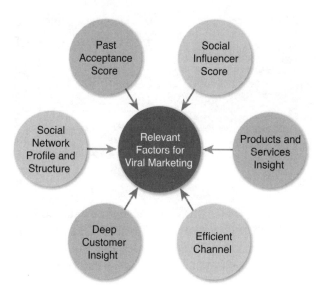

Figure 7.6   Relevant factors for viral marketing

The role of MDM in the context of viral marketing campaigns consists of provisioning a pervasive and complete customer record that also includes knowledge on products purchased and services subscribed to. This knowledge may be easier to capture in some industries and more challenging in others. In the financial services sector or the telecommunications industry, for instance, enterprises have knowledge on who has purchased which product or who is subscribed to which service. In the retail, media, and entertainment industries, this knowledge is already more challenging to obtain. The information captured in the MDM system is related to the *deep customer insight* factor and needs to be made available to the selection engine that determines the initial target set of customers and websites (instances in general).

As mentioned previously, the MDM system should also capture insight on customer demographics and other metrics, such as sentiments, opinions, and channel preferences. Ideally, the MDM system stores additional information, such as the *social influencer score* and the *past acceptance score,* that is highly relevant to viral marketing topics. Then the MDM system functions as a central information hub for the customer profile and linkage to relevant products and services. Figure 7.7 provides a high-level depiction of this central MDM role within the viral marketing context.

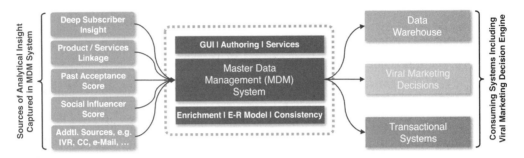

Figure 7.7   Role of MDM in viral marketing

Additional data sources are leveraged to enrich the MDM customer profile, such as interactive voice response (IVR) data, call-center (CC) transcripts, emails from customers and other parties, and other customer interaction-related data. The relevant analytical insight that is collectively derived from these data sources is captured in the MDM system and can thus be efficiently and consistently made available for the viral marketing decision engine.

As we have mentioned previously, the decision strategy to determine a most suitable initial target set of customers is based on correlating the viral marketing factors. This is especially true in analyzing the social network profile and structure in the context of available scores (for example, social influencer score, past acceptance scores), and products purchased or services subscribed to. In Chapter 6, we covered graph theory as a means to understand types of social networks.[17] Bipartite and complete bipartite graphs are interesting models to analyze this correlation between the viral marketing factors. Because of space constraints, we cannot dive into the mathematical representation; however, we would like to illustrate this correlation via the example shown in Figure 7.8.

The first set of vertices, or nodes, in Figure 7.8 are parties (for example, customers, subscribers, employees, and citizens) that are separated in two groups, or segments: the customer segment A and the customer segment B. The second set of vertices are products, services, or offerings of the company or competitors. The products in focus belong to the gold product group X; however, there also exists a second silver product group Y, which is out of scope for the viral marketing campaign. The edges between the customer vertices and the product vertices relate, for instance, to products purchased or services subscribed to by customers, but also relate to social media content and consumption, and interaction between customers and the products, services, and offerings. This allows an efficient linkage of the social network structure to the content of the viral marketing message (for example, promotion of a product, service, or offering). It allows determination of problems, sentiment, buzz, competitive insight, and perception that enriches the MDM party and product profiles and, most importantly, provides relevant insight for the viral marketing decision component.

17. See Table 6.2, "Types of Social Networks," in Chapter 6.

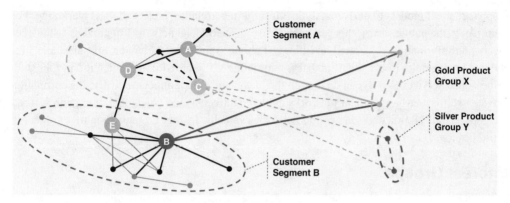

Figure 7.8   Relationship of viral marketing factors

In this example, customers A and B, as members of their respective segment, not only have the strongest linkage to the gold product group X, but also represent the strongest influence in their respective segment. Customer C, for instance, has a much lesser linkage to the gold product group X but a strong linkage to the silver product group Y, which, however, is out of scope of the viral marketing campaign. Customers D and E represent the linkage between the two customer segments; but they are neither strongly influential in their respective segment, nor are they linked to any of the products in question. Subsequently, customers A and B are chosen as the initial customer target set.

This model can be used for other use case scenarios that are not necessarily related only to products and services. A good example is a viral marketing campaign of government agencies, communities, or health associations designed to promote a healthier lifestyle of citizens (such as a campaign to reduce or even completely stop smoking). In such a scenario, the first set of vertices, or nodes, are again the citizens, and the second set of vertices are, for instance, documents or information on the health-related terms or themes (for example, smoking). The edges represent a sentiment, a tweet, a blog, or whether the citizen posts a document or consumes content. This allows determination of interests, preferences, and lifestyle details that correlate insight of the social network to the intent and content of the viral marketing campaign, and thus support the decision process to determine an initial set of citizens to reach out.

IBM has a set of products[18] and research[19] assets available that can be used as a foundation to implement some of the capabilities described previously. Graph theory and especially bipartite

---

18. You can find more information on predictive analytics and viral marketing in [18] and [19].

19. To find more information on IBM Research, see [20].

graphs are great models to derive analytical insight in correlating factors of viral marketing. For example, in the public sector, this can be used to correlate social networks of citizens with documents and information consumed and blogged about to influence behavior, attitudes, and lifestyles. For example, in the telco industry, correlating CDR-based communication graphs with value-added services (VAS) can do this. In the media and entertainment industry, the correlation between subscriber-based social networks and content consumed (such as movie genres, news and reports, talk shows, and soap operas) provides valuable insight for launching new content in "viral fashion."

Interest Groups

In the context of social media marketing, an *interest group* refers to any cluster of parties (for example, customers or citizens) that share, lobby, promote, or advance a common message. This message could be related or identical to a product, a service, an offering, a theme, or an area of knowledge (such as social welfare, healthy lifestyle, soccer or sports in general, good cigars) that can be characterized by sentiments and opinions.

With this in mind, the following list briefly describes possible social media and other related data sources that can be used to discover interest groups:

- **Facebook postings, tweets, blogs, newsgroups, forums, and so on:** To receive content of contributions from parties—for example, customers and potential customers.

- **Weblogs:** Log files that capture customer visits to derive insight regarding the "visitor journey"—for example, when, how, and by whom a web server was visited.

- **Telco CDRs and probe data:** Specifically, application data usage that provides insight on usage patterns, location information, and URL information.

- **Customer touch points:** Data from IVR transcripts, emails, and so on that can be used to understand product issues and the customer sentiment.

- **Media and entertainment logs:** For instance, data from set-top boxes (STB) to understand details regarding media content consumption.

Customer segmentation and clustering are well-known data-mining[20] techniques that can be used to determine interest groups. There is an emerging trend to capture different marketing personas to represent marketing segments, which can be used, for instance, to derive to relevant interest categories.[21] In this section, we do not intend to review the existing data-mining techniques, methods, models, algorithms, and so forth, and how they can be applied to customer

---

20. For more information on data-mining concepts, models, methods, and so on, see [21], [22], and [23].

21. For more information, refer to http://blog.bufferapp.com/marketing-personas-beginners-guide (accessed April 25, 2014).

segmentation and clustering in general. Instead, our intention is to highlight the possible augmentation and refinement of customer segmentation and clustering through social media analytics and discovery of interest groups. The relevance of social media networks and data to discover interest groups to optimize social media marketing initiatives is obvious.[22]

The segmentation of the customer base may not merely be done purely on the interest areas, such as fashion, sports, politics, and entertainment, but rather in conjunction with the clustering of the customer base. This may even lead to significantly new insight, adjusting the existing customer clusters or simple segments that may be rather broad, static, and generic to evolve into microsegments that can be used to efficiently market a message, a product, a service, or an offering to relevant interest groups or, in some cases, even to a small group of individual customers or parties in general.

In this section, we furthermore address the following questions:

- Which segments of subscribers usually exist, and how should these segments be adjusted based on social media–based insight?

- What new microsegments can be identified to improve social media marketing for subscribers and potential customers?

- How can interest groups be derived through weblog analytics, including enterprise-owned and public websites?

- What are the possibilities to derive the next best offer on an individual customer base (personalized recommendations)?

Depending on the specific use case scenarios, data from these sources should be integrated with available information from the MDM system (such as trusted demographics), the data warehouse system (such as credit card usage statistics), and transactional systems (such as service billing information).

Following is a list of analytical insight that can be derived from the preceding data sources that helps to discover special interest groups and further characterizes them:

- **Interest:** Recognizing the variety of interest areas that can further characterize existing customer segments and clusters and help determine interest groups

- **Like-mindedness:** Identifying like-mindedness and opinions as one possible attribute to derive to and further characterize the interest group

- **Influence:** Discovering influencers, advocates, and followers within an interest group for consumption in, for instance, viral marketing campaigns

- **Sentiment:** Analyzing the sentiment within interest groups to adequately respond to specific customers or adjust service offerings specific to interest groups

22. You can find more information on customer segmentation and clustering leveraging social media information in [24] and [25].

- **Emerging topics:** Understanding hot, emerging topics or the buzz and excitement in regards to a product, theme, and so on that further characterizes that interest group

In addition, members of the marketing team need to understand the structures of the interest groups (as outlined in Chapter 6). Depending on the use case scenario and the data source, not all input may come from existing customers, potential customers, or other parties.

As illustrated in Figure 7.9, additional tasks need to be performed. They include mapping interest areas to existing customer segments and clusters or further enriching knowledge of discovered interest groups with existing information from the MDM and data warehouse systems. For example, we might use demographics, product and services mappings, and analytical insight such as churn propensity scores.

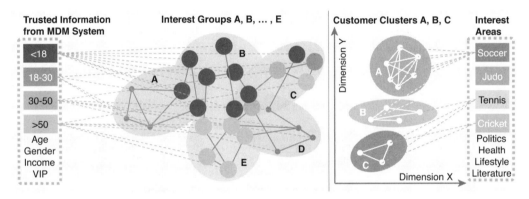

Figure 7.9   Enriching customer clusters and interest groups

The methodology uses bipartite graphs to map two sets of vertices along defined edges. However, the challenge is less associated with the edges but rather with the discovery of interest areas and groups and the customer clustering.

The left part of Figure 7.9 depicts five interest groups A through E, which may overlap in a certain way, with some parties belonging to several interest groups. Trusted information from the MDM system, such as age, gender, income, customer categorization (for example, VIP, gold, platinum); linkage to products and services; and analytical insight from the data warehouse systems, such as money spending and credit card usage behavior, geospatial patterns will be mapped against the identified interest groups. It is illustrated with the age demographics attribute: the interest group B is predominantly characterized with customers below 18 years old; there are just a few customers in other overlapping interest groups that belong to other age categories. Interest group E is associated exclusively with the age group greater than 50 years old. Interest group C, in contrast, is characterized with mixed age. This mapping should be done by leveraging two sources of information: (1) an adequate subset of the available trusted core information from the MDM system and (2) analytical measures from the data warehouse system.

The right part of Figure 7.9 depicts three customer clusters—A, B, and C—which may be derived along several dimensions. Identified interest areas are now mapped to the customer clusters. In the figure, you can see that cluster A seems to be excessively occupied with soccer. Cluster B is mixed, where not all members are into sports. In Cluster C, members are either into tennis and cricket, or no sports at all. The predefined customer segmentation can be adjusted, refined, and possibly even reduced to just a few customers to enable highly targeted marketing campaigns or next best offers.

The following high-level industry examples underpin the applicability and monetization aspect of the methodology to link interest areas to predefined party clusters:

- **Government and politics:** This method can be applied to clusters of citizens along demographic dimensions (for example, age, gender, income, address, employment status, and family status) that can mainly be derived from the trusted MDM system that a government agency or community office operates. The interest areas, derived from social media and citizen interaction points, are social themes (for example, health insurance coverage, pension system challenges, unemployment insurance issues). The linkage enables optimized election campaigns by targeting relevant themes. The anonymity of social media may require advanced text analytics to associate demographics information to identified interest areas. In some cases, this may be possible only in coarse-grained fashion.

- **Media and entertainment industry:** This method can be applied to clusters of subscribers along dimensions of service packages subscribed to, media content consumption patterns, and demographic information from the MDM system. The interest areas are, for instance, news and reports, music and entertainment, and movies. The linkage can lead to optimized subscription and services packages and optimization of content provisioning and targeted marketing campaigns.

- **Telecommunications industry:** This method can be applied to predefined clusters of subscribers and interest areas that are derived from analyzing CDRs and application usage data—for example, URL data—complemented with analytical insight from social media data. The linkage can lead to deeper customer insight with optimized service provisioning, reduced churn, and highly targeted mobile advertisement.

Summary

Marketing is evolving to become more personalized, targeted, and relevant to individuals. Social MDM serves as a foundation that helps us to improve and better understand individual interests. It helps us to link identity information from multiple sources. These capabilities are increasingly important across the range of marketing techniques as they are used independently or together.

In this chapter, we covered a range of marketing styles and techniques. Most importantly, we described the vital role and contribution of MDM for social media marketing initiatives and the emerging trends that characterize digital marketing. Social MDM, with its 360 degrees of party insight, provides the foundational capabilities for any emerging digital marketing initiative.

In discussing the range of marketing styles and techniques, we used the following three dimensions: (a) latency, meaning the time sensitivity of a campaign; (b) activity, behavior, and analytical insight; and (c) the geospatial knowledge that is related to where something is located or happening. These three dimensions are essential in understanding the role of Social MDM for any kind of marketing initiative:

- **Social media marketing:** This type of marketing gives enterprises the information they want, especially related to the process of gaining website traffic or attention through social media sites. Social media marketing programs use social media to create a social media presence and to establish a relationship with parties for a specific business purpose.

- **Contextual marketing:** This type of marketing is essentially the combination of locality and timing where contextual aspects could also take into account the family and household structure or the knowledge about interest areas. Contextual marketing is a good example in which Social MDM provides 360 degrees of customer insight that relates to the latency and geospatial requirements of a marketing campaign.

- **Mobile marketing:** For this type of marketing, we have provided a depiction of the key components of the mobile marketing and advertisement solution that is underpinned with an example from a communication service provider (CSP) implementing an "improved mobile advertisement solution."

- **Viral marketing:** This type of marketing requires the MDM system to capture insight on customer demographics and other metrics, such as sentiments, opinions, channel preferences, *social influencer score,* and *past acceptance score*—knowledge that is highly relevant to viral marketing campaigns.

- **Interest groups and personas:** The purpose of this type of marketing is to gain an in-depth understanding about clusters of parties (for example, customers or citizens) that share, lobby, promote, or advance a common message, where this message could be related or identical to a product, a service, an offering, a theme, or an area of knowledge, which can be characterized by sentiments and opinions.

The next chapter discusses emerging technical trends in Social MDM and the importance of ethical considerations in MDM programs.

References

[1] Baird, C. H., and G. Parnasis. *"From Social Media to Social CRM. The First in a Two-Part Series,"* IBM Institute for Business Value. Retrieved 4/28/2014 from http://public.dhe.ibm.com/common/ssi/ecm/en/gbe03391usen/GBE03391USEN.PDF.

[2] Baird, C. H., and G. Parnasis. *"From Social Media to Social CRM. The Second in a Two-Part Series,"* IBM Institute for Business Value, Retrieved 4/28/2014 from http://public.dhe.ibm.com/common/ssi/ecm/en/gbe03391usen/GBE03391USEN.PDF.

[3] Roth, J. *Mobile Computing. Grundlagen, Technik, Konzepte.* (dpunkt Verlag, 2005).

[4] Sauter, M. *Grundkurs Mobile Kommunikationssysteme: UMTS, HSPA und LTE, GSM, GPRS, Wireless LAN und Bluetooth.* (Springer Vieweg, 2013).

[5] Sauter, M. *Communications Systems for the Mobile Information Society.* (Wiley, 2006).

[6] Tuten, T. L., and M. R. Solomon. *Social Media Marketing.* (Prentice Hall, 2012).

[7] Barker, M., D. I. Barker, N. F. Bormann, and K. E. Neher. *Social Media Marketing: A Strategic Approach.* (Cengage Learning, 2012).

[8] Macarthy, A. *500 Social Media Marketing Tips: Essential Advice, Hints and Strategy for Business: Facebook, Twitter, Pinterest, Google+, YouTube, Instagram, LinkedIn, and More!* (CreateSpace Independent Publishing Platform, 2013).

[9] Lee, N. R., and P. Kotler. *Social Marketing. Influencing Behaviors for Good,* 4th ed. (SAGE Publications, 2011).

[10] Weinreich, N. K. *Hands-On Social Marketing: A Step-by-Step Guide to Designing Change for Good,* 2nd ed. (SAGE Publications, 2010).

[11] IBM. "IBM Enterprise Marketing Management (EMM). Social Media Marketing Solution." Retrieved 10/10/2013 from http://www-01.ibm.com/software/sg/marketing-solutions/social-media-solution/.

[12] Varnali, K., A. Toker, and C. Yilmaz. *Mobile Marketing: Fundamentals and Strategy.* (McGraw-Hill, 2010).

[13] Pasqua, R., and N. Elkin. *Mobile Marketing: An Hour a Day.* (Sybex, 2012).

[14] Krum, C. *Mobile Marketing: Finding Your Customers No Matter Where They Are.* (Que Publishing, 2010).

[15] Scott, D. M. *The New Rules of Marketing & PR: How to Use Social Media, Online Video, Mobile Applications, Blogs, News Releases, and Viral Marketing to Reach Buyers Directly,* 4th ed. (Wiley, 2013).

[16] Goldsmith, R. *Viral Marketing: Get Your Audience to Do Your Marketing for You.* (Financial Times Management, 2002).

[17] Penenberg, A. L. *Viral Loop: From Facebook to Twitter, How Today's Smartest Businesses Grow Themselves.* (Hyperion, 2009).

[18] IBM. "Integrating Social Media and Advanced Analytics for Richer Customer Insight." Retrieved 10/24/2013 from http://www.spss.com.ar/MKT/Promos/2012/0512_redessociales/integrate_socialMedia_PA.pdf.

[19] IBM. "Minimize Customer Churn with Analytics." Retrieved 10/24/2013 from http://public.dhe.ibm.com/common/ssi/ecm/en/ytw03085usen/YTW03085USEN.PDF.

[20] IBM Research and N. Modani. "Good Vibes from Social Networking." Retrieved 10/24/2013 from http://ibmresearchnews.blogspot.sg/2013/07/good-vibes-from-social-networking.html.

[21] Linoff, G. S., and M. J. Berrt. *Data Mining Techniques: For Marketing, Sales, and Customer Relationship Management,* 3rd ed. (Wiley, 2011).

[22] Kantardzic, M. *Data Mining: Concepts, Models, Methods, and Algorithms,* 2nd ed. (Wiley-IEEE Press, August 2011).

[23] Witten, I. H., E. Frank, and M. A. Hall. *Data Mining: Practical Machine Learning Tools and Techniques,* 3rd ed. (Morgan Kaufmann, 2011).

[24] Tsiptsis, K., and A. Chorianopoulos. *Data Mining Techniques in CRM: Inside Customer Segmentation.* (Wiley, 2010).

[25] Hansen, D., B. Shneiderman, and M. A. Smith. *Analyzing Social Media Networks with NodeXL: Insights from a Connected World.* (Morgan Kaufmann, 2010).

CHAPTER 8

Mobile MDM

For Social MDM, the touch points of your enterprise information systems (for customers, employees, and other users) have been recast as "systems of interaction." Mobile devices (cell phones, smart phones, tablets, watches, and so on) are rapidly being adopted as a primary system of interaction. There is a natural synergy between mobile systems and master data: MDM can inform mobile applications of key information about customers (preferences, account information, product information, and so on), and MDM can leverage information from mobile devices (device and user identity, location, and other sensor data) to improve customer satisfaction and increase employee productivity. A mobile device, as seen in Chapter 7, "Social MDM and Marketing," can obviously also be the target to deliver individualized marketing ads to customers. Mobile devices have some unique characteristics (limited form factor and bandwidth, in particular) that require a different architectural approach for integration with MDM.

Evolution of Interaction with Consumers

Since the explosion of the World Wide Web, there has been an evolution in the nature of systems of interaction. Prior to the Web, the standard applications were employee-facing green screen or PC programs accessing internal back-end systems. When the World Wide Web emerged, it brought with it the ability to reach out directly to customers with simple HTML-based customer-facing applications. In the past decade, systems of interaction have moved on to now include a multitude of applications targeting computers, tablets, phones, smart phones, cars, and other devices, engaging with customers and employees in ways that embrace the mobile and social nature and technology of today's environment.

Mobile devices are the newest of the channels that tie into existing and emerging ways of accessing enterprise data, and one of the faster growing ones. According to [1], there are now more mobile devices than people on the planet. With the rise of mobile devices, first in the consumer market, enterprises strive to extend their IT capabilities to encompass the mobile platform.

Apple and IBM recently announced a partnership[1] to deliver enterprise mobility. The ubiquitous nature of mobile devices opens some new opportunities for enterprises:

- Enterprises can now conduct business directly with people who don't have computers (emerging markets) but have cell phones or tablets. This capability is particularly of interest for banking and payment systems (because many residents of emerging markets may not have access to banks) and for social services provided by governments (for the same reasons). One interesting twist is that many people in emerging markets often share mobile devices, so applications cannot assume that one device is tied to a single individual (for profiling or authentication). From an MDM perspective, customer demographics of the individuals might not be completely known and less trusted since the identity can't be always assured.

- Consumers can interact with enterprises anytime or anywhere. The Web erased the notion of needing a storefront that is open a set number of hours to conduct business, but now the ability to place an order, get a notification that the order is ready, and pay for that order using a combination of computer, text messaging, and smart phone applications (or just one of those) dramatically simplifies and streamlines customer experience. Customers can also quickly use their mobile device to post a review to a social media site telling their friends and others how wonderful the product and the purchasing experience was, which will attract more customers.

- Knowledge workers can conduct business on the go, with access to the right information without needing a full computer. Employees out in the field, such as stockers searching for products, insurance agents taking claim data, case workers collecting information, and drivers delivering products, can use tailored applications that exploit mobile capabilities (for example, location and camera) to more quickly and easily do their jobs. Even traditional applications, such as travel expense reimbursement, are morphing in a mobile environment: employees can take pictures of their receipts and attach them to a request submitted via tablet or phone.

- Mobile is directly tied to immediacy of opportunity, action, and reaction. Targeted sales promotions, as discussed in Chapter 7, can be sent out to consumers in the vicinity of a favorite store, enticing them in, and then additional promotions can be delivered while in store, increasing the amount of money spent during the shopping trip. Exceptions requiring action, such as fraud alerts for worrisome credit card transactions, are now sent to mobile devices (typically text messages or calls) for validation—with a simple call or click needed to address the alert. Employees can also be informed in a similar fashion of an immediate business situation that they need to resolve and act directly on their device.

---

1. On July 15th 2014, Apple and IBM announced their partnership for enterprise mobility. More details can be found in [2].

Master Data and the Mobile Revolution

All the solutions and integration points of master data, social data, and systems of interaction we presented in previous chapters (next best action, customer care and insight, and so on) apply to the mobile channel. The same master data that feeds into existing applications can power mobile applications: customer, sentiment, house-holding, products, accounts, and so on—all can be consumed in a mobile application.

In particular, mobile applications benefit from master data profile information about users that is shared across systems of interactions:

- Name
- Language
- Cultural settings (date, time, structure of names)
- Privacy preferences
- Payment preferences
- Contact preferences
- Lifestyle preferences

Profile master data creates a cleaner experience with the end user, which is critical on mobile devices. The limited screen sizes and more restrictive text input drive an imperative to show only data that the user asks for and not to ask for data you should already know—two characteristics that master data enables.

Combining Location and Sensor Data with Master Data

Location, location, location—it not only is the mantra of real estate agents but also is a key component of mobile and MDM-powered applications. To match the old saying, MDM and mobile use types of location data to drive business value:

- Where is the user right now?
- Where are the enterprise products and services?
- Where is the normal location (mobility patterns) of the user?

The first two location characteristics (where is the customer, and where are the products?) can be combined with microsegmentation to create real-time offers based on customer profile data gleaned through analytics and stored in MDM or an offer system. The micro-segmentation mobility patterns could be factored in as well on top of traditional customer segmentation techniques. For example:

```
MDMGuru: Hey, I'm downtown and want a good pizza - does anyone have any
recommendations?
SuperFabulousPizza: @MDMGuru - come in to our location at 500 Wilkinson
Way before 9PM and we will give you $1 off any medium or larger pizza!
```

Location can be scraped from a post or tweet, but also retrieved from device characteristics. What makes these real-time offers even more interesting is that it is easy to measure the effectiveness of such campaigns (*MDMGuru* shows the response to the restaurant) and then tailor or update the campaign globally or for an individual based on response. More sophisticated campaigns can see who are attracted as new customers, what offers improve retention and basket size, and which customers don't need offers to buy your products. These analytics can be run inside a store while the customer is shopping (if the customer has given the right permissions to do so, as we discuss in Chapter 9, "Future Trends in MDM").

The third type of location (where is the customer's normal location?) typically surfaces for fraud detection. If *MDMGuru* lives in New York City but suddenly starts making purchases at an electronics store in Bangkok, this would generate a fraud alert to the customer. The antifraud system would leverage the master data on the customer's home to see if an alert was warranted and then leverage the information on mobile contacts to send an SMS (or call) the customer's phone asking if the transaction is legitimate.

Mobile devices can provide other useful sensor data that can be paired with master data. Pictures, fingerprints, and voiceprints (biometric data) combined with classic biographic data (name, address, social identification number, date of birth, and so on) yield better entity resolution (matching and merging of records), especially when the biographic data is incomplete or weak. Pictures can match product master data. For example, a smart phone camera can take a picture of a product and send it to an app to retrieve the information about that product—information from the store, other vendors, price ranges, social reviews, and more.

Here are some application scenarios where Mobile MDM provides new capabilities and business value:

- **Energy & Utility industry:** Here are a number of different scenarios enabled through Mobile MDM. Service technicians can retrieve relevant product and spare part documentation details through Mobile MDM while performing maintenance work on gas, water and electricity networks. Mobile MDM delivers service technicians in such a scenario access to the right information at the right time. Smart metering infrastructure for smarter homes can capture which customer is operating which device (e.g., internet-connected dryers or washing machines) establishing customer to product relationships in a Mobile MDM scenario.

- **Building maintenance:** Large office or manufacturing buildings have complex infrastructure such as lightning systems, water systems or air conditioning systems. Making every light bulb, every pump in the water system, etc. connected to the Internet allows maintenance firms to receive alerts that a certain piece of the infrastructure requires replacement. Having an MDM system managing the customer location (the building) with the relationship to the assets (light bulbs, water pumps, etc.) through mobile MDM, a service ticket can be sent to the closest service technician after obtaining an alert that an asset is broken.

Again, mobile MDM for asset maintenance delivers new capabilities in this scenario simplifying building maintenance.

- **Employee enablement:** In various industries such as automotive, insurance, or banking sales representatives, case workers (e.g., for insurance claims) or service technicians (e.g., road side assistance providing a spare part replacement for a broken part of a car) can leverage mobile MDM capabilities working with master data. For example, the service technician providing road-side assistance might want to review if the driver is entitled for this service. A sales representative might want to update master data to add a new contact met in a meeting for an organization customer.

- **Marketing:** Ads and promotions being pushed to customer's mobile devices at the right time at the right location, improving cross- and up-sell and thus improving revenue.

As shown through these scenarios, mobile MDM can be leveraged for customers as well as for many applications for employees improving business operations.

Empowering Knowledge Workers on the Go: Data Stewardship

We gave some examples earlier in this chapter about how mobile plus MDM increases employee productivity. There are some other scenarios we didn't discuss; specifically, employees can update critical master data whenever an issue is detected. So if an insurance agent is looking at prospects and sees some overlap with existing customers, or notices that there are multiple entries for the same customer, that agent can quickly resolve the issue from a mobile application. Just as alerts can be sent out to customers for potential fraud, MDM systems that detect exceptions in master data can notify stewards about exceptions via their mobile devices. If a link is included in the notification, a steward launches a mobile app to immediately fix the problem. With mobile enablement of enterprise business process management applications, the governance side of MDM comes into play by having all updates go through a consistent stewardship process. Stewardship is not limited to customer data but can also include addressing product data quality problems (such as duplicate entries for the same product) and location data quality problems (for example, delivery drivers can update addresses when they drive to a given address and find that it is wrong).

IT Impact of Mobile MDM

As the preceding section showed, a mobile channel offers businesses a wide range of new opportunities to engage with their customers and also allows customers with a means of interacting with an enterprise and their customer data. Similar things were said when online channels were established with the rise of the Internet and PCs got connected initially using dial-up modem connections and later on (broadband) DSL. So what's the big deal setting up a mobile channel from an IT perspective? To illustrate the point, we pick an example from the banking industry comparing online banking done from a PC or laptop from home to mobile banking done from a smart phone device. In both cases, customers want to see their customer profile or account status, issue electronic money transfers to pay bills, and so on. Let's introduce some architecture and application basics first before studying the impact of a mobile channel.

Architecture Overview for Mobile MDM in the Banking Industry

Figure 8.1 shows an architecture overview diagram for a multichannel banking architecture based on our Social MDM reference architecture.

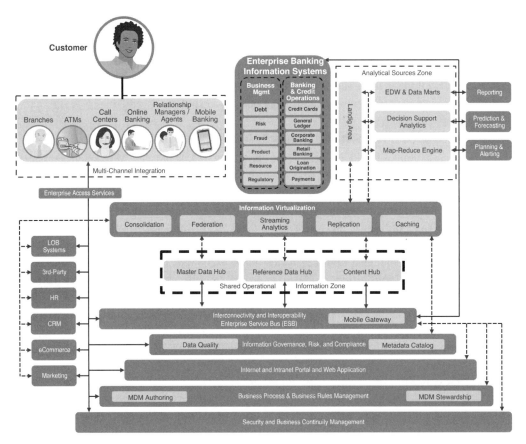

Figure 8.1   Multichannel banking architecture overview

A customer expects a unified end-to-end customer experience across all channels, including:

- Branches
- ATM

- Call center
- Online banking
- Relationship managers/agents
- Mobile banking

From an IT perspective, these locations are outside the core corporate IT center and thus require access through enterprise access services. For online banking, the corresponding entry point provided by the enterprise access services for the web application would be through a demilitarized zone (DMZ). Some mobile device platforms such as Android[2] prefer REST-based services over web services using the SOAP/HTTP protocol. Mapping back-end service interfaces to more appropriate and seamlessly consumable service interfaces is one of many useful functions a mobile gateway server can provide. Thus, such a component is needed and is part of the ESB, as shown in Figure 8.1, to extend MDM to mobile platforms. The mobile gateway can also be used to provide appropriate service mappings for services provided by the enterprise banking information systems so that they are also seamlessly consumable by mobile banking applications.

Because iOS[3] and Android dominate as operating systems for smart phones (see [3] and [4]), any enterprises developing and deploying mobile applications are well advised to have their applications support both of these operating system platforms for smart phone devices. Thus, a mobile application platform seamlessly supporting multiple native operating systems is needed. IBM Worklight is such a platform, which we explore in the next section. This approach is targeted toward on-premise deployments. However, such mobile back-end functionality can also be delivered as a software as a service (SaaS) solution through a public cloud model.

IBM MobileFirst

A key technology of IBM's MobileFirst strategy, the IBM Worklight platform (see [5], [6], [7], [8], [9], and [10]), is a comprehensive software solution for the development and deployment of mobile applications. It also allows you to store master data in an encrypted database on mobile devices. The IBM Worklight platform is composed of the following major components, as shown in Figure 8.2:

- **Worklight Studio:** The Worklight Studio represents the design-time component used by application developers developing mobile applications. Using the Worklight Studio, a developer can build different types of applications such as HTML5-based web applications or native applications. HTML5 applications require only a web browser on the mobile device. The key advantage of HTML5-based applications is the fact that they can be deployed to different mobile platforms such as iOS and Android. Native applications are written with the device-specific SDK and are unable to run on other device

---

2. Android is the operating system running on smart phones from Samsung, HTC, and so on.
3. iOS is the operating system running on smart phones from Apple.

applications. Hybrid applications use HTML5 and native functions. A WYSIWYG editor improves time to value for the mobile application developer.

- **Worklight Server:** This component is the runtime server of the mobile application platform. It provides unified push notification features so that one push implication works for different mobile device platforms. An adapter library provides mapping functions to expose, for example, SOAP/HTTP web services either from back-end systems within the enterprise or public clouds as REST services to mobile applications.

- **Worklight Console:** This is the administration console for the Worklight Server.

- **Worklight Application Center:** Mobile applications available for the users of the mobile devices are managed through the Application Center.

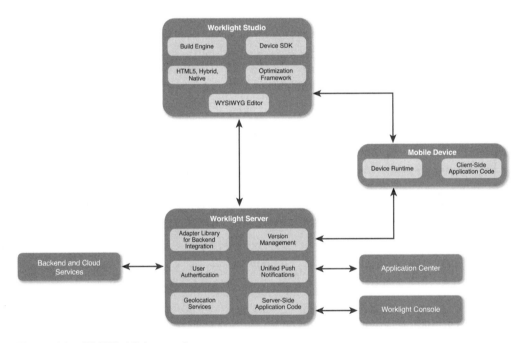

Figure 8.2   IBM Worklight overview

Mobile Banking Applications

In this section, we explore a bit of the functionality expected from a mobile banking application running on smart phones. Here are some of the key functionalities:

- **Start Screen:** On the start screen for a mobile banking application, typical functions include an entry point to search for nearby branches; entry points to the various social media platforms such as Facebook and Twitter, where the bank has a presence; an entry point for the contact touch points of the bank such as the call center; and obviously a login screen.

- **Contact Screen:** Here, customers find contact information for the various services the bank has to offer, such as mobile support, checking and savings, and credit cards. A typical implementation triggers the dial function of the phone when a contact phone number is tapped.

- **Locations:** If the search function for nearby branches is triggered, a screen with a map appears, showing the current location of the user and the closest local branches of the bank. Note that the geolocation functionality of the smart phone devices is used, along with APIs such as Google Maps API. Tapping over a nearby branch usually triggers a pop-up showing relevant information such as address, phone number, opening hours, and URL to website.

- **Login Screen:** On this screen, users must authenticate to log in before using banking services.

- **Home:** After users are successfully authenticated, a screen showing the various options available for banking customers appears; it usually provides entry points for all the functions listed in the subsequent bullets.

- **My Profile:** This functional area of the mobile application allows customers to change their customer profile information such as address, contact details, preferences, and privacy settings. These master data services are exposed to the mobile application.

- **My Accounts:** This functional area of the mobile banking application usually allows users to review accounts, their balances, and the transaction history.

- **Transfer Funds/Pay Bills:** This functional area of the mobile banking application usually allows customers to transfer money between accounts and support the payment of bills.

- **Markets:** Here, banking customers can review stocks, bonds, and so on and trigger appropriate actions.

- **Deposit Check:** Using the built-in camera function, banking customers can create a photograph of a signed check (the front and back of the check must be photographed). Using font recognition routing information, information is taken from the check and shown to the user for confirmation (and if needed correction). After the data is correctly shown and the images of the check are attached to the transaction, customers can trigger the deposit of the check.

This list gives you a high-level summary of typical functions of a mobile banking application. Next, we explore the impact of mobile applications.

IT Impact of a Mobile Channel

Mobile applications have a number of characteristics that make them different compared to in-house applications such as programming models (for example, DevOps), operating system platforms, and numbers of users (for example, millions of customers versus an in-house application for a few thousand or, for some really large enterprises, a few hundred thousand employees). Although each of these characteristics must be addressed, we want to focus on something that had been underestimated by the first enterprises going mobile: a drastic increase in *transactions and traffic*. To understand this better, take a look at Table 8.1, which shows the differences between an online and a mobile channel. The major difference between online and mobile banking is that online banking is done from devices such as PCs (and laptops), which are not always connected versus mobile banking where smart phone devices are always connected. To keep Table 8.1 simple for the key messages, we don't consider some cases such as online banking with a laptop where the user sits in a café with Wifi-based internet access. Similarly, a person can't carry a PC while being on the road but a smart phone is always possible. This affects of course the timing when banking services can be used (all the time with the smart phone doing mobile banking versus only at home before or after work using a PC for online banking).

Table 8.1   Comparison of Online and Mobile Banking Channel

	Online Banking	Mobile Banking
Access	From home	Anywhere
Offline and online operations	Online only	If master data is stored locally, online and offline operations can be supported.
Regular full-time employee	Primarily evenings, weekends	Anytime
Part-time employee	Partial time during the day when home, evenings, weekends	Anytime
Device	PC, laptop, tablets	Smart phone
Risk of device loss	PC—very low (burglary); laptop/tablet—depends on how often carried outside the house	Smart phone—compared to PCs, more frequently lost or stolen
Geolocation services	Usually no	Yes. Smart phones are location aware.
OS	Primarily Windows for PC and laptops (small footprint of Linux and Mac OS); primarily iOS and Android for tablets	Android, iOS, Windows Mobile

One of the banks we worked with added a mobile channel complementing its existing online banking channel. The bank's assumption was that the total number of incoming transactions across online and mobile channels remains the same, which means each transaction coming in through the mobile channel is one transaction less on the online channel. However, that turned out to be a poor assumption. When the mobile channel was launched, it was initially made available only to approximately 10% of the customers, who also represented 10% of the users of the online channel. The customer group starting to use the mobile channel created the same number of transactions as all the users of the online channel, which means roughly a tenfold increase of transactions per user. A root cause, once analyzed, was the ubiquitous nature of mobile devices such as smart phones allowing customers to access the banking services offered through the mobile channel *anywhere at any time*. As indicated in the previous section, a mobile banking application offers users self-service functionality on customer master data. As a result, the increase in service transaction requests hits not only the back-end banking systems but also the MDM system. Note that not all service transactions are equal. Some of them are high-frequency service transactions such as retrieving the customer profile or the account balance. Other service transactions might require immediate responses, whereas still others might be queued for asynchronous processing. Consequently, we need to identify techniques for high-frequency service transactions requiring immediate real-time responses.

Now take a look at Figure 8.3.

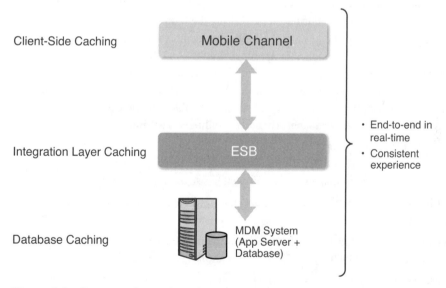

Figure 8.3   Conceptual overview of caching options

From an end-user experience, the services requested by the mobile banking application through the mobile channel need to scale consistently. This means the screen change time should not grow if the number of concurrent service transactions against the MDM system is scaled up drastically. This works only if the entire stack, including the MDM system, scales accordingly or if appropriate caching techniques are applied. Given that before updating the customer master data, the customer profile (or parts of it) is reviewed by the customer before the update is issued, one idea for load reduction is caching the customer master data. For caching, conceptually three options exist:

- **Client-side caching:** For this approach, caching technologies (for example, embedded databases able to run on mobile devices) that reside within the consuming mobile platform are used. Ideally, if master data is stored on the mobile device, it's protected through encryption. The advantages are as follows: It obviously has the lowest latency for the end-user experience because data access is possible on the device, avoiding network latency. It also supports offline scenarios (for example, when the user is on a flight, a network might be unavailable). From a cost perspective, this is likely the lowest-cost option. As user, data, and demand grows, not all read service requests are hitting the integration layer and the MDM system, and during periodic synchronization, all changes can be processed as a delta batch instead of many individual update requests. This enables much easier scalability since the number of service requests is lower. The major disadvantage of this approach is the creation of a bidirectional data synchronization requirement between locally cached changes and changes in the MDM back end. This bidirectional data synchronization also needs to resolve conflicting updates, which is a nontrivial problem in itself. Furthermore, making the bidirectional data synchronization between locally cached updates and the MDM back end resilient against error situations complicates matters. Although this approach might work for some types of data (for example, parts of the customer profile), for other parts it might not be desirable from a business perspective (such as transactions affecting balances and credit scores). Another disadvantage is that this approach is realistically feasible only on certain channels such as mobile but not for other channels (branches, online, ATM, and so on).

- **Integration layer caching:** For this approach, caching technologies[4] that reside within the bank can be deployed. Usually, they are within the ESB technology stack used to implement the integration layer. This approach has several major advantages:

  - **Ubiquitous applicability:** This technique can be used across all channels and applications.

  - **Transparency:** This technique can be implemented transparently for everything above the cache, which means for all applications and channels.

  - **Independence:** The cache in the integration layer can be scaled independently from all other infrastructure and applications.

4. The caching technique in the integration layer can be built using IBM Integration Bus features such as extreme scale and global cache. For more details, see [11], [12], [13], and [14].

- **Improved resilience:** This technique provides an additional layer of resiliency. For example, customers can access cached data even if the underlying back-end systems such as MDM would be offline for maintenance.

- **Support for all data types:** This approach can be used for virtually any kind of data (relational, columnar, key-value pairs, and so on).

- **Cost:** This approach is likely less expensive to scale compared to database-level optimization with caching.

  One disadvantage of the approach is the bidirectional data synchronization problem between the cache in the integration layer and the MDM system (or other back-end systems for which data is cached). This problem is similar to the problem with the client-side caching approach. A second disadvantage is that this approach does not allow for offline access.

- **Database caching:** For this technique to work, either the database used by the MDM system is moved to a more scalable platform (such as DB2 pureScale), or the infrastructure of the database system is increased to improve throughput and reduce latency by database tuning. There are two main advantages of this approach. First, it avoids a bidirectional data synchronization problem by design. Second, the approach is transparent for all consuming applications and can thus be easily used across all channels. However, this approach also has some significant disadvantages. First, it's very likely that this approach requires substantial migration work if the original MDM system design had not been in a way to scale seamlessly if service transactions increase by factors of ten or more. Second, from a latency and availability perspective, all the network hops from the mobile device to the MDM system are still part of the roundtrip. So, for example, if the integration layer does not perform as well anymore with increased service transaction volumes, the end user might not benefit from the performance improvements done in the MDM system. Finally, for nonvolatile data addressing, throughput and latency can be likely addressed with the other options at lower cost.

To select a solution from these techniques to make sure master data is available for consumption through a mobile channel, you need to analyze them on a case-by-case basis. However, architecturally, these are the three major options. Note that for a particular solution, a combination of these techniques might be used to address different concerns. For example, for high-frequency, read-only service transactions, integration layer caching might be used to avoid the load on the MDM system for them. For update service transactions, the MDM database might be tuned. This approach avoids the tricky issue of bidirectional update synchronization with conflict resolution, while offloading read-only access from the MDM system to the integration layer with improved performance for the read-only lookups.

Finally, to put the increase of service transactions against the MDM system into a historic perspective, consider the following: in 2004–2006, a large MDM installation for a major bank had to deal with 300–600 concurrent service transactions per second with an expected average response time below 200 ms. Today, we have seen production installations with 3,000–6,000 concurrent service transactions with subsecond response time requirements, and we are working with customers who are considering scaling beyond 15,000 concurrent service transactions per second with response times in the double-digit millisecond range. A performance benchmark showing that even more than 20,000 concurrent service transactions are possible with IBM Info-Sphere MDM is published in [14].

Security

If you expose master data through a mobile channel, another dimension is security. Mobile devices such as smart phones are more easily lost or stolen compared to a PC at home. So you certainly want to minimize unauthorized access to master data through a mobile channel by putting appropriate security in place. There are several considerations for mitigating these risks:

- Minimize the number of master data attributes exposed to the mobile channel to the bare minimum required for the business functions that are absolutely needed. For example, although the Social Security number might be part of the customer profile, it might be an attribute that should not be exposed through the mobile channel due to its sensitivity (and such identifiers are rarely if ever updated anyway).

- Apply encryption to the storage on the mobile device and the communication channels between the mobile devices and the MDM back-end system.

- Try to minimize the number of master data attributes that can be updated through a mobile channel to the minimum required for the necessary self-service functions.

- Apply audit on the MDM system to monitor who accesses master data and when. Apply secure engineering principles during development of mobile applications.

- Use geolocation services to validate if a read or change request is suspicious. For example, if a person lives at a certain address, accept read or write requests only if the location of the request is "close enough" to the default living area of customer. Otherwise, either ask for additional identification such as an additional security question the customer should be able to answer if it is a valid request and not a thief using the device, or buffer the request for human inspection into a stewardship process before allowing it into your MDM back-end system.

Conclusion

An MDM system is the natural source system for services, allowing customers to interact with their master data also from mobile devices. However, as shown in this chapter, extending the MDM solution into the mobile area creates a new set of challenges—scalability being one of the biggest. We have shown several architectural options regarding how this problem can be addressed.

References

[1] Hepburn, Aden. "Infographic: 2013 Mobile Growth Statistics." Retrieved 07/21/2014 from http://www.digitalbuzzblog.com/infographic-2013-mobile-growth-statistics/.

[2] IBM Mobile First strategy and partnership with Apple: Retrieved 07/21/2014 from http://www.ibm.com/mobilefirst/us/en/.

[3] BusinessWire. "Android and iOS Continue to Dominate the Worldwide Smartphone Market with Android Shipments Just Shy of 800 Million in 2013, According to IDC." Retrieved 4/26/2014 from http://www.businesswire.com/news/home/20140212005399/en/Android-iOS-Continue-Dominate-Worldwide-Smartphone-Market#.U1uIBBBim3Y.

[4] Kerr, Dara. "Android Dominates 81 Percent of World Smartphone Market." Retrieved 4/26/2014 from http://www.cnet.com/news/android-dominates-81-percent-of-world-smartphone-market/.

[5] IBM, "Experience the IBM Worklight Developer Edition." Retrieved 4/26/2014 from http://www-03.ibm.com/software/products/en/worklight.

[6] Dannhauer, A., S. Hanson, M. Z. Huang, P. Idstein, T. Kaplinger, H. Katory, C. Kirsch, K. McPhersion, and L. Olivera. *Extending Your Business to Mobile Devices with IBM Worklight.* (IBM Redbook, 2013). http://www.redbooks.ibm.com/abstracts/sg248117.html?Open.

[7] IBM. "Getting Started with IBM Worklight." Retrieved 4/26/2014 from http://www.redbooks.ibm.com/abstracts/tips1009.html.

[8] IBM. "Enabling Mobile Apps with IBM Worklight Application Center." Retrieved 4/26/2014 from http://www.redbooks.ibm.com/abstracts/redp5005.html?Open.

[9] Mousliki, Saad. "Build a Mobile Hybrid App Using IBM Worklight: Part 1." Retrieved 4/26/2014 from http://www.sitepoint.com/build-a-mobile-hybrid-app-using-ibm-worklight-part-1/.

[10] Mousliki, Saad. "Build a Hybrid Mobile App Using IBM Worklight, Part 2." Retrieved 4/26/2014 from http://www.sitepoint.com/build-hybrid-mobile-app-using-ibm-worklight-part-2/.

[11] IBM. "A Powerful Enterprise Services Bus for Any Size Project." Retrieved 4/26/2014 from http://www-03.ibm.com/software/products/en/integration-bus-advanced.

[12] IBM. "Introduction to the WebSphere Message Broker Global Cache." Retrieved 4/26/2014 from http://www.ibm.com/developerworks/websphere/library/techarticles/1212_hart/1212_hart.html.

[13] Hart, James. "What's new in the Global Cache in IBM Integration Bus v9." Retrieved 4/26/2014 from https://www.ibm.com/developerworks/community/blogs/ c7e1448b-9651-456c-9924-f78bec90d2c2/entry/what_s_new_in_the_global_ cache?lang=en.

[14] IBM. "IBM Integration Bus Technical Review." Retrieved 4/26/2014 from http:// pic.dhe.ibm.com/infocenter/wmbhelp/v9r0m0/index.jsp?topic=%2Fcom.ibm.etools. mft.doc%2Fab20551_.htm.

[15] IBM. "High Scale Benchmark Using IBM InfoSphere Master Data Management." Retrieved 4/26/2014 from https://www14.software.ibm.com/webapp/iwm/web/signup. do?source=sw-infomgt&S_PKG=ov17262&S_CMP=is_mdmwp81.

CHAPTER 9

Future Trends in MDM

Although Social MDM itself is a significant step in the way that MDM is currently used, it represents only one step in the ongoing evolution of Master Data Management. In this chapter, we explore some of the emerging technical trends that will enhance and enrich MDM implementations with new capabilities and new ways in which to realize business value from MDM technologies.

In the first section, we start with the heart of most MDM systems: entity resolution and matching. We also discuss how we are extending our ability to accurately match entities with additional sources of information, in particular how we can operate at lower likelihood values typical in associating social media data with structured, information rich data and how we can scale out matching to address challenges previously viewed as infeasible. As matching becomes ever more sophisticated, we can apply the same basic techniques not only to recognize identities, but also to discover relationships between identities. This brings us to the next section around what we call Semantic MDM. Semantic MDM leverages emerging capabilities in knowledge representation and semantic processing that allow us to represent information in ways that can improve our understanding of individuals and their relationships. Relationships exist not only between people, but also between individuals and their environment. This contextual understanding helps us to also develop a better view of individual behavior.

The final section of the book introduces the topic of ethics in the context of Social MDM and the consideration of ethical principles in the collection, management, and analysis of information. In light of recent controversies involving data collection and utilization, we need to ask the question, "Just because we have the technical capability to do something, should we?" The ethics of information use is an area that will get increasing attention as the technology for integration improves and the amount of available information increases. We explore some of the challenges in this evolving area and suggest some basic guidelines.

Entity Resolution and Matching

Matching is a key component of most MDM solutions. Its primary function is to join together records that represent the same real-world entity (person, organization, household, and so on) and as such is sometimes referred to as *entity resolution*. As you have seen in prior chapters, however, the use of matching in Social MDM has uses beyond resolving entities in creating associations between known entities and less trusted objects, such as social media profiles. Using matching to relate these new sources of data will only increase as we move to other data domains, and this creates new requirements for this fundamental component of MDM. The fundamentals of MDM matching are discussed in Chapter 5. Here we concentrate on the future requirements driven by Social MDM.

Social matching uses a combination of probabilistic and deterministic matching. Starting with a customer profile in MDM, we use probabilistic matching to determine a set of profiles that are a likely match and then use rules to determine if a social profile is associated with the customer profile. These rules consider such items as location (for example, is the user tweeting from a location known to MDM such as a home or work location?), cardinality (for example, is a similar social profile already attached to this customer?), and existing linkages (for example, does this social profile link to another customer with higher likelihood?). These additional steps allow us to link (not resolve) profiles at significantly lower levels of certainty than required in classic entity resolution. However, as we encounter new data, our matching techniques will need expansion. The key areas for expansion are as follows:

- **Fusion with biometrics:** One key feature of social media data is that it incorporates image information. Currently, these images are most useful for matching if they have been "tagged" by users. However, as facial extraction and recognition technology improves, these images can be used in matching. This will be especially useful for organizations that already collect images as part of their customer profiles (for example, law enforcement and health care).

- **Geographic and temporal information:** The spatial and temporal patterns generated by social media users can provide information that aids in identifying them. As mentioned previously, geospatial information from mobile devices can be compared to known locations in the customer profile. This data can also be used to develop new "known" locations. In addition, several of the attributes used in matching have temporal dependencies. These attributes can be relatively long term, such as a residence address, or short term, such as using one email account during working hours and a different one during non-working hours. Exploiting this data will challenge new matching solutions.

- **Uncertainty models:** Many of the unique features of social matching result from the fact that we are using them for data with higher uncertainty than standard matching for entity resolutions. One example of this is the notion of transitivity in matching. In standard entity resolutions, we employ transitivity, which says that if A resolves to B and B resolves to C, then A resolves to C. This transitivity is applicable only when we have near certainty in resolution. Transitivity fails when we replace "A resolves to B" with "A *might* resolve to B." If you are only 85% certain that A resolves to B and similarly certain that B resolves to C, then we are at most 72% certain that A resolves to C. To continue to work at the lower certainty inherent in social data, we need to augment our entity models to include uncertainty.

- **Big data:** Today, it's not uncommon for large MDM deployments to manage on the order of 100 million customer records. As we begin to include social media data, the volumes required by matching technologies easily moves into the billions of records. To scale to these volumes, we need to move matching algorithms to horizontally scalable systems such as map/reduce on Hadoop.

In addressing this broad set of Social Matching use cases, we find that stewardship surrounding the matching process remains important for two reasons. First, given that we are often dealing with uncertain and sparse information, human expertise may assist in resolving or validating questionable linkages. Clearly there is a need to automate matching and linking as much as possible—but sometimes we need a bit of human help to improve our confidence in the results. The second reason follows the first, if people are able to detect additional patterns and signals from the data, then perhaps there is knowledge that we can capture to better train the matching and linking algorithms to do a better job. So rather than view stewardship as simply a cost, we can view it as an opportunity to continually improve automated processing. As new kinds of social information emerge, or customer profiles continue to change, the stewards will likely be the first to detect the changing data and can often offer insight into how to adjust the processing to accommodate these changes. In essence, the action of data stewards, either as a dedicated effort or "on the edge" review, enable the machine learning essential to scale data improvement in the big data environment.

In summary, we need to evolve matching solutions to address four fundamental problems inherent in Social MDM:

- Volume of data to integrate/master requires high-capacity matching solutions.
- Variety of data requires multiple simultaneous integrations of different kinds of data.
- Velocity of data requires near real-time integration to customer/prospect data.
- Veracity of data requires advanced matching algorithms.

Semantic MDM

As organizations continue to look for new technologies and approaches to improve customer care, service, and retention, the notion of applying semantic web technologies to master data has evolved. Semantic web technologies have evolved over the past 20 years or so as a way to improve search and navigation of information across the World Wide Web (WWW).[1] Fostered,

---

1. An example for a semantic web standard by the W3C can be found in [1].

encouraged, and standardized by the World Wide Web Consortium (W3C), semantic web technologies enable people to store, link, and query information in flexible and powerful ways. Two key features of semantic web technologies are the ability to easily create complex graphs of relationships between objects and the ability to classify objects based on their characteristics. Both of these features can be applied to Master Data Management to help us derive and apply new kinds of insight. Semantic MDM is the application of semantic web technologies to MDM.

Semantic MDM recognizes the increasing importance and sophistication of relationships between entities and how we discover, represent, and utilize these relationships. Relationships exist not only between people, but also between an individual and the context encompassing their situation—including products they own, their physical location, and perhaps even their activities. This contextual understanding helps us to develop a comprehensive individual profile.

Discovering, understanding, and utilizing relationships between and among people and organizations are key elements of social MDM systems. Current MDM systems support direct relationships, hierarchical relationships, and grouping of parties. Direct relationships provide a typed relationship between two parties. Examples of direct relationships include:

- Individual spouseOf Individual
- Individual manages Individual
- Organization isSupplierFor Organization
- Individual isPhysicianTo Individual
- Individual owns Product
- Individual hasAn Account
- Organization employs Individual

Hierarchies can be used to represent organizational structures and parties within organizations. Starting from an individual party, we can easily navigate both up and down the organization to, for instance, identify who the individual works for and her employees. Groups that provide a flexible mechanism used to represent individuals have something in common—for instance, members of the same household or individuals with the same hobby.

Each of these mechanisms is useful for understanding parties and their relationships with other parties. However, many MDM systems today are limited by the kinds and complexities of relationships that we observe. Relationships also extend across entities. For example, a person owns multiple products, lives at a given location, and has financial relationships with organizations and other people. The collections of these and other relationships is important in understanding the individual, his needs, and his interests.

Semantic MDM allows us to address business questions that may otherwise be difficult to understand. Figure 9.1 shows an example of the family relationships around a small household. The household has two parents (Abraham and Betty) and two children (Gil and Ethan). Betty is divorced from Claude, and they had two children, Ethan and Fran. Although it is hard to tell from the diagram, Abraham is a widower. He and Hilda had one child, Gil. In this example, there are only a few kinds of relationships:

- marriedTo
- divorcedFrom
- parentOf
- childOf
- siblingTo

Even with these few relationships represented in this small household, the diagram is somewhat complex. Yet even with this level of complexity, if you are a bank or insurance company—or even a retailer or telecommunications provider—there are a lot of unanswered questions that may be important to your business.

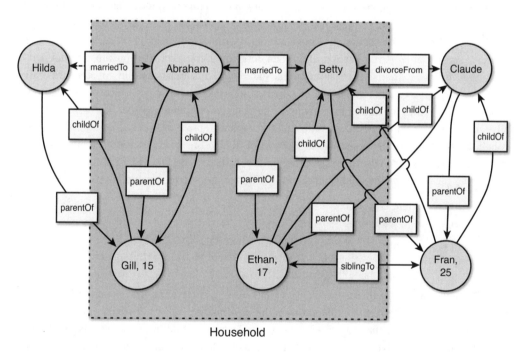

Household

Figure 9.1 Complex household relationships

When Betty and Abraham married, did Abraham legally adopt Ethan and Betty legally adopt Gil? This information could be important if Abraham and Betty were taking out a new insurance policy. In the United States, Ethan is of college age. If he's applying for scholarships, all his familial and financial relationships may be pretty important. Fran has a steady job and is looking to buy an apartment. She applies for a mortgage, and the bank sees that she has recently received money from Abraham. Should the bank be concerned? If Abraham is a high net worth customer of the bank, should it look on her mortgage application more favorably? There are lots of interesting questions to ask and many ways to use the answers. Relationships between people are complex, some of them change over time, many of them are sensitive, and some of them may not be openly acknowledged. Cultural, religious, and political differences are critically important and may dictate what relationship information can be collected, how it should be used, and how it can be used. We address some of the ethical considerations in the section "Ethics of Information."

Now that we have established the value of representing and understanding relationships, how should we implement them? MDM systems today are capable of representing each of the relationships, but depending on the MDM implementation, it can become awkward to store, query, and understand. It can require complex navigation through multiple queries to understand, for example, how Abraham and Fran are related. Using traditional MDM, we could resolve this question programmatically with a detailed understanding of the available services and data. It would require significant analysis and some development. However, there may be a better way.

Over the past 20 years, there has been a significant amount of experimentation with graph databases and semantic processing. Representing information in a graph is certainly not a new concept, and it can be particularly useful when describing complex relationships around people and organizations. Perhaps the most important standard in this area is a family of standards called the Resource Description Framework (RDF) that was released as a W3C Recommendation in 1999.[2] RDF provides the ability to show how one object is related to another through a conceptually simple syntax: Subject-Relationship-Object. Each statement of Subject-Relationship-Object is called a *triple*. We can persist triples either in a file (in one of many representations) or in a managed triple store such as the Graph Store in IBM DB2.[3] Using DB2 v10.5, the triple store feature allows the relationships for Hilda shown in Figure 9.2 to be represented in pseudo-RDF as:

- Hilda marriedTo Abraham
- Hilda parentOf Gil
- Gil childOf Hilda
- Abraham marriedTo Hilda

Note that although these statements seem sensible, there is no true meaning behind each relationship beyond how an application uses the information. So, for instance, there is nothing that would restrict us from adding this statement: Abraham childOf Hilda. For us to add more meaning, and in fact to be able to derive new information, a broader set of standards such as OWL was introduced. OWL allows us to classify both individuals and relationships and to represent properties and constraints on both. Using an OWL-like notation, the *marriedTo* relationship is represented as shown in Figure 9.2.

2. You can find the W3C specification on RDF in [2].
3. IBM released this feature in DB2 v10.1. You can find a presentation on this feature at https://www.ibm.com/developerworks/mydeveloperworks/blogs/nlp/resource/DB2_NoSQLGraphStore.pdf.

```
:marriedTo rdf:type owl:IrreflexiveProperty,

          owl:ObjectProperty,

          owl:SymmetricProperty;


    rdfs:range:marriedPerson;


    rdfs:domain:marriedPerson.
```

Figure 9.2   OWL notation for relationship marriedTo

This figure says that *marriedTo* is a relationship (in OWL, this is called an object property) and that this relationship is symmetric—meaning that if person A is married to person B, then person B must also be married to person A. The relationship is also "irreflexive," meaning that an individual cannot be married to himself or herself. We can also see that the relationship can only be between two *marriedPerson*s. Here, *marriedPerson*s is the class of all people who are married. A relationship such as this in Owl is a very powerful statement because it not only describes a relationship between two individuals, but also allows us to reason or infer additional facts. An additional logic engine, called a Reasoner, can be used to review a set of statements in OWL and infer additional facts. For example, if we just represented the relationship between Hilda and Abraham as an RDF triple, we would state (as we did previously) both that Hilda is married to Abraham and that Abraham is married to Hilda. The additional semantics that OWL provides mean that we only have to specify either that Abraham is married to Hilda or that Hilda is married to Abraham. Once we specify one direction of the relationship, the other direction can be inferred because we have indicated that the relationship is symmetric. OWL also allows us to express that a relationship must have an inverse relationship. We can specify that the *childOf* relationship is the inverse of the *parentOf* relationship. So if we state that Gil is the *childOf* Hilda, then we can infer that Hilda is the *parentOf* Gil.

In the previous example, we touched on the OWL notion of a class when we discussed *marriedPersons*. Classes in OWL are like sets in Mathematics. An individual entity (in our example, a person) can be a member of one or more sets. We can state that an individual is a member of a class. Using a Reasoner, we can also dynamically infer what classes an individual belongs to. For instance, in the definition of the *marriedTo* relationship, we find that it is between two *marriedPersons*. If we state that Abraham is *marriedTo* Betty, then we can infer that both Abraham and Betty must be members of the *marriedPersons* class. Classifying entities can be dynamic: as we learn more facts, we may be able to infer additional classifications, as shown in Figure 9.3.

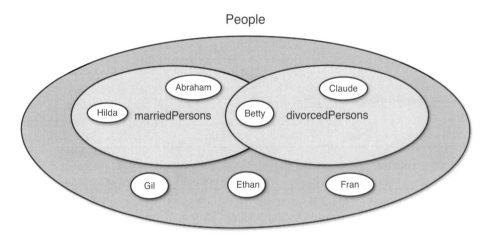

Figure 9.3   Classifications

    Classification may be inferred from relationships and from other attributes about an individual. Many of these relationships can be discovered through the advanced matching techniques described earlier in this chapter. Classification is a very useful and powerful mechanism, but it can also be a bit tricky. One of the interesting things about OWL is that it follows what is called "Open World Reasoning," whereby things are assumed to be true unless stated otherwise. In our example, we can see that the children—Gil, Ethan, and Fran—are not specified as being married. But unless we explicitly state that they are not married or have additional constraints that prevent them from being classified as married, the system could assume that because there isn't anything preventing them from being married, they should be classified as married. Now, although in reality, this doesn't make a lot of sense for Gil and Ethan, who are underage, it could be quite possible that Fran is married and we just don't have information about her spouse.

    Semantic technologies are very powerful, can be very useful, but also require care and understanding. We see great promise in these technologies, but it is more for extending and enriching existing MDM architectures than replacing them. Exploring these techniques in the context of Social MDM, where we consider broader sources of information and leverage the techniques for entity resolution, matching, and social analytics is an area of active research and development.

Ethics of Information

In this book, we have focused on how to use the techniques of Master Data Management, of social analytics, and of Big Data, to improve an organization's ability to attract, serve, and support its customers. This is good for the customers as well as being good for business. But as more information becomes available, as analytic methods improve, as we look to get more value from information, it is inevitable that the opportunity for ethical boundaries to be stretched increases.

In this, the final section, we felt it important to discuss the ethics of information, to share some stories, provoke some thought, and provide a bit of a framework for thinking about the ethics of information systems. Whole books[4] have been dedicated to the ethical use of information and analytics, especially in the context of the Big Data movement. In this section, we highlight a few points around key themes and recommend further reading, thinking, and actions.

Technology is inherently ethics-agnostic, but it pushes the art of the possible to new limits. Thus, consider:

- The availability of a wide range of data from many sources
- The ability to cheaply process and link this data together to understand a bigger picture
- The accuracy with which an individual can be identified and targeted
- The ability to pinpoint location for contextual insight and surveillance
- The application of this new insight to a wide range of activities and actions
- The operation of the insight in real-time or near real-time

Knowingly or unknowingly, intentional or not, information and insight can be used inappropriately, leading to sometimes unpredictable (and undesirable) results. We have seen many examples of this—from the ability of retailers to detect changes in shopping patterns that signal that a women might be pregnant[5] to making hiring decisions in part based on an applicant's social media profile. Deciding what is an appropriate or ethical use of information and analytics requires a consideration of possible outcomes, and an understanding of potential positive and negative consequences.

Technology isn't ethical or unethical. It is the *use* of technology that may become problematic. It is our responsibility as technologists, as data scientists, as business analysts, as individuals, to actively consider the implications of our actions—or lack thereof. Ethical behavior begins with situational awareness and the actions we take in these situations.

Legal regulations and business practices are different throughout the world. Cultural, generational, and political expectations on the rights and relationships between individuals, businesses, and governments vary throughout the world. Fundamental notions of identity and privacy are changing as new technologies and capabilities emerge. Fortunately, ethical and legal standards and practices are beginning to emerge to address a variety of concerns—from general topics such as privacy to more specific topics such as the handling of mobile location in analytics. Ethical standards are being discussed across different industries, including retail, automotive, banking, insurance, and health care.

As we look to apply these ethical frameworks to our own situations, our role is to understand the emerging frameworks, to consider what we can influence and change, to develop

---

4. [12] and [13] are good starting points for interested readers; [14] provides a nice overview.
5. See [11] for the *New York Times Magazine* article that highlighted the potentially intrusive nature of analytics.

reasoned practices that reflect the ethics of all of our stakeholders, and to follow these practices on a daily basis. We need to develop processes, checklists, and technical capabilities to ensure that our ethical standards are met.

To develop and apply these practices, let us look at examples of the three basic phases of the analytics lifecycle, as shown in Figure 9.4. First, we need to find or collect and then prepare information for analytic processing. Next, we can explore and analyze the information for insight and then apply this insight to decisions that alter future actions. The following sections discuss these phases in more detail, laying out opportunities for ethical considerations in each.

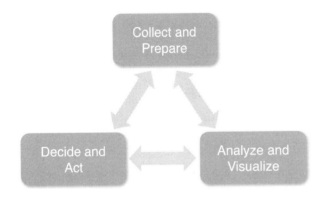

Figure 9.4   Information collection, preparation, and management

Information is not intangible; it is a tangible representation of people, places, things, actions, and events that has significant meaning and value. To hold information is a responsibility that we must honor. After we have obtained information, been entrusted with data, we need to ensure that we protect and prepare the information appropriately. This goes beyond standard best practices of securing and protecting information. We often need to understand something about the information itself and how we want to use it to select and implement appropriate protections and controls. In many cases, legal frameworks such as the Health Insurance Portability and Accountability Act (HIPAA) [10] or the U.S. Federal Trade Commission Privacy policies [3] define how information of a particular kind must be collected, managed, and used. In most cases, this is left to organizations to create and apply reasonable practices.

The most fundamental step is gathering and preparing data that we think might be useful for analysis. Here, we need to consider how the data was obtained, the provenance of and ownership of the information and, perhaps most importantly, our belief that the information is accurate enough for us to process. We can summarize these factors with the term *confidence*. If we are confident in using data for a particular purpose, then we will be more confident in the insight that we are able to derive. Conversely, if we don't have confidence in using information for a particular purpose, how can any insight we derive be trusted?

There are many examples of questionable gathering and use of information. Notions of privacy are fluid; they are not standardized legally or ethically. What information should never be shared? What information can be shared in strictly limited ways? What information is public? Society, governments, and industry are all struggling to answer these questions, and both the questions and answers continue to change. For instance, in Chapter 6, "Social MDM and Customer Care," we discussed how telecommunications service providers collect information about phone calls. Is it ethical for them to use this information to market their services to you? If they observe that you make a lot of calls to a specific country, they may want to offer you a tailored rate that would reduce your costs. Most people would view that this is an ethical use of data. If, on the other hand, a phone company noticed that you were calling a competitor and then used that information to make you a special offer, is that okay? Let's consider an even more interesting example: when you use a cell phone, the telecommunications provider knows where you are. Is it ethical for the provider to sell that information to nearby retailers so that they can entice you with specific offers? Many believe that this is not ethical—unless the customer has given explicit, informed consent. Yet if this same customer had an emergency and called emergency services, he or she would expect (and in some places the law requires) that location information would be shared with the emergency services provider.

If you have a smart phone, the phone itself may contain a GPS that not only can inform local applications running on your phone but also send that information to remote applications that you may or may not be aware of. Most people would view that sharing of their location information without their explicit consent is unacceptable. Many phones now offer users the ability to control which applications can receive location information, but is even this enough? Should location sharing be enabled or disabled by default?

These examples highlight the responsibility of information consumers to understand both where the information came from and if and how they are entitled to use it. In the preceding example, location information from a smart phone application that a customer has explicitly authorized is very different from similar information that may be gathered implicitly and without a customer's explicit understanding or permission. To summarize, entitlement and provenance of the information are foundational to the ethical use of information. Master Data Management provides a mechanism to store, manage, and use such customer preferences and thus can help organizations manage their use and communications with their customers.

Ethical frameworks for collection and handling of personal and contextual information are emerging. For example, a best practices paper from the Global Association for Marketing at Retail [4] provides the following summary statement:

> While technology imposes few restrictions on data collection in retail settings, marketers should safeguard consumer privacy. This document provides recommendations to marketers on maintaining ethical boundaries with consumer data and suggestions on how consumer observations and marketing insights should be collected and used.

The paper goes on to highlight some key tenets for ethical data collection that we can summarize as follows:

- Obey the laws. For instance, in the U.S., collecting information about minors is regulated.
- Collect the minimum of information in the least intrusive way possible.
- Disclose that you are collecting information.
- Collect personally identifiable information only with explicit consent.
- Protect personally identifiable information carefully.

Most of these principles may be viewed as common sense; however, as we encounter more specific scenarios across industries and geographies, careful consideration is required.

In many situations, an organization already has collected information that may be useful for a new project. This presents a different set of factors to consider and often requires a bit of investigative work. For example, do we understand where the information came from (the provenance) and who owns the information? In other words, do we have the rights to use it? What is our confidence in the information? Confidence depends on a number of factors, including quality, currency, and relevance.

Let's say we have a new project to understand product buying patterns across different sales channels. As we collect or find data sets that we want to use together, we most likely will need to prepare these data sets for analytical processing. This is exactly what we do today in preparing a data warehouse or mart. We develop a set of extract-transform-load (ETL) jobs using a tool such as IBM InfoSphere Information Server,[6] to cleanse, integrate, and restructure information from multiple sources into a consistent representation that is suitable for analyses. A warehouse is often a great source of pre-integrated, high-quality information. But sometimes the information we need isn't in the warehouse and may not even be represented as well-structured, relational information. Here, we may need to prepare the information with additional tools and leverage systems such as Hadoop to both prepare and store this information. No matter the source of the information, selecting and preparing the information for a new project requires careful consideration of the confidence that we have in using this information for this use.

So far, we have discussed how to develop a trusted data set. But how do we manage and protect sensitive data? We have many options available to us depending on the kind of sensitive data we have, the kinds of analyses we need to perform, and the system controls we can establish. Data scientists and analysts often want to create their own private experimental "sandbox" in which they can try out and evaluate different analyses. Allowing users unfettered access to sensitive data is generally not a good idea, so many organizations enforce policies to transform the data set using masking algorithms to hide the personal identity of the information but attempt

---

6. You can find more information about IBM Information Server at http://pic.dhe.ibm.com/infocenter/
   iisinfsv/v9r1/index.jsp?topic=%2Fcom.ibm.swg.im.iis.productization.iisinfsv.home.
   doc%2Ftopics%2Fic_homepage_IS.html.

to preserve key statistical characteristics. For example, one technique would jumble names, addresses, and phone numbers. Masking strategies can get quite sophisticated, and specialized tools such as the IBM Optim Test Data Manager[7] are useful to implement and manage this support. Research and development of masking techniques is ongoing; finding masking algorithms that preserve privacy without degrading the integrity of the analytic results can be challenging.

We must, of course, secure and protect information and especially personally identifiable information from unauthorized use and visibility. Well-known practices for access control, encryption, database auditing, and other forms of governance should be followed. Secure engineering practices for vulnerability assessment and remediation and for the physical and computing infrastructure are well known. All too often we hear of data leaks and break-ins that could have been prevented by following well-known industry practices.

Ethically managing the collection, preparation, and management of information not only requires the standard best practices that we apply to building and contracting warehouses and marts, but also requires being thoughtful about what data is needed for what purpose, understanding ownership rights, confidence, and sensitivity of the information. Collecting new information offers us new opportunities to gain consent, be transparent, and be careful in how we steward the information we are entrusted with.

Explore and Analyze

Developing accurate and meaningful insight into a dataset requires the skills and experience of an experienced data scientist or statistician. Data scientists use their skills to derive insight from the information and help others understand that insight, discussing both the degree of confidence as well as the uncertainties in the results. Many forms of analytics provide their results in terms of likelihood, error analysis, and confidence. Confidence derived from analysis depends on our confidence in the combination of people, tools, and processes used to perform the analysis in addition to our confidence in the suitability of the information we are operating on.

It is sometimes easy to forget that analytics is inexact. Data scientists explore data and run experiments to elicit meaning from a data set. Validating the experiments means finding or collecting additional data, sometimes constructing new experiments to test previous ones, or attempting to generalize the insight. When repeatable results have been obtained, the analyses may be transitioned from an exploratory process to an operational process that is automatically executed as part of normal business operations. When a set of analyses is in production, it is periodically revalidated to maintain confidence in the accuracy and effectiveness of the analyses.

To bolster trust in analytics practitioners and to set expectations on best practices, the data scientist community has developed codes of conduct and ethics. Numerous associations and organizations represent this growing community, and many have developed not only codes of

---

7. You can find more information about IBM Optim Test Data Management solutions at http://pic.dhe. ibm.com/infocenter/idm/v2r2/index.jsp?topic=%2Fcom.ibm.optimd.install.doc%2FInfoCenterTopics %2Ftopics%2Finstalling_optim_dg_dp_tdm_solutions.html.

conduct but also offer training and certification. The ethical guidelines recognize both the scientific nature of analytics and the professionalism expected in deriving, communicating, and applying results. They also recognize the rapidly evolving nature of data science and the importance of both keeping abreast of emerging technologies and trends but also awareness of bad science and short-lived fads.

Analytics is no longer just an offline activity used to provide scheduled performance feedback. Analytic processing is becoming increasingly integrated with operations. Retailers want to make targeted offers to you based on your interests and profile, as you move around within a store. Analytics supports customer service agents in helping them assist customers. Insurance companies make real-time offers based on the customers' profiles and input. As analytics is increasingly integrated into all kinds of processes, the ethical considerations for both the insight and the use of the insight become intertwined.

Decide and Act

The application of the insights that we derive is where ethical considerations are perhaps the most critical. Just because we suspect that something may be true, should we take action based on this? What are the ramifications if we are wrong? What if we are right? For example, if we observe a purchasing pattern that indicates that someone in a household may be pregnant, is it ethical to change the marketing offers made to that person? Is this exposing information that individuals would rather be kept private or information that they are willing to share with potentially interested neighbors? What if our analytics indicated that someone in a household had an incurable disease?

We need to think carefully about how we use the insight that we ascertain. What kinds of decisions and actions are appropriate, responsible, and ethical based on our belief and confidence in the information that we have? Whether it's deciding to hire someone, treat a patient, or rent a house, analytics over more and more sources of information provides new kinds of insight that can influence more kinds of actions faster. As analytics pervades more and more operational processes, the impact—both positive and negative—increases. Considering ethics in how we apply the insights we gain through analytics helps us to consider and hopefully avoid negative consequences and maximize the mutual benefit of derived insight.

The boundaries of what is considered ethical vary within organizations, geographies, cultures, and industries. Few things are always right or wrong—until you get to extremes that offend the majority of a population—and even there, what offends one population may not offend another. Deciding if and how to use analytical insight depends on each situation, the stakeholders, and the possible consequences.

An Ethical Framework

The ethical challenges, considerations, and potential consequences that we have explored hopefully leave you wondering how you can make ethical considerations part of your organization's practices. Awareness of these ethical considerations is perhaps the first and most important step. Putting an effective ethical framework into place takes planning and expertise that go beyond the scope of this book. However, as we implement Social MDM and other systems, we can identify some approaches to getting started.

Implementing such systems starts with comparing current practices with best practices, as we discussed earlier in this section and can be reviewed more extensively in the work we reference in the "References" section at the end of this chapter. Are there gaps that need to be filled? There may be gaps in both technical implementations and processes to document and implement as part of an ongoing improvement plan.

Evolving processes is especially important in creating and maintaining an active approach toward considering ethical issues. The process for evaluating new project proposals is a good example. Figure 9.5 provides a simple process flow for considering a proposal for a new analytics project, and Figure 9.6 illustrates it for a telecommunication provider use case. Each organization would customize this framework by developing:

- A template for defining solution attributes
- A statement of the organization's values and principles
- A set of questions to assist in evaluating the ethical considerations of executing the project

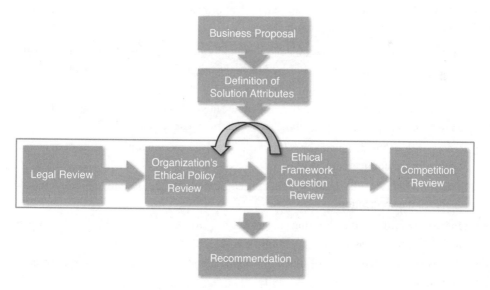

Figure 9.5   Ethical framework process flow

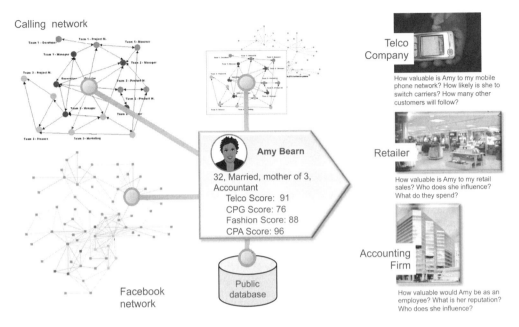

Figure 9.6   Ethical framework process flow considering the analytics outcome

Solution design attributes include questions about the data, the analytics applied to that data, and how the results will be used. MDM plays a key role in the collection, preparation, and management of the data, especially personal data. Ethical framework questions focus on how we apply an organization's documented values and ethical principles to the solution characteristics defined for the proposed project. Sample questions are

- **Context:** For what purpose was the data originally surrendered? For what purpose is the data now being used? How far removed from the original context is its new use?

- **Consent and Choice:** What are the choices given to affected parties? Do they know they are making a choice? Do they really understand what they are agreeing to? Do they really have an opportunity to decline? What alternatives are offered?

- **Reasonable:** Is the depth and breadth of the data used and the relationships derived reasonable for the application it is used for?

- **Substantiated:** Are the sources of data used appropriate, authoritative, complete, and timely for the application?

- **Owned:** Who owns the resulting insight? What are their responsibilities toward it in terms of its protection and the obligation to act?

- **Fair:** How equitable are the results of the application to all parties? Is everyone properly compensated?

- **Considered:** What are the consequences of the data collection and analysis?
- **Access:** What access to data is given to the data subject?
- **Accountable:** How are mistakes and unintended consequences detected and repaired? Can the interested parties check the results that affect them?

Implementing process frameworks such as this helps illuminate often-overlooked questions that will foster discussions and negotiations among many parts of the organization. The results of this discussion can be a much higher degree of clarity over what the organization values, and a mutual understanding of the costs, benefits, and consequences of enforcing (or not) these values.

A desire to implement Social MDM reflects a desire to deepen our relationship with prospects and customers: we strive to understand them better so that we are better able to serve them, win their business, and hopefully enhance their desire to do business with us. Establishing open and ethical practices is key to developing and maintaining these relationships.

Conclusion

Master Data Management continues to be an active, interesting, and vibrant area for innovation in both technology and how we apply that technology to enterprise practices. As technologists, we continue to explore new ways to derive additional meaning and insight from information—to deepen our understanding of individuals, products, and organizations and to discover and represent new and interesting kinds of relationships. We do this in the pursuit of improving customer service and experience, to improve the operations of our organization, and, frankly, to benefit businesses.

In this last section, we also showed the importance of developing ethical frameworks that go beyond legal requirements to meet the privacy and fairness expectations of our customers, employees, and colleagues. Collection and use of information must be governed by high standards that reflect the brand promise of the organization.

References

[1] W3C. "Semantic Web." Retrieved 12/10/2013 from http://www.w3.org/standards/semanticweb/.

[2] W3C. "Resource Description Framework." Retrieved 4/16/2014 from http://www.w3.org/rdf.

[3] Federal Trade Commission, Bureau of Consumer Protection. "Consumer Privacy." Retrieved 6/12/2014 from http://business.ftc.gov/privacy-and-security/consumer-privacy.

[4] POPAI—The Global Association for Marketing at Retail. "Best Practices: Recommended Code of Conduct for Consumer Tracking Research." Retrieved 5/28/2014 from http://www.popai.com/docs/DS/2010dscc.pdf.

[5] National Association for Retail Marketing Services. "Code of Ethics." Retrieved 6/12/2014 from http://www.narms.com/about/narms-legal-administrative/code-of-ethics/.

[6] National Automobile Dealers Association. "Code of Ethics." Retrieved 6/12/2014 from http://www.nada.org/Publications/CodeOfEthics/.

[7] Gallagher, Callahan, & Gartrell. "Effective Code of Conduct for Banking." Retrieved 6/12/2014 from http://www.gcglaw.com/resources/financial/codeofconduct.html.

[8] International Association of Insurance Professionals. "Code of Ethics." Retrieved 6/12/2014 from http://www.internationalinsuranceprofessionals.org/?page=code_of_ethics.

[9] Limentari, Alexander E., Director of Health Policy and Public Health, East Kent Health Authority. "An Ethical Code for Everybody in Health Care." Retrieved 6/12/2014 from http://www.ncbi.nlm.nih.gov/pmc/articles/PMC1113129/.

[10] Department of Health and Human Services. "General Overview of HIPAA." Retrieved 5/06/2014 from http://www.hhs.gov/ocr/privacy/hipaa/understanding/coveredentities/generaloverview.html.

[11] Duhigg, Charles, *How Companies Learn Your Secrets*, *New York Times Magazine*, 2/16/2012.

[12] Davis, Kord & Patterson, Doug, *Ethics of Big Data*, ISBN-13: 978-1-4493-1179-7, O'Reilly, 2012.

[13] Buytendiijk, Frank, *Socrates Reloaded: The Case for Ethics in Business & Technology*, ISBN-13: 978-1478316343, 7/27/2012.

[14] Chessell, Mandy, *Ethics for Big Data & Analytics*, http://ibmdatamag.com/2014/03/ethical-use-of-big-data-and-analytics/, 3/21/14.

Index